THE CULTURE OF QUEERS

For around a hundred years up to the Stonewall riots, the word for gay men was 'queers'. From screaming queens to sensitive vampires and sad young men, and from pulp novels and pornography to the films of Fassbinder, *The Culture of Queers* explores the history of queer arts and media.

Richard Dyer traces the contours of queer culture, examining the differences and continuities with the gay culture which succeeded it. Opening with a discussion of the very concept of 'queers', he asks what it means to speak of a sexual grouping having a culture and addresses issues such as gay attitudes to women and the notion of camp.

Dyer explores a range of queer culture, from key topics such as fashion and vampires to genres like film noir and the heritage film, and stars such as Charles Hawtrey (outrageous star of the Carry On films) and Rock Hudson. Offering a grounded historical approach to the cultural implications of queerness, *The Culture of Queers* both insists on the negative cultural consequences of the oppression of homosexual men and offers a celebration of queer resistance.

Richard Dyer is Professor of Film Studies at The University of Warwick. He is the author of *Stars* (1979), *Now You See It: Studies in Lesbian and Gay Film* (Routledge 1990), *The Matter of Images* (Routledge 1993) and *White* (Routledge 1997).

THE CULTURE OF QUEERS

Richard Dyer

London and New York

First published 2002
by Routledge
11 New Fetter Lane, London EC4P 4EE

Simultaneously published in the USA and Canada
by Routledge
29 West 35th Street, New York, NY 10001

Routledge is an imprint of the Taylor & Francis Group

Typeset in Garamond
by Wearset Ltd, Boldon, Tyne and Wear
Printed and bound in Great Britain
by Biddles Ltd, Guildford and King's Lynn

British Library Cataloguing in Publication Data
A catalogue record for this book is available from the British Library

Library of Congress Cataloging in Publication Data
Dyer, Richard.
The culture of queers / Richard Dyer.
p. cm.
Includes bibliographical references and index.
1. Gays in popular culture. 2. Homosexuality in motion pictures.
3. Homosexuality in art. 4. Homosexuality—Public opinion.
5. Gay men—Attitudes. I. Title.
HQ76 .D9 2002
306.76'6—dc21

2001048303

ISBN 0-415-22375-X (hbk)
ISBN 0-415-22376-8 (pbk)

CONTENTS

ILLUSTRATIONS

INTRODUCTION

All people in all societies inherit and bequeath frameworks of understanding and feeling about themselves and everyone else. These frameworks include various kinds of categories of persons. We find and refuse to find ourselves in these categories, live with, within and against them, but never actually without them. They provide locations and a vast set of codes wherein and with which we can speak, create, doodle, in short, make culture. The essays in this book deal with aspects of the culture produced by and/or about men in the category queer.

Queers

Between the mid-nineteenth and mid-twentieth centuries in Western society, there was a notion of sexual attraction between men characterised by three features: that such attraction indicated a sexual category to which a man either did or did not belong, that it went along with other, non-sexual qualities and that it was humanly (morally, medically, socially) problematic. Men of this kind were queers (or fags, froci, poofs, Schwule, tapettes, etcetera).

We could identify the period in which this conceptualisation held sway as 1869–1969. In the earlier year, the Hungarian Károly Mária Benkert published in Leipzig a pamphlet calling for the repeal of laws against sex between men, in which he used, it seems for the first time anywhere, the term 'homosexual'. In 1969, denizens of the Stonewall bar in New York City resisted a police raid, sparking a riot. Dates, especially when they so prettily embrace a century, are never more than vivid emblems of the much more ragged processes by which ideas come to prominence and ebb away. Benkert was one of several people developing ideas about homosexual persons in the 1860s, ideas that themselves have roots in Romantic and Enlightenment thought, and earlier still, and that are related to the development of actual homosexual social groupings, both elite and otherwise, in probably all developed urban societies. Equally, the Stonewall events, par excellence a phenomenon of urban homosexual grouping, also gained their force both from the growing homosexual campaigning of previous decades and the concurrent development of ideas and publications about queerness and sexual freedom more widely. Moreover, while Stonewall is felt by many to inaugurate, symbolically, a new era, of gays rather than queers, the establishment of that era has been uneven and insecure, even in North America, Western Europe and Australasia – it's by no means clear that we're entirely out of the age of queers and into that of gays. Yet with all these provisos about the flaky boundaries of periods, I am concerned in these essays with culture produced in a rough hundred year period under the sign of queerness.

The point of looking at the historical boundedness of a notion is not that of periodisation for its own sake but rather because having a sense of other ways in which something has been thought and felt about allows us to see the specificity of the way we think about any particular manifestation of it. In the process of doing this with sexual attraction between men, there is a danger that one may overstate a claim for the utter uniqueness of the concept of queers (and an even greater one of assuming that because there was not the concept there was not the reality). Nonetheless, it does seem probable that without this era, while sexual attraction between men is universally known, the three characterising features of the notion of queers are less commonly found, if at all. In most periods we can find examples of men whom everyone knew to be habitually attracted to other men but it is less clear that people in other periods necessarily, commonsensically, extrapolated from that to the idea that such individuals belonged to a type of man defined by these tastes. Again, the accounts of certain men in the past – the outrageous Monsieur at the courts of Louis XIII and XIV, for instance, or, at the other end of the social scale, the *fanchonos* persecuted by the Portuguese Inquisition or the mollies in male brothels in Elizabethan England – seem to evoke a queenly type rather familiar to us, whose non-sexual manners and mannerisms nonetheless indicate a type of sexuality. It is certainly reasonable to see such men as part of the pre-history of queers, but it's not so certain that, as the notion of queers requires, they were taken to be representative of the generality of men having sex with men or that having sex with men was presumed to entail being like that. Finally, in relation to the third characteristic of queers – that they are humanly problematic – it seems to be the case that the overwhelming official view of sex between men in Western tradition has been that it is something monstrous (even if it has been, to various degrees, in practice tolerated and even found amusing, and in probably rare instances idealised). However, though a language of monstrosity does persist in the age of queers, it expresses a view much more terrible than modern notions of queerness, which are more inclined to speak of moral weakness, mental sickness or personal inadequacy. In particular, the notion of queers stresses an idea of impulses that the individual has no choice over having (though he may have choice over acting on them), which enables notions of pity, cure and toleration, as well as resignation and defiance, to come into play.

The queer, then, is an historically bounded notion, albeit trailing clouds of glory and ignominy back into at least the late Middle Ages, and still with us, maybe even hegemonically, today. Its first characteristic, that there is a male sexual type that consists in being attracted to other men, has always been affirmed in a context where, in fact, a vast range of other instances of sex (to say nothing of sexual attraction) between men occurs. Just to indicate the sheer range and fluidity of human experience, consider the following cases: men whose lives divide into first a queer and then a straight period (or vice versa) and who variously understand this in terms of their changing (being first one thing then another), having really all along been one thing without knowing it or being permanently bisexual, but choosing to live exclusively as either hetero or homo for reasons of, for instance, convenience or a commitment to monogamy; men who have one intense sexual relationship with a man or a woman at a certain point in their lives but are sexually involved otherwise only with, respectively, women or men; men who see themselves as bisexual, but then in various proportions between the impulse towards men and towards women; men who have only had or ever wanted to have sex with either men or women.

Actual sex with another man can thus be for the individual man exclusive or occasional, permanent or temporary, and this is likely to be even more complex, fluid and variegated, fleeting and even unnoticed, in relation to sexual attraction, fantasy and speculation. A strong notion of queers runs counter to this – queer is something you are, constitutively, rather than something you might do (have done), feel (have felt), mainly, sometimes, once, maybe. It is this latter range and fluidity (which goes far beyond another fixing notion, the bisexual) that analytical notions of homo-eroticism and Queer seek to address (and throughout my discussion capital letter Queer will indicate the latter conceptualisation). Both attempt to capture the wide range of impulse and feeling beyond the fixed and exclusive sexuality posited by queer, but with different emphases and implications.

Homo-eroticism tends to stress libidinal attraction without sexual expression, sometimes even at the level of imagination and feeling. While in some usages homo-eroticism can be a wider term which includes homosexuality, or can be a euphemism for homosexuality, it importantly indicates a sense of male pleasure in the physical presence of men, or even sometimes in their spiritually or ethically masculine qualities, which cannot be contained by (or, discourses of homo-eroticism would tend to say, reduced to) the idea of queerness. The notion of homo-eroticism may thus connect queers to a broader sense of attraction between men and it is often so used with a polemical force (queers are just part of a continuum that includes contact sports, stag nights, all-male clubs and best friends). However, it may also be put to exactly the opposite end, to distinguish queers from this higher form

of attraction (relations of mateyness and brotherhood, bonding and vener-
ation, have nothing to do with sex). The emphasis on a higher affectivity has
been interpreted as a way of accommodating libidinal attraction between
men, by giving it expression while simultaneously limiting and containing
it. Equally, in certain periods, such ideas might be used to argue for a preferred form of homosexual expression, as is notably present in some *mannmännlich* (man-manly) German imagery in the early twentieth century or in
the homophile discourse in 1950s France (see Chapter 9).

Homo-eroticism can be a generous and inclusive notion, but its tendency
to contain and desexualise also made it problematic, both for queer but also
for Queer. The latter, notably as manifest in Theory, also looks beyond an
exclusive and fixed sexuality (being a queer), but in order both to stress the
continuity with anyone who is only homo and to retain the dangerous,
troubling dimension of the genital. Queer Theory is especially interested in
manifestations of male–male sexual attraction where you wouldn't expect to
find it, where it's been diverted or repressed or else obliquely expressed or
unknowingly sublimated, but it does not focus on these to separate them
from queerness and nor does it buy into the notion of an erotic that is distinguishable from a sexual. In some versions, homosexuality is discovered to be
so pervasive as to constitute a defining element of all sexuality, of the very
notion of sexuality – that's what's Queer. In Queer rhetoric, this process of
sexual constitution tends to be viewed as always in some manner dissonant,
disturbing, subversive, transgressive – while the notion of the homo-erotic
points to the way male–male attraction may nourish the affective life of
society as a whole through accommodation to and by it, Queer is more likely
to find such attraction stimulating the social construction of affect by prick-
ing and unsettling it.

The focus of the essays here is on queers, but in at least five cases I have
been interested in Queer-related issues: the awareness of the constructedness
of queer identities in avant-garde film (Chapter 2), the problem of reading
homosexuality in film noir (where obvious queers may be married and
straight guys may be queer on occasion), the uneasy discourse of homophilia
and friendship in *L'Air de Paris*, the way knowing about Rock Hudson's
homosexuality may allow one to see the unsettling of heterosexuality in his
films, and the putative straightness of male porn stars who live by having
sex with men under the eyes of men. Even focusing, as most of the essays do,
on queers proper involves looking at a range of expressions and representations, since there are historical variations and specificities even within this
less fluid category.

As soon as we consider those expressions and representations, it is also
clear that we are talking about something more than sexuality in the most
literal sense. This takes us to the second feature of the notion of queers,
namely that this homosexuality goes along with other personality traits.
Primary among these is the relation to gender. If a queer is not like a hetero-

4

sexual man in terms of his sexual object choice, then he must not be like one in other ways. From this stems the commonest form of obvious queerness: being in some way or other 'like' a woman, fey, effeminate, sensitive, camp. Nearly all the examples discussed here are informed by this, from the screaming queenliness of camp taste and Charles Hawtrey to the so-sensitive vampires and sad young men. However, queers' relation to women is complex. On the one hand, you cannot discuss male queer culture without reference to both femininity (cf. 'politics', camp, clothes, Hawtrey, Fassbinder) and relations with and attitudes towards women (cf. misogyny, noir, the sad young man, *L'Air de Paris*, Rock Hudson, heritage movies). On the other hand, there is a structural ambiguity in queers' relation to women – they are more despicable or derisory than women (of whom, misogyny notwithstanding, there are proper, accepted and idealised ideas), yet at the same time, as men, they are more privileged. The treatment of queers may acquire its more vicious or contemptuous forms from the degree to which queers are not real men, from the cognitive dissonance between masculinity and queerness – and yet in practice queers can practice an exclusionary or domineering masculinity, often control those woman-centred sectors of employment that make space for them (hairdressing, fashion, dance, some clerical work and caring professions), are by no means free from misogyny, in short, can be men, be perceived to achieve manhood, in spite of being queers.

Less common than the perceived femininity of queers is the opposite assumption, that two men together constitute an intensified form of manliness. One may find this in some versions of 'Greek love' (referenced in *Maurice*, discussed in Chapter 14), in the virile bonding canvassed by some in Germany before the 1930s, in the contrast between the central male couple and the obvious queen in *L'Air de Paris*, in the hyper-masculine imagery of post-1960s homosexual fashion and pornography (touched on in Chapters 5 and 13). Some of these examples overlap with instances of homo-erotic and Queer men, because, while a queen or a sissy is at once distinguishable from a regular man, virile queer guys are not. However, even where no gender inflection or exaggeration is involved, no sissiness or man–manliness, relations between men always take place in a world where distinctions are drawn between men and women – it is virtually impossible to live, imagine or represent sexuality between men as if it is not informed by awareness of the difference between men and women.

Where there is no explicit gender reference, notions of the queer still entail other non-sexual characteristics that are held either to account for or flow from a different sexuality. These are much more various and diffuse than the gender constructions, but include ideas of body type, physical and mental weakness, decadence, attitudes of irony, disdain or 'attitude' *tout court* and propensities towards superficial performance and display.

Many of these notions (weakness, irony, display) have femininity concealed within them but they also have class and ethnic connotations. The notion of queers has tended to be associated with elite and white men. The traditions of proletarian and non-white queer sub-cultures and lifestyles are indisputable and, as already noted, were foundational for the development of idea of queerness, yet they keep disappearing from view in dominant constructions of queerness.

Irony, decadence, fashion and 'attitude' can all be understood as signs of a vein of snobbism in the queer personality, whether by virtue of birth or aspiration. The core term 'queen' evokes social superiority (or the performance of it), and although the prime instance in these pages, Charles Hawtrey, is in fact utterly without middle- or upper-class associations, still the queen is more usually upwardly mobile in pretension. The image of queers as upper class and white is seldom utterly secure but nor is it often dislodged from centrality. Oscar Wilde, the queer par excellence, was a socialist but this is eclipsed in the popular imagination, perhaps rightly, by his flaky Irish aristocratic origins, social climbing and aesthetic snobbery. In their different ways, two who have subsequently carried the Wildean flame, though both in fact of lowish class origin, Noël Coward and Quentin Crisp, have moulded queer personalities through refinement of accent and condescension of attitude. Not for nothing did Crisp, a pauper most of his life, still play on the snob resonances of queerdom by calling himself one of the 'stately homos of England' (evoking thereby not only the National Trust but a Coward song). In the widespread image of aristocratic and white men pursuing working-class and/or Latin, Arab, Indian and Africano men, it is the former who tend to be thought of as the queers, not the latter.

These class and ethnic associations are not fixed and inevitable. The fact of a Hawtrey, Wilde's socialism, the way class origin is implied in the aspiration beyond it, the enthusiasm of bourgeois white men's non-bourgeois, non-white lovers, all unsettle the primary identification of queer as upper class and white. Just as there were Black Nationalist discourses saying that queerness is a white problem, so there were white racist theories seeing homosexuality as a sign of the inherent weakness or inferiority of other races, citing notably the effeteness of Indian cultures and the acceptance of the berdache in Native American nations. In short, while the relation of queerness to gender, and especially the feminine, is inescapable, the class and ethnic associations are weaker and more contradictory but, all the same, still there.

Most of the secondary queer characteristics are negative: effeminacy, sickness, attitude, superficiality, snobbery. This is the third feature of being a queer – that it is a bad thing. As already noted, the language of monstrosity has by and large disappeared, but notions and feelings of immorality, deviance, weakness, illness, inadequacy, shame, degeneracy, sordidness, disgust and pathos were all part of the notion of queerdom. Queer Theory and politics have sought to reclaim the word queer, not so much to cleanse it of its negative associations as to challenge the assumption that these associations are in fact negative – thus immorality may be a challenge to repressive morality, deviance a rejection of the straight and thus narrow, and what is considered sordid and disgusting may in fact be exciting, risky, a life lived to the full on the edge. The case is selective – I don't sense a desire to reclaim weakness, inadequacy and pathos, for instance – but Queer does resist a view of queerness as unrelieved frightfulness.

What Queer is turning on its head – the negativity of queer – was already being challenged throughout the age of queerness. The notion of homosexual was, after all, an invention of queers, just as were the long, albeit intermittent traditions of urban sub-cultures. These were defiant assertions of male–male sexuality, refusals of pathology, enthusiastic embracings of difference. Just as queerness was always jostling with the range and fluidity of actual sexual practices and with the fact that men attracted to men did not necessarily display the secondary, non-sexual characteristics of queerdom, so too the age of queers was not one of unmitigated misery and subjection, of men simply believing and accepting they were awful. Yet this negativity was, I'm suggesting, the dominant attitude, the one you had to deal with and fight against. The theory of Queer tends to overplay notions of transgression, resistance and the ludic in the age of queers; while other, often older commentators lament the passing of the age of queerdom, when suffering brought intensity to love and secrecy demanded indirection, ambiguity and elaborate double entendre in expression. It is not that any of the elements indicated in the last sentence are untrue, that there was no subversion, play, passion or irony, but that they may either mask the reality of the oppressiveness of the category queer or accept too high a price in the name of intensity of feeling and refinement of expression.

The essays that follow were not written to redress the balance, to put back the negativity in queer. However, allowing for the different contexts for which they were written (see p. 12), they should be judged on how well they manage to hold together a sense of oppression *and* resistance, negativity *and* play. When I say that, for instance, noir queens are seen as sick deviants but are also a lot more fun than the straight heroes, or that the melancholy of the sad young men could be transmuted into sexy romanticism, I hope I have not appeared to say that the fun and the romance make up for the sickness and sadness or that they had equal power under the sign of queerness.

One further term, used a couple of times already, needs addressing: 'gay'. In fact, the notions of 'queer' and 'gay' are often not far apart. Both – queer by design, gay in practice – designate persons rather than acts or aspects of personality. 'Gay' is more flexible – to speak of a gay man does not always imply that a whole other set of personality traits comes in the train of his sexuality. However, the difficulty 'gay' has had with 'bisexual' is instructive. Quite apart from elements of political resistance on both sides (gays seeing bi as a dilution of homosexuality, bis seeing gay as a diminution of their heterosexuality), it is telling that one solution for organisations and events has been to add 'bisexual' (and 'transgender') on to 'gay'. This both preserves gays and bis as separate categories and also retains both as categories of persons, defined by their sexual choices – like queer.

The real difference between 'queer' and 'gay' is that of negativity, though even this has to be formulated with some care. It would in fact be perfectly possible to write the history of the age of queers as that of the slow birth of gay. Benkert, after all, was affirming the rights of homosexuals and we can chart other such heroic moments and trends leading up to Stonewall: Wilde's 'love that dare not speak its name' speech at his trial in 1895; the development of homosexual rights organisations, beginning in Germany with the foundation of the Humanitarian Scientific Committee in 1897 and taking off again from the 1940s on; Radclyffe Hall's publication of *The Well of Loneliness* in 1928 (with indubitable implications for her queer brothers); the 1948 Kinsey report on male sexuality; the making and publishing of homo-erotica; the outrageousness of queens throughout the period and at all levels of society (think Barbette, Quentin Crisp, Antonio Iacono, José Sarria, Sylvester, Ernest Thesiger, to suggest only some with a foot in show biz[1]). The negativity of queer was always resisted, contested, evaded or flouted. However, the notion of queer always had an awareness of negativity, had always to bear the weight of it. 'Gay' sought to think and feel without a consciousness of negativity.

Culture

The culture of queers dealt with in this book belongs within a somewhat narrower definition of culture than that sometimes deployed. Thus there is no discussion here of, for instance, scientific discourses or patterns of behaviour, of the geographies and codes of cruising, the negotiation and playing of roles in relationships or the presence of queerness in business or sport, and I only touch lightly on language (in the discussion of camp). There are discussions of clothes, as actually worn and as they figure in representation, and of misogyny and camp as attitudes, but by and large my focus is on culture in the sense of the arts, from the popular (pulp novels, Hollywood, a French melodrama, an English comedian, pornography) via the middle (heritage cinema) to the high brow (avant-garde and arthouse cinema).

The essays are about culture, in this narrower sense, produced by men who were queers. Queers of course produced a great deal of culture that, while readable as Queer, was not in any evident sense queer. The essays here though are about queer made culture that is in some sense explicitly queer, whether, as with camp, insistently deriving from a queer perspective on the world, or, in clothes style, signalling the fact of queerness, or, mostly, representing queers and queer relations. There are also a couple of cases concerned with culture less evidently produced by queers but which does represent them, such as film noir and the heritage film. All these constitute a number of queer frameworks of understanding and representation of queers. What I want to consider here is the status and value of such frameworks in regard to what we may take them to tell us about actually being a queer.

Culture is not for the main part done in order to say something or make a point, and queer culture is in this no exception. The processes of cultural production in Western society are primarily concerned with pleasure, with making things that are enjoyable and giving vent to the need to speak, to express and communicate; they are also most often undertaken to make a living. Moreover, all such processes are, for the most part, a not much reflected on reproduction of ways of doing things, languages, habits and conventions that carry production along, only gradually altered by the needs of the moment or where this or that detail feels like it doesn't work. You have to include all that in the account before you start assuming queer cultural production is about things like self expression and representation. Like all other cultural production, only occasionally is queer cultural production done in order to say something about queers and the world in which they find themselves, though inadvertently it may suggest ways of making sense of these.

Queer cultural production – like queers – can only exist in the society and culture in which it finds itself. Queer culture had to occur in the institutional spaces available and certain spaces were more propitious than others for queer cultural production. I have not traced this for every case discussed, but I do address it in relation to the film avant-garde, fashion and film noir, instances of places where there was a bit of give in the cultural system. Equally, some men – a Clifton Webb, Marcel Carné, Rainer Werner Fassbinder – acquired a certain amount of cultural clout that allowed them to do queer things within the straight inclined structures they perforce worked within.

It is of course not just a matter of institutions but also of the languages and forms available. These delimit and deform what can be done, culturally – but they are also what makes doing possible at all. To understand queers in film noir or heritage cinema, say, we have to understand noir and heritage more generally. This means that there is no pure expression of queeritude, uncontaminated by an equally unalloyed straightness surrounding it. Thus camp in its many variants, clothes style, irony, the masculinities of homosexual porn and heritage movies all work with and within the wider culture, of which they are an ineluctable part. This with and within is even true where there is little or no question of marginality within a sector of cultural production, of heterocentric market presumptions or of hostility built into the very forms deployed: none of these apply to the self-consciously queer/gay and artistically independent films discussed in Chapter 2, yet they too do not float free from the mesh of queer and straight cultures in which they find themselves.

9

However, if there is no pure queer culture, straight constructions of queerness are also not so easy to find, if at all. At one level, it turns out to be hard to identify straight imaginings of queers in which no queers had a hand. The texts looked at in these essays are often situated within mainstream cultural production: *L'Air de Paris* is in many ways a run of the mill 1950s French movie drama, the *Carry On* films that provided Charles Hawtrey's main claim to fame were a huge national box office success story with a long afterlife on television. Yet the director of *L'Air* and Hawtrey were homosexual. Equally one would not wish to underestimate the importance of James M. Cain, Clifton Webb or Cornel Woolrich to film noir or of Merchant-Ivory to heritage cinema. Even when producers in the mainstream were not homosexual, leave alone queers, and often of course we just don't know such matters, they were nonetheless basing themselves on what some other queers had produced or assented to as their culture.

Just to make matters yet more complex, even saying what is mainstream is difficult and perhaps especially with texts featuring queers. Film noir for instance has some partially valid claim to being, as I discuss in the essay on it, an alternative cinema within Hollywood production; cheap paperback fiction of the type that featured sad young men is low both in critical prestige and in the best-seller stakes; heritage movies are at once nationally popular, internationally middle brow and critically despised. These examples suggest that the mainstream has many outer or insecure tributaries. On the other hand, some queerish production has its own form of mainstreaming – gay porn is a huge business, perfectly respectable within the confines of all porn's contested respectability, while Fassbinder is the defining figure in the international arthouse success New German Cinema.

The analysis of the relation between queer and straight traditions involves much fine tuning in every given instance, both in relation to questions of personnel and in relation to the languages and cultural frameworks available. Just as queer traditions were bricolaged in part out of straight, so straight culture was indelibly structured by queer. This does not mean that it's all mixed up and everything is everything. There is a felt difference – of weight, emphasis, tone, rather than sharply drawn contours or rigid formal differences – between queer and straight cultural production, and straight retains the prestige of normative sexuality, its felt centrality and taken for grantedness.

All this means that culture does not give us unmediated access to an uncontaminated queerness, because no culture is there to do that about anything and because queer and straight are neither exclusive nor equal categories. Culture does however tell us what was available to be thought and felt about being a queer.

All culture is always produced by relatively few people and of that only a tiny proportion gets even moderately wide circulation or has any staying power. Although part of the idea of queers was that they all tend to be artistic, the culture of queers too was, in fact, the product of a handful. At the same time, it was the available face of queerness, it was what was identifiable as queer. It did not actually represent all queers (as indeed nothing can actually represent all of anything) – but it was the public representation of queerness, it was what could be taken to be speaking for queers, expressing their/our perspective and sensibility, showing their/our lives and ways. Again, as it did not actually represent all queers, a fortiori it did not represent all men attracted to men – but it was available to be taken as doing so and probably was the dominant understanding of sexuality between men in the period.

There is no starting point in the processes of cultural construction. The culture of queers drew on the lifestyle, language, geographies and traditions of queers without being the only or full expression of these, and these things were themselves developed and moulded in response to the public representation of queerness. In some measure queers acted in certain ways because that's how the cultural imaginings of them proposed they/we act, but at the same time those imaginings were based on actual practices. Again, if queers acted, and even felt and thought, to some extent like the culture suggested they should, it was only to a certain extent, and the ways in which they broke with, undermined and played with the culture became, in turn, part of the raw material from and with which they handed on queer culture and others produced imaginings of them.

Actually living as a queer was always more than what was culturally constructed as queer. The latter always, like all imaginings, fell short of the complexity, fluidity, sheer extensiveness of reality. Yet just as it is wrong to think either that culture sets about telling you about life or that there is nothing outside culture, no nature, no givens, still it is the case that there is nothing cultural outside of culture. What is beyond culture is glimpsed and sensed, but the moment we even think about it to ourselves, leave alone speak, frame, perform it, it becomes cultural. The glimpse and the sense are the reasons culture is always being revised, toyed with, given fresh performances – culture never 'gets' life but it's also the only means we have to make any kind of sense of living at all.

For all the richness and complexity of queer culture, then, it also has to be seen as limited, partial, impure. In other words, typical culture.

In putting these essays together, I was drawing on essays that dealt either (the majority) exclusively with male homosexual culture or with male and female combined. I have retained the lesbian aspects of the essays on authorship, vampirism and Fassbinder, but I have not wanted to pass off the collection as a whole as dealing equally with lesbian culture in the age of queers. Much of what has been said above could be applied, *mutatis mutandis*, to lesbians, though, as my discussion of queers and gender has averred, no sexuality exists independently of constructions of gender and thus discussions of

11

lesbian queer culture could never be collapsed into discussions of an over-arching, ungendered queerness.

The book is organised as follows. The first three essays deal with general issues: the contours of queer culture, bringing out the differences and conti-nuities between it and later gay culture; the theoretical issues raised by talking at all in terms of a person's sexuality in relation to the culture he or she produces; the ways in which gay men are misogynistic. The next three are about topics (camp, fashion, vampires) that run throughout the age of queers. Thereafter the essays are presented in roughly chronological order according to subject matter. The last two deal with culture produced after Stonewall. One, on self-reflexivity in gay pornography, though I guess you could make arguments about its roots in the days of queers, is included because I would like to make it available to a wider audience. The last, on the other hand, on homosexuality in European heritage cinema, is a discus-sion of films made after Stonewall about gay/queer life before Stonewall and thus seems a nice way in which to conclude essays themselves written about queers in the light of the movement towards gay. It will be readily apparent that there is no claim to complete coverage and nor are the particular topics covered meant to be cases of some overarching philosophy or map of the culture of queers. (Film features disproportionately because that is what I know most about.)

At least two different ways of organising the book offered themselves. One was according to the kind of publication they were written for. In prac-tice the assigning of each to particular categories of publication and decid-ing the order in which to present them would have entailed all sorts of invidiousness. However, it is important to say something about it, for the essays are certainly very different in terms of tone, address and scholarship. The publishing contexts range from popular gay journalism (the 1970s soft porn magazine *Playguy* (camp), the 1990s lifestyle magazine *Attitude* (mis-ogyny, Charles Hawtrey)) through gay political publications (the Canadian monthly *The Body Politic* (Rock Hudson), a book produced by the Gay Left Collective ('Politics') and another coming out of the 1990s campaigning organisation Stonewall (fashion)) to more strictly academic contexts (vam-pires, noir, sad young men, *L'Air de Paris*, Fassbinder, pornography, her-itage). These distinctions though don't work perfectly. Many of the academic articles, for example, were also either originally developed for or else presented at lesbian and gay film festivals (noir, sad young men, Hawtrey, Hudson, porn, heritage), while the vampires were discussed at a lesbian and gay writers' festival. The essays on camp and Hudson have been reprinted in scholarly collections and one might characterise the Gay Left and Stonewall publications as trying to operate on the cusp of scholarship and politics (a cusp not to be confused with impenetrable academic work advertising its own political transgressiveness). It has been increasingly diffi-cult for British academics to operate on this cusp because of the pressures to produce work that 'counts' according to particular notions of intellectual respectability, but the ideal is still to bring scholarship to bear on popular writing and to allow the virtues of plainness and vivacity to inform academic writing.

A second way of organising the essays would have been in terms of when they were written.[2] However, while I have not interfered with the tone or argument of the essays, I have, where it seemed necessary, brought them up to date (corrected factual errors, incorporated more material) and also added suggestions for further reading. Some of the latter may move the argument on, sometimes in explicit disagreement with me, but I have not altered the essays to answer these points. Nonetheless, for the most part and accepting that all writing is historically contingent, I think the essays stand as valid in their own right and so I have not arranged them in order of composition.

Two essays though are more than usually caught up in the moment in which they were written. One is the essay on Fassbinder, which has not been brought up to date through a consideration of the films he made after the time the essay was written (1979) nor the welter of subsequent scholarship. This does not of itself invalidate the argument, but the essay is perhaps most significant for the account it gives of debates within the gay cultural criticism of the period. These relate to the other essay clearly marked by the moment of its composition, 'The Politics of Gay Culture', whose very title dates it – no-one writes about the politics of this or that nowadays. It explicitly addresses what it refers to as 'traditional gay culture' (the 'culture of queers' of this volume) from the perspective, and in the white heat, of gay politics. The essay was written in collaboration with Derek Cohen, and his contributions in particular (signalled in the essay) convey the excitement and importance then of culture and representations of being gay.

My own contribution to the 'Politics' essay is explicitly written by someone who grew up as a queer but went through gay liberation, and this perhaps indicates the position from which all the essays are written. I hope I have, to the degree to which one can, checked, corrected and tempered my accounts against the textual and contextual evidence of the topic at hand. Nevertheless, the essays are marked but also made possible by this: I remember being a queer and have never been entirely convinced that I ever became gay.

I should like to thank here those who commissioned or encouraged these pieces: Roger Baker, Diana Fuss, Susan Hayward and Ginette Vincendeau, Emma Healey and Angela Mason, Isaac Julien and Jon Savage, Pas Paschali, Susannah Radstone and Tony Rayns. My thanks also to Ann Kaplan, who twice commissioned pieces on women and film noir, which led to the essay here, and very special thanks to Derek Cohen, for allowing me to reprint our joint article, the product of a very happy collaboration.

Notes

1 Barbette was a drag trapeze artiste with the Barnum Circus in Paris in the first decades of the twentieth century, Crisp an artist's model in Britain in mid-century and later a celebrity through the success of the film based on his life, *The Naked Civil Servant*, Iacona is most famous internationally as one of the upfront queens in *La Dolce vita* (1960) but has been a personality on the Roman scene since the 1950s, Sarria was a drag artiste who ran for mayor in San Francisco in the 1950s, Sylvester was the falsetto star of 1970s disco, Thesiger was an actor more famous for doing needlepoint with Queen Mary and other such regal hobnobbing.
2 Two – noir and heritage – were written especially for this book. Noir does incorporate one or two passages from earlier writings on the topic.

Further reading

Bravmann, Scott (1997) *Queer Fictions of the Past: History, Culture and Difference*, Cambridge: Cambridge University Press.

Bronski, Michael (1984) *Culture Clash: The Making of a Gay Sensibility*, Boston: South End Press.

Butler, Judith (1991) 'Imitation and Gender Insubordination', in Fuss, Diana (ed.) *Inside/Out: Lesbian Theories, Gay Theories*, New York: Routledge, 13–31.

Castle, Terry (1996) *Noël Coward and Radclyffe Hall: Kindred Spirits*, New York: Columbia University Press.

Chauncey, George (1994) *Gay New York: Gender, Urban Culture and the Makings of the Gay Male World 1890–1940*, New York: Basic Books.

Cleto, Fabio (ed.) (1999) *Camp: Queer Aesthetics and the Performing Subject: A Reader*, Edinburgh: Edinburgh University Press.

Creekmur, Corey K. and Doty, Alexander (eds) (1995) *Out in Culture: Gay, Lesbian and Queer Essays on Popular Culture*, Durham, NC: Duke University Press.

Dall'Orto, Giovanni (1986) 'Omosessualità e cultura. Può esistere una "cultura omosessuale"?', in Delfino, Gianni (ed.) *Quando le nostre labbra si parlano*, Turin: Edizioni Gruppo Abele, 47–56.

De Lauretis, Teresa (1991) 'Queer Theory: Lesbian and Gay Studies, an Introduction', *Differences: A Journal of Feminist Cultural Studies* 3: 2, iii–xviii.

Doty, Alexander (1993) *Making Things Perfectly Queer: Interpreting Mass Culture*, Minneapolis: University of Minnesota Press.

Doty, Alexander (2000) *Flaming Classics: Queering the Film Canon*, New York: Routledge.

Gross, Larry and Woods, James D. (eds) (1999) *The Columbia Reader on Lesbians and Gay Men in Media, Society and Politics*, New York: Columbia University Press.

Jay, Karla and Young, Allen (eds) (1978) *Lavender Culture*, New York: Harcourt Brace Jovanovich.

Sedgwick, Eve Kossofsky (1990) *The Epistemology of the Closet*, Berkeley: University of California Press.

Sinfield, Alan (1994) *The Wilde Century: Oscar Wilde and the Queer Movement*, London, Cassell.

1

THE POLITICS OF GAY CULTURE

(co-written with Derek Cohen)

There are few moments of our lives when we are not assailed by the myriad forms of popular and select culture. Much of this is deemed superficial or a mere distraction, but whether it be television, theatre, music or advertising, culture at once shapes our identity, tells us about the world, gives us a certain set of values and entertains us. The purpose of this article is to examine gay culture and its politics.

Before doing this however we want briefly to consider a prior question – what are the *politics* of culture? All too often this phrase, familiar enough in recent years on the left, simply means drawing up a balance sheet as to how right-on such and such a work of art is. But this still leaves culture inert – an expression that we approve of (or not) from our political perspective, but not something that actually does political work in the world, alongside leafleting, demonstrating, lobbying, picketing and so on. Yet while culture cannot, as some cultural workers fondly hope, by itself change the world, as part of a programme of political work it has certain key functions to perform. To begin with, it has a role that necessarily precedes any self-conscious political movement. Works of art express, define and mould experience and ideas, and in the process makes them visible and available. They thus enable people to recognise experience as shared and to confront definitions of that experience. This represents the starting point for a forging of *identity* grounded in where people are situated in society, in whatever strata. This sense of social identity, of belonging to a group, is a prerequisite for any political activity proper, even when that identity is not recognised as political. This role for culture has perhaps a special relevance for gay people, because we are 'hidden' and 'invisible'. For many of us, reading about, say, David and Jonathan, or seeing *The Killing of Sister George*, is one of the few ways of identifying other homosexually inclined persons. Without that moment of identification, no other political practice is possible

Secondly, culture is part of that more conscious process of making sense of the world that all political movements are involved in. This process is the social group's production of *knowledge* about itself and its situation. Cultural production is more orientated to the affective, sensuous and experimental, whereas theory and research are more concerned with the analysis of situation, conjuncture, strategy and tactics – but both are forms of knowledge. Traditionally, analytic work is upgraded relative to cultural production, usually because the latter is considered to produce less useful knowledge. We do not need to detail here how crippling this restriction of knowledge to the analytical and cerebral has been – for our purposes, it is enough to insist on the role of culture in a group's total political intelligence.

Thirdly, all cultural production is some form of *propaganda*. We should not flinch at this word. While in practice much propaganda is simplistic and manipulative, it is not defined by these qualities. Rather propaganda is *committed* culture, which recognises its own committedness, and enjoins the audience to share its commitment. Political work is unthinkable without it. (All culture is committed, but most makes out that it is uncommitted. To be committed to non-commitment is at best fence-sitting and at worst acceding to the status quo.) Finally, related to but distinct from propaganda, culture is in general pleasurable. We tend to ignore *pleasure* as part of the business of politics – at our peril. At a minimum pleasure clearly allied to politics keeps us going, recharges our batteries. More positively, the pleasure of culture gives us a glimpse of where we are going and helps us to enjoy the struggle of getting there.

We shall be using these four concepts of the politics of culture – identity, knowledge, propaganda and pleasure – in the rest of this article. We begin by suggesting some working definitions of culture, and their particular relevance to homosexuality. In the next section, we look at what we term 'traditional' (predominantly male) gay culture and then in the following section consider contemporary 'radical' gay culture. In the final section we look at the relationship between these two modes of gay culture and what each has to learn from the other.

The distinction between 'traditional' and 'radical' gay cultural modes, though conceptually and historically valid, also springs from our two different experiences. This difference can best be indicated by the contrast in how we come out as gay – one of us by learning and adopting camp behaviour and taste before the advent of the gay liberation movement, the other coming out straight into the gay movement and the already altered gay world. For this reason, in the section on 'traditional' gay culture (largely written by Richard Dyer) and 'radical' gay culture (largely written by Derek Cohen), we draw on our respective personal experiences of growing up and coming out into these different cultural situations. As the area we are dealing with needs considerable research to move beyond the tentative ideas put forward here, we hope these personal accounts may serve as testimony for more sustained work in the future.

Any full definition of culture encompasses the products and practices of what Raymond Williams calls 'a whole way of life' (1961: 56). However here we confine ourselves to that area more or less loosely referred to as 'the arts'. These tend to be those things that are either produced (e.g. sculpture) or performed (e.g. dance), rather than experienced or transmitted (e.g. ways of talking).

There are two qualifications. First, we want to use the word 'culture' to avoid the snob connotations of the word 'art'. Second, culture in the narrow sense in which we are using it nevertheless depends upon and is part of culture in the wider sense of a whole way of life. Specifically in relation to gays and culture, and gay culture, what particular artefacts and performances mean, how they feel, depends upon how they are situated within the gay subculture(s). Drag acts depend for their appreciation upon an understanding of the semi-closeted gay atmosphere of many of the pubs and clubs where they are performed, and the ambiguous relationships of the men in the audience to the man/pseudo-woman on the stage. Many lesbian singers refer to aspects of gay life in their songs, and the powerful resonances come from the way they are touching on the lives of women in the audience.

In trying to do a review of gay culture it becomes apparent that there are other divisions within society which overlay gay people. The differences between lesbian and gay male culture reflect the different positions of women and men in society. Gay men have, for all their oppression, gained practically all the advantages of men generally. Men's work is valued above the work of women, even when that work is identical (men are chefs, women just cook), and this is also true of cultural production. Men have always had greater access to culture, both as producers, where their greater material assets have enabled them to have a greater access to resources, and as consumers, with men having more leisure time as compared with the all-consuming domestic labour of women. Thus while we may be able to identify, through history, homosexual tendencies in artists, sculptors, writers etc., these are far more often men. Lesbian culture has suffered from the same invisibility as women's culture generally, and is emerging within that framework.

Class is another largely determining factor in culture. If we use definitions of culture which preclude those things which are at the same time associated with work, which concentrate on the fine arts, theatre, opera, ballet etc., working-class culture becomes invisible. Once we extend into work-associated culture, we find many examples of working-class culture, from barge-painting to ornamentation in architecture to street cries and drinking songs. We know about the historical development of culture by what lasts, and by and large what is made to last is élite culture. Gays seeking their roots are bound to use élite cultures as part of their so-called heritage, and the lack of working-class culture in this heritage reinforces the tendency to upwards mobility among gay men.

Traditional gay male culture

If one turns to the centre pages of *Gay News*,[1] one finds the 'culture' section. Anyone unfamiliar with the gay scene might be forgiven for finding this section puzzling in some regards. It's obvious enough why there should be reviews of plays, books and films that deal with homosexuality in their subject matter, or else are known to have been produced by gay people. But why all these other reviews, page after page of reviews of classical records, ballet, cabaret artists etc.? Although it is certainly the case that gays have no more instinct for culture than any other group in society, *Gay News* moved swiftly and unerringly to this broad coverage of its pages, as indeed have other gay publications. Such publishing ventures grew out of the tastes of a metropolitan male gay milieu; *Gay News* and the rest helped to solidify and define this culture as gay culture itself, and hence to reinforce the notion that this culture, very narrowly rooted in social terms, is what gays turn to spontaneously.

In literature, the characteristic mode of gay cultural production has been that of the minor literati, e.g. Christopher Isherwood, Robin Maugham, J. R. Ackerley. These are gay men working within established middle-class literary modes, and writing very 'well' within them, but always restricting their literary ambitions to the small-scale and exquisite.

The arts of opera, ballet, certain painters and sculptors and antiques, have for so long been thought of as gay preserves that, for instance, Noel Coward could make a risqué reference in his adaptation of Cole Porter's song 'Let's Do It' by singing 'Nice young men who sell antiques/Do it'. These arts have, like that of the minor literati, an ambiguous place in bourgeois high culture. Recognised as Art, and subsidised as such, there is still a strong current of opinion that does not quite take them seriously as Art – not compared to the kind of non-musical theatre subsidised by the Arts Council or the kinds of art hung and displayed in national and municipal galleries. Ballet – with its association with women as well as gay men – has suffered particularly from this ambiguity.

Not all traditional gay male culture is highbrow, however. Show business traditions, especially cabaret and musicals (stage and screen), are part of the canon. Among the most characteristic icons here are the flamboyant/tragic singers such as Judy Garland, Diana Ross *et al.* (compare the repertoire of Craig Douglas in the film *Outrageous!* (Canada 1977)). Central here are drag and camp, the most well-known and obvious aspects of traditional gay male culture in its showbiz inflection. Finally, somewhere between highbrow Art and showbiz come the areas of 'taste', such as couture, coiffure and interior decoration.

Before proceeding, it is worth stressing that this set of cultural artefacts and practices is not identical with the work of gay artists and cultural workers. On the contrary, some of the above may have been produced by non-homosexual women and men, while much culture produced by gay men clearly stands outside, or in an ambivalent relationship to, the gay subcultural mainstream under discussion here. The many gay male ballet dancers and choreographers do not seem to have made many inroads on the heterosexual assumptions of most ballet scenarios and forms of movement. Traditional gay culture essentially refers to a distinct way of reading and enjoying culture, and hence involves both gay and non-gay products.

For me, growing up gay and getting into this sort of culture felt like the same process, namely the process of establishing an identity. It was summed up for me in the word 'queer'. Being queer meant being homosexual, but also being different. It is easy to see how easily I formed an equation between this and being interested in culture. In an all-boys school in the late fifties and early sixties, culture was as peculiar, as 'other', as being queer. To begin with, the connection between culture and queerness was spatial: culture seemed to be a place where you were allowed to be queer. This is partly because I had picked up on the folklore about cultural milieux being full of, or tolerating, queers. Ballet and hairdressing above all, but coteries of painters and writers, for instance, were supposed to be very queer. At a minimum, the world of culture just seemed to be a place you could go if you were queer.

My sense that this was a place for me was confirmed by three people. One was a teacher at school, whose shelves were full of books like *Mr Norris Changes Trains* and *Death in Venice*, books which he lent me and I read avidly as I have never read books since for their revelations of decadence. But the real point was that they were Penguin Modern Classics – they were Art, not just books. This teacher also implied a knowledge of gay cultural circles and when he got married (an event which rather confused me) I went to the wedding party and met a poet, a composer, an actor, all queer. The culture-queerness connection was made, and it was confirmed by the first man who ever picked me up. He took me home to a flat in Chelsea full of books and paintings. He and his flatmate discussed cultural matters that meant nothing to me, but impressed me. Eventually I asked him what he did for a living. 'I'm a writer,' he replied. 'What sort of things do you write?' I asked. 'Novels.' 'What sort?' 'Surrealist.' (Again, not just books.) 'What's that mean?' 'Do you know Kafka?' 'Ye-es.' 'Well, it's like that.' Third, my first real friend who was gay had been in the theatre, although he then ran a coffee bar. In a way, Michael was different because what he was really into was showbiz, but the point was that he was from the world of culture. All queers were in those days.

Culture was the place to go – and a way out. The attraction of culture, to begin with, was just that it was an apparently liberal, tolerant milieu, where you could be queer. That much I had picked up from gossip and the mass media, as well as my few encounters with other queers. (The gossip included the usual dirt on Shakespeare, Wilde, Tchaikovsky, Gielgud and the rest;

but I also remember eagerly reading Freud's book on Leonardo da Vinci, without any knowledge of psychoanalysis, while on a school trip to Italy.) Homosexuality was also the subject-matter of a fair amount of literature, to an extent that was not true of the kind of films I had access to, or of television. (I remember the curious sense of pride I felt when in my first term at university the lecturer spoke about the importance of homosexuality in understanding André Gide.) There was no place else that I could identify as 'riddled with it', no place that seemed at least to accord queerness recognition.

Culture was also attractive in ways that went beyond the fact that its practitioners and subject-matter were queer, but ways which were still crucially related to queerness. Culture was beautiful, sensuous, fun. This is true anyway, as is people's use of it as escape. My involvement in culture certainly included enjoyment and escape, but the kind of culture I got into accorded more precisely with what I thought about being queer. I was into high culture. Actually, I found this quite an effort – I was really into the *idea* of high culture, while in practice preferring Michael's showbiz. I didn't come from an artistic or even particularly cultured background, and although I got myself into 'serious' music and literature, I never had any spontaneous response to painting and sculpture. But nevertheless I thought of myself as someone capable of appreciating high culture. I would sit painfully through Antonioni films and assure everyone of how 'beautiful' they were. I was keen on things being beautiful.

All this was connected to being queer; indeed, it was part of being queer. Queerness brought with it artistic sensitivity – it gave you the capacity to appreciate and respond to culture. It was a compensation for having been born or made queer; it was a positive to set beside the negative of being queer, with which it was inextricably bound up. Being into beauty was also part and parcel of the mechanism of self-oppression, because I defined my cultural sensitivity as a compensatory product of being queer. It also made you doubly 'different' – queer and cultured. And how splendid to be different! Even if you were awful.

This sense of being different certainly locked me into ways of thinking about myself – as queer, as cultured – which reinforced my self-oppression, for further reasons that I will explore in a moment. But it did have relatively positive consequences, too. It made me feel myself as outside the mainstream in fundamental ways – and this does give you a kind of knowledge of the mainstream you cannot have if you are immersed in it. I do not necessarily mean a truer perspective, so much as an awareness of the mainstream as a mainstream, and not just the way everything and everybody inevitably are; in other words, it denaturalises normality. This knowledge is the foundation of camp, to which I took like a duck to water, since camp is so much about the exaggeration and send-up of normality. Camp's roots in showbiz also gave it a vitality that saved it from the rather anaemic qualities of some of the high gay culture. Feeling different also gave me identity, a real sense of queers as a social group – an advantage later on when I got into the gay movement, although actually a rather problematical concept, since homo-sexuality is so much more fluid an aspect of human beings than class, gender or race.

One other thing needs to be said about the attractions of the artistic = queer = different equation, namely, its snobbism. As best, being different and proud of it gave me a defence against the blandishments of the middle-class, masculine society around me – who wants to be like *that*? But because it involved getting into high culture, at least notionally, it meant getting into bourgeois culture, and of the most apolitical sort. This was ulti-mately the problem for me and perhaps why I never took this gay route out all the way. I loathed the middle classes in a way that only those brought up by them can; and culture is curiously placed in relation to them, despised and honoured at the same time. I found too that gay men who were really into high culture could be extraordinarily reactionary and snobbish. I do not want to give the impression that I was a worked-out, right-on socialist from the cradle; but I did 'care about' the poor and the starving, about war and privilege. I could not sort it all out – being into culture and against privi-lege – but I was never able to hold both things together, and in the process high art lost out, somewhat.

Culture was not just an attractive place to go, it also seemed the right place. I have already mentioned that artistic sensitivity seemed to be part of what being queer was all about. It gave one a sense of beauty, a sense of being outside – and a sense of pain. The kind of poetry I liked at the time was full of the melancholy recognition of the awfulness of the world. A. E. Housman was the perfect poet for me to come across (introduced to me by a closet gay French teacher who kept quoting him in lessons) with its melan-choly allusions to being queer, along with other sad things. 'Melancholy' was one of my favourite words; I felt it summed up my condition, for it caught – and here is the real trap – that peculiar mixture of pain and beauty that I took to be the 'condition' of homosexuality. In other words, artistic melancholy, part of being queer, reconciled me and even bound me to that very definition of homosexuality encapsulated in the word queer.

But the rightness of being cultured and hence queer, or vice-versa, went further into an area I still have not disentangled. Somehow to me cultural sensitivity was 'feminine'; and being queer was not being a man – that was why the two went together. This obviously involves a particular conception of male homosexuality (and of course of femininity); it also involves a particular conception of culture, precisely by linking it to femininity. It stresses culture as concerned with social manners and domesticity (not work, or Big Subjects); culture is expressive, not useful or instrumental; culture is affective, sensuous, even passionate, but not intelligent or, perhaps, finally serious. This way of seeing culture – which means attending especially to certain kinds of culture – raises theoretical and empirical questions and political ones. The former require elaboration and research, to come to grips with how culture is placed in relation to gender in this society. The political questions are contradictory. It is clear that, as I experienced it then, the equation of artistic queerness with femininity downgraded both femininity and me. I negate myself by identifying with women (hence refusing my bio-logical sex), and then put myself down by internalising the definition of female qualities as inferior – for the values I was brought up with were those of work, instrumentality and seriousness, values I still feel the pull of. Yet, with the women's and gay movements, it became possible to turn these values on their heads while preserving that art-gayness-femininity link. Only now one was asserting the inherent seriousness of 'small' subjects (in the slogan, 'the personal is political'), identifying the repressiveness of a life so focused on instrumentality and seriousness, so afraid of or unable to handle emotion and sensuality.

The traditional gay male culture was never knowingly political, and fully effective political movements have to be self-conscious movements. Never-theless, this traditional culture did and does have political significance. It provided a space and, however maimed, a definition/recognition of homosex-uality, and thus constituted one homosexual identity. There is real know-ledge there, too. Directly, traditional gay culture has the capacity to see and feel the constructedness of gender identities, role play and sexual behaviour, to respond to sensuousness and fun. We can also gain knowledge from it (if we pose the right questions of it) about how self-oppression works, the rela-tion between culture and gender and so on. Finally, and not opportunisti-cally, the fact is that many gay men are into this form of culture, for better or worse, and thus it is in a manner part of the constituency of gay politics. It is one of the languages in which propaganda can speak; it is one of the grounds in which the pleasure of politics can be rooted. Whatever its limita-tions, we have to work with it in order to move beyond it.

Radical gay culture

The same period which saw the emergence of a self-defining, self-asserting gay identity, as opposed to a furtive or concealed homosexual one, also saw the beginnings of attempts to bring together the isolated experiences of les-bians and gay men that had for so long been separated. Visual, written and performance arts were seen as channels through which those who had 'come out' and who had some positive things to say about their experiences as homosexuals could communicate to others, whether they were gay or not.

This self-conscious culture differs from the traditional one, even when this is on rare occasions affirming of homosexuality, in its ability to look critically at our experiences without being condemning, to be self-aware rather than descriptive from the outside. The reason for this lies, most obviously, in the fact that the (homo)sexuality of the artists is an integral, rather than incidental or hidden aspect of the work. In the film *Word is Out* many of the lesbians and gay men who spoke about their experiences talked of the role-playing that used to go on between gay couples, and as a viewer I felt that these gay people were not putting down those experiences, but speaking from a more self-aware, less constrained position. The lesbian theatre group *Hormone Imbalance*'s satire of lesbian stereotypes extended well beyond their name (a reference to a supposed cause of lesbianism) to a chilling song by Lottie and Ada called 'You Don't Know What It's Like to Be Revolting', portraying the very worst fears of what lesbians are like: predatory, deranged, 'dildo users, child abusers . . .'. The Brixton Faeries' play about the Jeremy Thorpe case,[2] *Minehead Revisited*, was created not out of a sense of revelling in the misfortunes of someone famous, but because the case was having consequences in the daily lives of the actors. The company felt able to respond to the Thorpe affair, where gay activists felt caught between wanting to condemn Thorpe's tactics whilst not consequently putting down his homosexuality. Lesbian and gay male singers can assert that it's not enough just to come out, even to be a conventional commercially successful out gay rock star like Tom Robinson. One must, like Ova (a lesbian duo), challenge the very concepts of being successful in terms that are defined by male heterosexual values. Rather than try to compile some sort of list of alternative gay cultures, it seems more useful to look first at what marks off radical gay culture from non-radical treatments of homosexuality, and secondly to look at ways in which gays have tried to exploit cultural production and consumption in a political way.

Whereas much conventional handling of homosexuality in the arts works by introducing gay characters or images into an otherwise heterosexual milieu, radical gay culture defines its own situation. A lesbian or gay character in a TV play (or even soap opera series) does not constitute gay culture. We are presented there as objects to be consumed. Radical gay culture sees our *experiences* as being central. In a paradoxical sense, as one of the essentials of our experience as gays is our alienation from society, any culture which attempts in some liberal way to include us fails to portray our experiences accurately. That very assimilation, as if we were the same as everyone else but different in one minor way, shows a preoccupation with the surfaces, with the physicality of our homosexuality, and not the dynamics of our interaction with the rest of society. For if even literal straight culture were to recognise that interaction for what it is, an oppressive one, it would also have to recognise its own role in that oppression.

Even where an appreciation of the experience of being outside is allowed, it is compartmentalised, almost sanitised. This week a gay character, next week a black one. For example, the kind of fuss that attended the presentation of a television play about men (*Coming Out*[3]) reveals just the separation that we are challenging. We will know that we are gaining ground when serious presentation of our oppression on TV is such a commonplace that it coheres with the rest of the characterisations and presentations. At such time productions will only make sense if the forces we fight against are also presented seriously and accurately. However, commercially motivated arts do not present and endorse material that is critical of their own practice, including their contributions to gay oppression.

Radical gay culture can play a key role in the development of a gay identity. When I started coming out, one of the handicaps I had to overcome was having only a stereotypical view of what gays were like and how they lived. Thus I was quite fortunate that at that time the original 'Homosexual Acts' season started at the Almost Free Theatre in London. Those plays presented a number of scenarios of gay men's lives. They served a number of functions for me. First, they were informative, conveying the dynamics of gay men's lives – jealousy, seduction, loneliness, comradeship etc. While talking to other gay men might have given me some ideas about how they lived and conducted their relationships, unless I knew some of them quite well (which I didn't) I would not have gained much deep insight into the joys and conflicts of being gay and relating to other gay men. Those plays provided me with that privileged view of some (fictional) lives.

That season of plays also provided a focus for meeting other gay people. A season that was so blatant in its declaration of the subject of the plays was bound to attract a high proportion of gays, and there was a chance to feel, for that period at least, that there was something of a shared positive experience among the audience. The characters in some of the plays enjoined us to share their good feelings and their bad ones. As I remember, some of the plays involved sequences where the characters addressed either the audience as a whole or supposed members of it. Homosexuality was not something being examined in a test tube, separate from reality, but as an experience shared by the characters and the audience. In addition, the season was something I could take my non-gay friends to, an entertainment where, for once, *I* was on home ground.

The close link between performers and audience meant not just that culture was close to me, but also that I was close to culture. The easier access to these performers meant that I could bask, ever so slightly, in the glow of their fame.

This is not to idealise the season; all the actors denied that they were gay and some parts of the plays were extremely self-oppressive. The achievement and the power was in having a season called 'Homosexual Acts' – the word was on the streets not in the form of political sloganeering or snide media abuse, but as an integral part of entertainment.

When gay people define their own artistic environments, as opposed to slotting in to traditional ones, they can move beyond art which is purely description from the outside. An exhibit at a gay photographic exhibition contrasted a collage of photographs of naked men from porn magazines with a picture of a line of naked gay men arm in arm at a gay men's weekend. We could note more than the difference in posture, and reflect on the contradictions in our own lives as gay men between the objectification we often promote of other men's bodies and the pleasure we can experience in just being with other gay men in a close physical situation. The basic acceptance of homosexuality which permeates radical gay culture allows us to question ourselves and be challenged by that culture into new ways of thinking. For gays in small towns who cannot support many of their own gay cultural events, the visit of a gay theatre group or musicians, for example, can provide a focus for the start of further development of local activities. The small scale of much gay culture, arising partly out of financial necessity, enables it to be mobile and to counter the concentration of good events in the big cities.

Because radical gay culture is rooted in both a radical tradition and a cultural one, it can challenge us to reconsider the notions we have accepted of homosexuality (our own), politics and entertainment as being separate elements in our lives. Pleasure, propaganda and the personal can be combined in one experience.

The contemporary scene[4]

In order to make our point at all, we have had to pose the traditional and radical gay cultures as being utterly separate. They are distinguishable phenomena, but we need now to look at inter-relations, overlaps and blurred edges, especially in the contemporary scene.

For a start, the very terms 'traditional' and 'radical' need qualifying. The traditional culture is not necessarily reactionary (as its opposition to radical might seem to imply), it has simply been around longer and is not defined by its self-conscious political orientation. The traditional culture could be very radical, whether in terms of artistic innovation (e.g. Diaghilev, Eisenstein), political affiliation (e.g. Oscar Wilde, André Gide, Christopher Isherwood) or simply in being blatantly homosexual (e.g. Quentin Crisp, many drag acts). Equally, 'radical' as a term covers a multitude of differences. There is radicalism that links sexual politics to other kinds of politics (e.g. Tom Robinson, Lesbian Left Revue) and radicalism that confines itself to the assertion and development of gay identities (e.g. *Word is Out*,[5] *The Front Runner*[6]). There is radicalism that remains aesthetically conservative (e.g. *Outrageous!*,[7] *Bent*[8]) and that which is formally innovative (Virginia Woolf, Joe Orton). There is radicalism whose style and tone derive basically from other, not gay, forms of radical culture production (e.g. *The Dear Love of Comrades*,[9] Barbie Norden[10]), and radicalism that is deeply and/or ambivalently involved in traditional gay cultural forms (*As Time Goes By*,[11] the Brixton Faeries,[12] *Nighthawks*[13]).

These overlaps in the meanings of the terms 'traditional' and 'radical' tally with the actual inter-relations between the two streams, since the emergence of the radical culture with the development of gay liberation politics in the seventies. We will consider briefly here the use of the traditional culture by the radical, the impact of radical gay politics on the traditional culture, and the emergence of a third stream of gay culture.

As has already been noted, much radical gay culture has drawn on the traditional culture for its imagery. This can be traced back to cultural production before the advent of gay liberation, for instance in the underground films of Andy Warhol, Kenneth Anger, Jack Smith, Ron Rice and others. While by no means socialist, nor informed by gay liberation ideas (how could they be?), such films were rooted both in gay male imagery and lifestyles and in the concerns of avant-garde film-making, and the latter acted back on the former in different ways so that these films were not simply another example of gay culture but in a kind of dialogue with it, now ironic, now critical, now celebratory. It is this creative tension between the traditional and the radical forms that characterises some of the most interesting contemporary work. Gay Sweatshop's men's company from *Mister X*[14] to *As Time Goes By* remained ambivalently – but also productively – locked into certain traditions of theatrical and cinematic camp. Jan Oxenburg's film *Comedy in Six Unnatural Acts* (USA 1975) draws on a whole range of references, from camp, the lesbian subculture and the mass media, in an exploration of the definitions and understandings of that social category, the lesbian. Such examples are not only using a language many gay people can feel is their own, but are also working on it, examining it, helping us to reflect on it.

Not all the radical gay culture is informed by this, nor would we want it to be. Oxenburg notwithstanding, it does seem that lesbian radical culture in particular has developed in a rather different direction to gay male radical culture. Lesbian radical culture is a component of feminist culture, and particularly the adaptation of the confessional novel (e.g. *Rubyfruit Jungle*,[15] Marge Piercy) and contemporary folk songs (e.g. Holly Near, Chris Williamson) that characterise much feminist cultural production. These two forms lend themselves to a feminist inflection: the novel is one of the few art forms to which women have always had relatively greater access and which is to a large degree defined by a socially developed approach to the personal and the individual (as feminism is); contemporary folk songs not only had women stars from early on (Joan Baez, Judy Collins, Joni Mitchell) and deploys readily available artistic means (voice and simple guitar), but is associated with the peace movement and its receptivity to 'feminine' ideas (hippy lifestyle, flower power, etc.). One can even present this difference between lesbian and gay male radical culture as a polarisation of sensibilities: the emphasis on self-reflexivity and artifice in camp, the stress on authenticity (the hallmark of the confessional novel) and naturalness (the folk song ethos) in feminist culture.[16] While this would ignore key overlap figures, it is a real difference of tendency between the two.

The radical gay cultures relate in different ways to the traditional, now working on it, now ignoring it and finding a more valid reference point in progressive and alternative cultural modes outside the gay world. The kind of politics that informs this radical gay culture has also had an impact on the continued life of the traditional culture. It has even given the traditional culture a new confidence in itself. *Gay News*, *After Dark*, *Mandate*, *Q*, *Blueboy* and other such publications continue to find opera, old Hollywood and so on their most salient cultural reference points, but this goes along with a degree of campaigning (or at any rate complaint) and an acknowledgement that the readership is homosexual (though *After Dark* is still uneasy about this). Unlike the Brixton Faeries or *Comedy in Six Unnatural Acts*, this new confidence rarely extends to taking a critical distance from the traditional culture – it merely asserts the homosexual connection where previously it was implicit: it seldom asks why this connection is there, or what it means.

Between the growth of the radical gay cultures and the renewal of the traditional, and perhaps as a result of them, there has been the emergence of a gay mainstream culture, operating in neither the alternative modes of the radical culture nor the subcultural languages of the traditional. This mainstream culture signals the presence of gay expression in the wider general culture of the society, and it takes three forms in particular. First, there is the increased and confident use of straight artistic forms for gay content: the detective novel (e.g. Joseph Hansen), the sentimental/romantic novel (e.g. *The Front Runner*, Gordon Merrick), the thriller movie (*Dog Day Afternoon*, the TV movie *The Ice Palace*). These of course are no longer necessarily gay culture, in the sense of being produced directly out of a gay experience or perspective. Their value is hard to assess too – they do insist on the humanity of gay people, on the possibility of having gays as heroes or at any rate people you can identify with – but the price is often the avoidance of the gay liberation politics of experimentation with gender identities and lifestyles, and of a wider vision of social and sexual transformation. It is hard to know whether we can move beyond the immediate value the mainstream culture offers of helping us to feel good about ourselves and to see ourselves as having a social role, or whether this very quality does not precisely block off more completely the wider perspective.

Second, television programmes such as *Rock Follies* (Thames TV 1976–7) and *Soap* (ABC TV 1977–81), themselves relatively experimental in terms of television, have been able to include gay characters whose lives have been treated with the same seriousness (or lack of it) as the other characters, while at the same time always holding on to the specificities of being gay. Because these programmes have developed new forms of narrative and characterisation they are more easily able to sidestep the usual unquestioned heterosexist assumptions of what is good family entertainment.

The other mainstream development has to be disco culture. Although not always visibly gay – even Sylvester and Village People need not be perceived in that light – it has established not only a form of social recreation but an aesthetic that is unthinkable apart from notions of gay culture. It draws heavily on black music and dance, and on white (heterosexual) popular songs, but equally it is informed by the theatricalism, sensuality and fun of traditional male gay culture and something of the rethinking of sexuality occasioned by the sexual politics of the seventies (though it is not yet clear whether 'liberation', or its patriarchal capitalist version, 'permissiveness', is what disco ultimately asserts).

There is a sense in which all these developments – the radical gay cultures, the continuing traditional male gay culture and the new mainstream forms – are politically significant and even to a degree to be welcomed. At a minimum they further help establish homosexual identities, which we can work with, or if need be against, politically. They are all identifiably homosexual, while at the same time offering a variety of ways of socially expressing and communicating their different roots, and they provide us with a wider knowledge of how it feels – how it *can* feel – to be queer, lesbian, homosexual, gay, and hence a wider field for investigation of how people live out and make sense of their sexuality. It is important to listen to this variety of gay cultural voices, and not to think that the one we individually use most comfortably is *the* voice of gay culture. We must listen for the knowledge of each other and of social definitions that they contain; and we must use the voices, in propaganda, to widen the constituency of gay and sexual politics. We must acknowledge the different pleasures that each form offers, and hence embrace their manifold political potential. This is not to say that anything goes, that anything which comes vaguely under the banner of gay culture is fine and wonderful. Rather we would want to say that within the distinctions between the broad *kinds* of gay culture that we have outlined, there is politically effective and politically ineffective, reactionary and revolutionary cultural production. But at the most general level each has much to learn from the other: the political vision and daring of the radical culture and the mass appeal of the mainstream, the awareness of artifice of the traditional culture and the commitment to authenticity of the radical. It is starting within these terms, taking each mode at its strongest point, that a socialist gay culture is constructed.

Acknowledgement

From Gay Left Collective (eds): *Homosexuality: Power and Politics*, London: Allison and Busby, 1980.

Notes

1 British fortnightly gay and lesbian newspaper 1972–82.
2 Leader of British Liberal Party, who in 1979 was tried and acquitted on a charge of conspiracy to murder related to homosexual blackmail.

3 BBC 10.4.79; see Howes 1993: 135.

4 When originally written, all the references in this section were readily familiar to most readers. Here I have identified titles in footnotes (unless the context makes clear what they are), but only where I have judged them to be now particularly obscure have I identified names. On the lesbian and gay culture of this period, see Jay and Young 1978, and on film Dyer 1990: 211–286, on literature Woods 1998 and Zimmerman 1991, on music Gill 1995, on painting Cooper 1986: 238ff, 266ff, on theatre Sinfield 1999.

5 Documentary film, USA 1977, Mariposa Film Collective.

6 Novel, Patricia Nell Warren, 1974.

7 Feature film, Canada 1977, Richard Benner.

8 Play, Martin Sherman, 1979.

9 Play, Noel Greig 1979, performed by radical theatre group Gay Sweatshop.

10 Lesbian stand-up comic.

11 Play, Noel Greig and Drew Griffiths 1977, performed by Gay Sweatshop.

12 Radical theatre group, whose shows included *Minehead Revisited* (on the Thorpe trial) and *Gents* (on cottaging).

13 Feature film, GB 1978, Ron Peck and Paul Hallam.

14 Roger Baker and Drew Griffiths 1974.

15 Novel, Rita Mae Brown, 1973.

16 While some specific references in this article may now merely be obscure, this observation seems the most dated. The lesbian feminist culture alluded to here may have seemed or even been hegemonic at the time (and see Cooper 1986: 238ff, Dyer 1990: 174–210 for discussion of it), but the picture has vastly changed since (cf. Hamer and Budge 1994, Clark 1995, Graham 1995 and Smyth 1995).

References

Clark, Danae (1995) 'Commodity Lesbianism', in Creekmur, Corey K. and Doty, Alexander (eds) *Out in Culture: Gay, Lesbian and Queer Essays on Popular Culture*, Durham NC: Duke University Press, 484–500.

Cooper, Emmanuel (1986) *The Sexual Perspective: Homosexuality and Art in the Last 100 Years in the West*, London: Routledge & Kegan Paul.

Dyer, Richard (1990) *Now You See It: Studies on Lesbian and Gay Film*, London: Routledge.

Gill, John (1995) *Queer Noises: Male and Female Homosexuality in Twentieth-Century Music*, London: Cassell.

Graham, Paula (1995) 'Girl's Camp? The Politics of Parody', in Wilton, Tamsin (ed.) *Immortal, Invisible: Lesbians and the Moving Image*, London: Routledge, 163–181.

Hamer, Diane and Budge, Belinda (eds) (1994) *The Good, the Bad and the Gorgeous: Popular Culture's Romance with Lesbianism*, London: Pandora.

Howes, Keith (1993) *Flaunting It: An Encyclopaedia of Homosexuality on Film, Radio and TV in the UK 1923–1993*, London: Cassell.

Jay, Karla and Young, Allen (eds) *Lavender Culture*, New York: Harcourt Brace Jovanovich.

Sinfield, Alan (1999) *Out on Stage: Lesbian and Gay Theatre in the Twentieth Century*, New Haven: Yale University Press.

Smyth, Cherry (1995) 'The Transgressive Sexual Subject', in Burston, Paul and Richardson, Colin (eds) *A Queer Romance: Lesbians, Gay Men and Popular Culture*, London: Routledge, 123–143.

Williams, Raymond (1961) *The Long Revolution*, London: Chatto and Windus.

Woods, Gregory (1998) *A History of Gay Literature: The Male Tradition*, New Haven: Yale University Press.

Zimmerman, Bonnie (1991) *The Safe Sea of Women: Lesbian Fiction 1969–1989*, Boston MA: Beacon Press/London: Onlywomen Press.

2

BELIEVING IN FAIRIES

The author and the homosexual

A student once said of me to a colleague, 'Of course, Richard doesn't believe in authors – unless the author is a woman'. He or she might have added 'black' or 'lesbian/gay', but it was an acute remark. I'll happily teach *The Searchers* (John Ford) as a John Wayne movie about race, but as soon as it's *Dance, Girl, Dance* (Dorothy Arzner) or *Car Wash* (Michael Schultz) I'm wanting students to worry about whether you can tell they were directed by a woman and a black person, respectively, and how, and whether it matters. (Note already, however, the discrepancies: Ford is banished as Ford, but Arzner and Schultz come back emblematically as woman and black; then there's the unaddressed whiteness of Arzner, the maleness of Schultz, the white maleness of Ford, the sexualities of all three...) Equally most of my writing has been about images and representations, texts and readers, yet I have just finished a book on films made by lesbians and gay men (Dyer 1990), a book posited, that is, on the notion that it does make a difference who makes a film, who the authors are. In this essay I want to think through some of the implications of what that student observed, relating it to a further apparent paradox, a commitment to lesbians and gay men and an acceptance that being lesbian/gay is 'only' a social construction. I do this through an account of some of the problems and discoveries I had writing the book just mentioned.

The project was haunted by two politically and theoretically dubious figures: the author and the homosexual. Worries about these figures are most easily authorised by reference to the formulations of two homosexual theorists, Roland Barthes's pronouncement of the death of the author and Michel Foucault's labelling of the homosexual as a social construction. These texts crystallised wider intellectual and political misgivings about both figures, misgivings that I shared.

As far as the author is concerned, reference to him/her in the study of the arts privileged the individual over the social and in practice privileged heterosexual, white, upper-/middle-class male individuals over all others. Texts were often treated, at worst, as illustrations of the author's biography, at best as the expression of his inner life, flying in the face of both the evident discrepancy between most authors' persons and their texts and also the vast range of public functions cultural production performs. In the interpretation of texts, the author was used as a means of fixing and giving weight to particular interpretations, rather than acknowledging the multiplicity of meanings and affects that readers generate from texts. In short, the author was an authority concept, anti-democratic in its triumphant individualism, a support of existing social divisions, hostile to public discourses, and resistant to the creativity of the reader.

The homosexual, when treated as a universal figure in human societies, also posed problems of authority, if by contrast one saw him/her as a social construction, a personality type characteristic of and probably unique to modern Western societies. Work that sought to establish the continuity of lesbian/gay identity across time and culture seemed to be imposing the way lesbian/gay sexuality is for 'us' now upon the diversity and radical differences of both the past and 'other' (non-white, Third World) cultures and often to be eliding the differences between lesbians and gay men. The notion of the homosexual seemed to buy into the very operation of power through the regulation of desire that lesbian/gay politics and theory were supposed to be against. It also seemed to sail too close to the wind of the kind of biological etiologies of homosexuality that had been used against same-sex relations and, by holding up a model of what we inexorably are, to deprive us of the political practice of determining what we wanted to be.

This last misgiving gives the social constructionist position its political edge over the apparently more inspiring universalist positions on homosexuality. While the latter seem to have more immediate political power to mobilise people round an identity apparently rooted in an essential human type, social constructionism returns control over same-sex sexuality to those who live it. It does this by identifying the fact that the latter are not generally those currently in control of it and indicating the cases and ways in which they are or can be. Those cases and ways include forms of cultural production – but one can have no concept of socially specific forms of cultural production without some notion of authorship, for what one is looking at are the circumstances in which counter-discourses are produced, in which those generally spoken of and for speak for themselves.

I want here to suggest some of the ways in which I tried to work with a model of the author and the homosexual that takes on board the misgivings indicated above. I'll begin by sketching this model and suggesting the ways in which it is useful in trying to conceptualise lesbian/gay cultural production before looking at the ways I found it helpful in the historical analysis of lesbian/gay films and the ways in which the model itself informs and animates many of the texts of those films.

I'm not sure that I ever believed (since I left school) in either the author or the homosexual in quite the way attacks on them presented them.[1] If believing in authorship (in film) means believing that only one person makes a film, that that person is the director, that the film expresses his/her inner personality, that this can be understood apart from the industrial circumstances and semiotic codes within which it is made, then I have never believed in authorship. If believing in lesbians and gay men means believing that they/we have existed as particular kinds of persons at all times and in all places, that what they/we have been like has been pretty much the same in ditto, that being lesbian/gay automatically gives one a particular way of looking at the world and expressing that, then I have never believed in fairies. I sometimes underestimate the extent to which anyone at all believes either in authors or gays and lesbians in those ways, and am brought up sharp by people's readiness to credit a shot in a film to the director's sexual life or to assume that all lesbians identify with the Amazons and all gay men love Judy Garland. But I also think professional intellectuals are inclined to overestimate the extent to which those who went before them thought such things.

Not believing in sole and all-determining authorship does not mean that one must not attach any importance whatsoever to those who make films, and believing that being lesbian/gay is a culturally and historically specific phenomenon does not mean that sexual identity is of no cultural and historical consequence. The model I worked with was of multiple authorship (with varying degrees of hierarchy and control) in specific determining economic and technological circumstances, all those involved always working with (within and against) particular codes and conventions of film and with (within and against) particular, social ways of being lesbian or gay. The model is general but none of its particulars are; they always had to be worked out in each case.

In this perspective both authorship and being lesbian/gay become a kind of performance, something we all do but only with the terms, the discourses, available to us, and whose relationship to any imputed self doing the performing cannot be taken as read. This may be a characteristically gay (I hesitate to claim lesbian/gay) perception, since for us performance is an everyday issue, whether in terms of passing as straight, signalling gayness in coming out, worrying which of these turns to do, unsure what any of that has to do with what one 'is'. If the perception is gay, however, I am not arguing that the author-as-performer model applies only to lesbian/gay authorship – it's just that our social position tends to make us rather good at seeing authorship like that. All authorship and all sexual identities are performances, done with greater or less facility, always problematic in relation to any self separable from the realisation of self in the discursive modes available. The study of (gay/lesbian) authorship is the study of those modes and the particular ways in which they have been performed in given texts.

This model of authorship as performance hangs onto the notion of the author as a real, material person, but in what Janet Wolff (1981) terms a 'decentred' way. In other words, it still matters who specifically made a film, whose performance a film is, though this is neither all-determining nor having any assumable relationship to the person's life or consciousness. What is significant is the authors' material social position in relation to discourse, the access to discourses they have on account of who they are. For my purposes, what was important was their access to filmic and lesbian/gay subcultural discourses. In other words, because they were lesbian or gay, they could produce lesbian/gay representations that could themselves be considered lesbian/gay, not because all lesbians or gay men inevitably express themselves on film in a certain way, but because they had access to, and an inwardness with, lesbian/gay sign systems that would have been like foreign languages to straight filmmakers.

There are two advantages to retaining authorship in this form. One is that it allows one to have a notion of lesbian/gay cultural production without having to locate that notion only in the way the text is read or else only in the peculiarities of the text itself. I have nothing against either of these approaches for a full understanding of lesbian/gay culture. Neither the Amazons nor Judy Garland were meant to be figures in lesbian or gay culture, but they are and it is proper to analyse them as such.[2] However, we will miss much lesbian and gay cultural production if we restrict ourselves to what fits in with our own codes and conventions of lesbian/gay culture. Equally, some works may have textual properties pretty well unique to lesbian/gay cultural production – the campiness of Jack Smith's films, perhaps, or the clitoral celebrations of Barbara Hammer's – but such cases are unusual and often hard to make; if the poor old text alone has to bear the burden of being lesbian/gay, one will come up with few lesbian/gay texts.

Let me illustrate the last point in a way that will, I hope, also indicate why I think it matters. While I was thinking about this piece, I happened to hear a performance of Tchaikovsky's *Pathétique* Symphony on the radio. I had not heard it for quite a while, but it reminded me that virtually the first thing I ever did which could be construed as gay studies was while I was still in secondary school, when I gave a talk entitled, can you believe it, 'The Sick Genius of Tchaikovsky'. Then (1964) certainly I did talk about the beautiful tragic cadences of the *Pathétique* as an emanation of Tchaikovsky's inner despair at being a queer. Listening to it again, I still felt one could hear that feeling, though now I might choose to write about it in terms of constructions of queerness and self-hate. It would be hard, however, to argue that one can hear that feeling because of something about the melodic structures and orchestration of the *Pathétique* that could only embody a specifically homosexual despair. You can hear the homosexual feeling by putting together what you know of the circumstances of queerdom of the time with those sounds. This is different from simply choosing (as with camp) to make a cultural artifact work within a particular cultural register; there is warrant to hear the *Pathétique* in a homosexual way and it gives one a particular kind

of pleasure, that of fellow feeling, a pleasure of particular political importance to minority or marginalised people.[3]

There is another reason why there is some value in hanging on to authorship in some form. Jean-Paul Sartre (1968: 56) once aphorised of the French
poet Paul Valéry, 'Valéry is a petit-bourgeois intellectual, no doubt about it.
But not every petit-bourgeois intellectual is Valéry.' In other words, it tells
you a lot, where an author is socially placed (in my terms, what discourses
she/he has access to) but it still doesn't tell you everything. It doesn't tell
you how a woman with no experience of filmmaking, in a production team
under the control of a highly patriarchal man, is able to come up with a film
as subtle and affirmative as *Mädchen in Uniform* (1931), or how a 17-year-old
boy in his parents' house one weekend can make a film as sophisticated and
fascinating as *Fireworks* (1947). Placing will tell you a lot about both cases:
Leontine Sagan was a theatre director who had trained in traditions stressing
the use of light and performance, both crucial to the subtlety and affirmation of *Mädchen in Uniform*; Kenneth Anger had knocked about Hollywood
and knew some of the film students at USC, whence the sophisticated and
fascinating mix of extravagant and avant-garde elements in *Fireworks*; both
lived in periods and places of lively lesbian and gay culture – but if all that
were so clear as an explanatory model, why were there not many more
Mädchens and *Fireworks*? The very specific contribution of the key authors
need not be the starting point or an explain-all, but it is often needed if one
is to give a full account of how a lesbian/gay film came into being and why
it took the form it did.

Treating authorship as multiple, hierarchical, performed within material
and semiotic circumstances, turned out to be revealing as well as conceptually and politically necessary. It focused attention on the contradictoriness
and impurity of the work I was looking at and it suggested the way in
which these films were partly *about* authorship, or rather that authorship,
claiming images one produces as one's own, is often what is at stake for
lesbian/gay authors/identities. This section looks at the first of these points.

I took it as a starting point that the films I was looking at, as all cultural
artifacts, are not culturally pure, that is, are not lesbian/gay films uncontaminated by straight norms and values. Equivalent issues have been much
debated in relation to both women's and black writing. Elaine Showalter
(1985) and Nancy Miller (1988), among others, have discussed the problem
of conceptualising the position of the woman writer and are equally uneasy
with ideas of an *écriture féminine* existing outside of the language women
share with men and with any assumption that writing in that language is
the same for women as for men. Similarly, the work of Henry Louis Gates,
Jr. (1984) and others has tried to steer a path between approaches to
African-American literature that seek to affirm only one side of that appel-
lation, making it either purely African or only American. Likewise,

lesbian/gay cultural production must be understood to take place within, and to be a struggle about, both the cultures of the mainstream and lesbian/gay subcultures. (The latter are themselves in large measure a handling and rehandling, sometimes to the point of unrecognisability, of the former; nor do the cultures of the mainstream learn nothing from lesbian/gay cultures.)

This situation is perhaps particularly sharp with lesbian/gay film production, since lesbian/gay sub-cultures are especially clandestine (often illegal), despised and indirect, and filmmaking requires a scale of financial investment and technological know-how that means it is seldom left in the control of persons from socially subordinated groups. Because of all this, I took it as given that I would have to look, for instance, at the norms of the cycle of (straight) sex education films of which *Anders als die Anderen* (1919) was a part; or the conventions of the avant-garde that fed into US underground cinema and the work of Anger, Smith, Warhol, and others; or the developments in documentary that underpinned the talking heads movies of gay liberation. The whole history is complex – there was also, to varying degrees, a lesbian/gay input to the shaping of all the film traditions involved – but teasing out the interplay, the within and against, of lesbian/gay subcultural discourses and the relevant available filmic discourses was a point of departure. What I was less prepared for was the importance of considering the actual personnel who made the films, in terms of who among them did have access to lesbian/gay discourse from a lesbian/gay social position.

This was less of an issue, less problematic, in my later groupings (the US underground, the cultural feminism of the seventies, the films made under the banner of lesbian and gay movements), but with my earliest studies, on the two Weimar films, *Anders als die Anderen* and *Mädchen in Uniform* (1931), and on *Un Chant d'amour* (1950), things were less clear-cut. Neither of the Weimar films was directed by someone we know to have been gay or lesbian, but I felt I had to include them, chiefly because prima facie they felt so lesbian/gay-authored. To be true to my 'by' criterion I had to hunt for the lesbian-gay author, identify both who had access to lesbian/gay discourses and who had control, and in what way, over the films' textual properties. *Chant* presented a different issue, raised by the question mark over the relative importance of the two main gay men involved in its making, Jean Genet and Jean Cocteau, who performed in almost antithetical gay subcultural modes. In all three cases, looking in detail at these issues uncovered something of the power play of (lesbian/gay) cultural production and helped to draw attention to and clarify the contradictory pulls in the films themselves. Let me say a little more about each case to illustrate this.

Anders als die Anderen was directed by Richard Oswald and co-scripted by him and Magnus Hirschfeld, the leader of the most established gay rights organisation of the time, the Scientific Humanitarian Committee. Oswald was an established director and producer working for his own successful production company and specialising in both tales of the fantastic and what were known as *Aufklärungsfilme* (enlightenment films), dealing with social, and especially sexual, issues from a perspective of liberal tolerance. There is no reason to suppose he was gay.

The in-put of these two authors to different aspects of the film draws attention to and accounts for the oddness of this campaigningly 'positive' work which nonetheless contains strongly 'negative' feelings. *Anders* intersperses a narrative causal chain, of love, blackmail, suicide and resolve to fight to change the law, with lectures (by Hirschfeld) about both homosexuality and the law. The lecture elements are unequivocally positive about homosexuality, even if there are many quarters in which they would not find favour today (with, for instance, their interest in the biological basis of homosexuality and their roll call of the great and the good lesbians and gay men of the past) and these are the elements most obviously controlled, authored, by Hirschfeld. The narrative elements are more equivocal. There is no doubt that the central love relationship (between a violinist, Paul, and his pupil, Kurt) is to be celebrated, and Kurt's determination to avenge Paul's suicide to be applauded. Yet the *Aufklärungsfilm* genre constructs the issues it deals with, here homosexuality, as problems, the story places the cause of Paul's downfall in his visit to a gay bar where he picks up a rough-trade blackmailer, and the casting (notably of Conrad Veidt as Paul) and lighting bring in the tragic-sinister tones of the fantastic. In other words, in those elements that it is more likely Oswald controlled (simply by virtue of know-how), a rather different message about homosexuality comes across.

There is a further ironic twist to this. The 'positive' homosexual relationship shown in the film is that between Paul and Kurt, one with definite overtones of the *mannmännlich* 'Greek' love widely canvassed at the time, which was often equivocal about whether such eroticism involved genital acts. Although by no means politically straightforward, it certainly drew on discourses of respectability and manliness that were current in the period. It was not Hirschfeld's view of homosexuality, which tended more towards ideas of a Third Sex and was much more rooted in the ghetto culture of the time. This culture, and its androgynous denizens, is depicted in the film, but as the embodiment of unequivocal genital desire and resultant blackmail. In other words, in terms of narrative and imagery, the province of the experienced producer/director Oswald, the gay discourses exalted and denigrated by the film run counter to those generally favoured by Hirschfeld in his work. Far from presenting an unproblematic, unified image of homosexuality, the fragments of *Anders als die Anderen* indicate that what it means to be homosexual is always contested, within and without the cultures of homosexuality.

The case of *Mädchen in Uniform* is just as tricky in a different way. It was directed by Leontine Sagan, but under the 'artistic supervision', as the credit puts it, of Carl Froelich. He was a well-established film director who had moreover set up the company to produce *Mädchen* (which had been a hit as a play under different titles in Leipzig in 1930 and Berlin in 1931); Hertha Thiele, who played the part of Manuela, remembered him as being very much the boss on set. Neither he nor Sagan were, so far as we know, gay/lesbian. Of the key personnel involved, only Christa Winsloe was. She had written the original play (the second production of which had been directed by Sagan) and co-scripted (with a man, F. D. Andam) the film. However this is complicated, even before we relate the script to the film itself. In 1930 (that is, at the time of the production of the first play version, in which the element of lesbianism was almost entirely absent), Winsloe was still married. It was only in the next few years that she began to live openly as a lesbian and not until 1935 and her short story 'Life begins' that she wrote a work directly exploring lesbian life. In other words, *Mädchen* was written at a time of identity transition in Winsloe's life. This does not throw into question the validity of considering her a lesbian author – we cannot require that authors are card-carryingly out to themselves and the world – but it does mean that we have to be careful in how we understand *Mädchen*'s lesbianism, in how we relate it to prevalent discourses of lesbianism.

This problem is highlighted when we learn that it is only in the film that Manuela (the pupil in love with the teacher, Fräulein von Bernburg) does not kill herself and that this decision was Froelich's (on the grounds of taste). In other words, what seems to be the most triumphantly affirmative aspect of the film in relation to lesbianism cannot be credited to the only person we can reasonably presume was a lesbian among the key personnel. Yet the evidence of the film suggests we have a different case from that of *Anders*. Froelich was a far from liberal director, whose other films show sympathy with the authoritarianism that *Mädchen* attacks and who was perfectly happy working under the Nazis (who condemned *Mädchen* for its decadence). Yet, despite all that, *Mädchen in Uniform* undoubtedly celebrates lesbianism. Can we turn to Sagan to account for this?

Although we have no clear evidence of who made what directorial decisions, it does seem the case that the elements that most carry the celebration of lesbianism in the film are performance and lighting, elements that derive as much from theatrical as cinematic tradition. If Sagan might have had to follow Froelich's lead in relation to camera angles and editing, say, then she would surely have had the confidence and authority to control performance and lighting, especially as she had so successfully directed those in the Berlin production of the play. But still, we have no reason to consider Sagan lesbian. She was, however, of course, a woman.

It would be wrong to credit all women, and therefore Sagan, with special sympathy for lesbians and we have no evidence of what her attitude was. What we can argue, gingerly, is that the film is directed (especially performances and lighting) within the cultural codes of the 'feminine', valuing especially softness, diffuseness, delicacy, and roundness, and representing hardness and straightness as oppressive to women. This 'femininity' (noted by many critics, notably the doyenne of Weimar film historians, Lotte Eisner) is of a piece with the construction of lesbianism in the central relationship in the film, in two ways. First, the relationship is represented through delicate looks and touches, and through the suffused light that envelops both partners (unlike the contrast of lighting often found in the representation of heterosexual couples, sharp for him, soft for her); second, the structure of the relationship is seen to be identical with that of mother-daughter, pupil-teacher relationships. Indeed, one could posit (though there is no warrant for this either way) that for Sagan it was only that, and critics have often suggested the film is not about lesbianism but about a young girl longing for her mother (which she is, among other things) – but seeing the mother-daughter bond as the ideal form of relationships for women and thus as the very foundation of lesbianism was a widely held view in the period. In other words, Sagan's 'feminine' direction enriches and heightens the lesbianism of the film without necessarily being intended to, because it is in line with contemporaneous constructions of lesbianism.

The argument I have just elaborated can be made along similar lines about a number of other films I looked at, notably Maya Deren's *At Land* and many of the women's documentaries of the seventies. The former contains imagery suggestive of lesbianism in the context of a predominantly heterosexual exploration of consciousness; the latter often present lesbianism as part and parcel of women's liberation from male definitions. All are based on a perception of continuity between femininity, or womanhood, and lesbianism. A similar argument for men would be harder to make, because male gay identity has more often been constructed as oddly placed in relation to masculinity, seen as either departing from it towards effeminacy or else as play-actingly exaggerating it in clonedom.

Analysis of who exactly was and was not gay or lesbian among those who made *Anders* and *Mädchen* illustrates the problems of identifying and making sense of gay and lesbian authorship in contexts in which straight people had most control, and the consequences this has for the text produced. *Un Chant d'amour* is different in that no one questions that the two authors at issue, Jean Genet and Jean Cocteau, were both gay. The argument is about whether it is of any importance to mention Cocteau. For many years it was widely intuitively felt that it was relevant, until the producer Nicos Papatakis in an interview said that Cocteau had had no influence. We do not need to doubt Papatakis, either his veracity or his memory, to open the question up again. The intuitive sense that there is something Cocteau-ish about the film should be respected. Considering the authorial circumstances may account for it and draw attention to the rather different constructions of homosexuality at work in the film.

It may well be the case that Cocteau did not intervene by actively making suggestions, but he and Genet were extremely close at this period (ex-lovers and mutually involved in various artistic ventures), Cocteau was present almost every day at the shooting, was an established filmmaker and an embodiment of a certain tradition of playful, rarefied literary homo-eroticism. Genet, on the other hand, had never made a film and came from an underground, provocatively homosexual culture. It is hard to believe that Cocteau's charisma and cinematic know-how are of no significance in approaching *Chant* and indeed they may account for why the film, though it does have a great deal in common with Genet's other work, is also in certain respects unlike it. While unequivocally gay (unlike Cocteau's own work), it is much less radically perverse than Genet's novels and plays. It does have his characteristic play upon beauty and sordidness, sexuality and spirituality, but in Genet's other work these elements are always felt simultaneously and ambiguously (does he exalt the perverse or bring low the holy?), whereas in *Chant* there are passages, most notably chiaroscuro, abstracted love-making scenes and sequences of lovers in a wood, which are untouched by the sordid or perverse, in a way that is more Cocteau than Genet. Focusing on the mix of Cocteau and Genet as authors in *Chant* accounts for the way the film has something for everyone, delighting those who generally find Genet sordid and self-oppressive as well as those who find him exciting and subversively perverse (to say nothing of those who find Cocteau silly and evasive as well as those who find him subtle and sublime).

My central concern in the book was with the available and utilised filmic and lesbian/gay discourses, but picking over authorship down to its particu-lars in the way just described also allowed me to bring out in quite a con-crete way the realities of power and contradiction in lesbian/gay cultural production. However, constructs of authorship were not only useful for me, they were also part of the *raison d'être* of these films, and in terms of the very misgivings theorists had about them.

The idea of authority implied in that of authorship, the feeling that it is a way of claiming legitimacy and power for a text's meanings and affects, is indeed what is at issue in overtly lesbian/gay texts. They are about claiming the right to speak as lesbian/gay, claiming a special authority for their image of lesbianism/gayness because it is produced by people who are themselves lesbian/gay. They do this in different ways; their doing so reintroduces the problem of the social construction of homosexuality; and they also often indicate that they know something of that problem.

I was focusing on films made by people known to be, in whatever the par-lance of their day, lesbian/gay, and which dealt directly with homosexuality as subject matter. What was at stake in such texts was in part the act of pro-ducing lesbian/gay images that were owned by those who made them as being about themselves, an act with obvious parallels to the strategy of coming out so central to lesbian/gay politics. This marking of authorship could be achieved in various ways.

In film the burden of evident author(is)ing of the text most readily falls to those on screen. The lesbian or gay man filmed speaking about being lesbian/gay, to an audience or to camera, is the clearest statement of a lesbian/gay person owning what they say on film. Hirschfeld's appearance in *Anders als die Anderen* is one of the few early examples; the talking heads films of the seventies, including the marathon *Word is Out* (1977), are perhaps the most familiar. Documentary footage – in lesbian/gay bars in *Anders*; in the COC club in Amsterdam in *In dit teken* (1949); at the meetings, demos, and get-togethers that fill lesbian/gay documentaries of the seventies – also generally implies by the way it is filmed a consent to have been filmed and hence an owning of that consequently circulating identity (cf. Waugh 1988).

Less easy to make clear in film is the lesbian/gay identity of the filmmaker(s). There are a fair number of examples of texts which draw attention to their maker, sometimes just in credit sequences, more often in other ways. Quite common is the use of the filmmaker's voice interrogating the imagery: Jan Oxenburg reflects on the contrast between her father's home movies of her as a child and her own footage of lesbian gatherings in *Home Movie* (1973); Curt McDowell describes the process, and his feelings about it, of picking up straight men and getting them to undress and masturbate for the camera in *Loads* (1980). Others are still more elaborate: Susana Blaustein assembles people from her past and discusses on camera their reactions to her lesbianism in *Susana* (1979); Barbara Hammer frequently includes herself in shot filming, reflected in a mirror, say, or her hand or feet coming into the frame.

More often though, it is the context that indicates lesbian/gay authorship/authority, or at any rate heavily implies it. Coverage in the gay press has facilitated this, but even without that coverage something in the context may effect it. Genet and Cocteau were well known as gay writers. The underground tradition stemming from the forties was in general based on a model of the individual author expressing his/her individuality on film, so that anything in the films, including homosexual imagery, was to be read as issuing from the author's self. The cultural feminist cinema of the seventies was part of a political-artistic milieu which insisted on the connection between the artist and her work. Films explicitly promoting lesbian/gay liberation one pretty well assumes were made by lesbian/gay people. The same is true of gay male pornography, though lesbian-made lesbian pornography cannot make that assumption and achieves its lesbian identity perhaps in its imagery and construction (though it can be hard to distinguish this from lesbian imagery in straight male porn) and certainly through its marketing in lesbian magazines and networks, in gay and women's bookshops.

All these examples claim authorship, but the circumstances which make that claim possible and the nature of the consequent authority differ. At one end, as it were, there is the deliberate, promotional presence of the self-declaring lesbian or gay man. The clearest example is *In dit teken*, because it is an advertisement for the COC and as such more or less says, 'we are homosexual people, come and join us'. This is also implicit in the talking heads films, though what there is to join is rather more amorphous (the films often keeping quiet their base in the sexual political movements) and there is sometimes another address, a message of 'accept us', mixed in. At the other end, the makers of films such as *Fireworks* (Kenneth Anger 1947) or *Twice a Man* (Gregory Markopoulos 1962–3) might very well aver that these are not gay films, they are Anger or Markopoulos films – but it is precisely in so fiercely claiming them in individual terms when that individual is himself gay that they become, at any rate, films evidently authored by gay men. Somewhere between these two variants of the lesbian/gay author-text relationship comes cultural feminist cinema, explicitly grounded in the experience and vision of the particular women making the films but wishing to affirm the collective, trans-individual dimension of that experience and vision.

All these examples in their different ways are claiming the authority to speak – as representatives of homosexuality, as lesbian/gay individuals, as embodiers of lesbian community. What they are also often doing is attempting to fix identity: in the first and last case, they are (or can appear to be) attempts to freeze a certain construction of lesbian/gay identity and claim it as definitive; in the case of the second, they assert the individual as the source of authority. As has been said of coming out in general, in the very act of claiming, in the face of denial, the right to speak, these films are stemming the flux of identity. In countering the malignant distortions of the mainstream media, stating either 'this is how we are' or 'this is how I am', they seem to deny the historically contingent, provisional, incomplete and socially determined nature of being lesbian/gay. What is fascinating about so much of lesbian/gay films, however, is the degree to which some kind of awareness of this problem is apparent, either in the form of challenges to the work or as a feature of the work itself.

Gay/lesbian films, when they are not insistently individualistic, do, implicitly or explicitly, claim to speak for and on behalf of gay men and/or lesbians. This claim has always been vulnerable to criticism, in two forms. The first is that the claim to representativeness often turns out to be socially restricted: lesbian/gay films that are really only about the boys, others that are overwhelmingly white and middle-class. This criticism does not question the notion of lesbian/gay identity itself and the response to it has usually been to open up the representation, to recognise the importance of statements from non-white, non-middle-class lesbians and gay men, to make general films as socially inclusive as possible.

The second criticism is that the representative gay/lesbian identities shown exclude many lesbians and gay men and, even more, most lesbian/gay experience, even when they are sensitive to other social differences. Lesbian cultural feminism has perhaps been given the toughest time on this score. I

42

know many women who define themselves as lesbian and lead very out, open lesbian lives who cannot relate at all to the vaginal and nature/spirit iconography of lesbian cultural feminist cinema. This iconography, rooted as it is in notions of the ahistorical and archetypal, constructs a vision of authentic lesbianism in which many lesbians do not recognise themselves, a source of often bitter resentment. Certainly I had a problem in writing about this work, and not just as a man, but because of an irreconcilable contradiction between the implications of (literal) lesbian universality in the films and an approach (like mine) which stresses cultural-historical specificity and wants to celebrate this work as a particular construction of lesbian identity.

The criticism of the claim to represent lesbian/gay identity or a lesbian/gay self has not only come from outside the films themselves. A peculiarly sharp awareness of the debatability of lesbian/gay identity is central to many of them. I have already suggested that one can see within films such as *Anders*, *Mädchen*, and *Chant* intimations of competing lesbian/gay identities, but this is not really because the films themselves foreground them. However a tendency to do just that, to disrupt any implication that lesbian/gay identity is unified, unchanging, or natural, is found in many of the films, as in so much gay/lesbian culture.

The underground film tradition, for instance, is much more complex in relation to authorship and identity than I have so far indicated. While the earlier films (Anger, Markopoulos), and later ones following on from them, do operate with a notion of self-expression, what characterises this most repeatedly is a notion of the fragmentation of self, often a source of anxiety, generally only healed by reference, in Anger especially, to transcendent forces. Moreover, this impulse within the underground was displaced by the mid-sixties by the approach of filmmakers such as Jack Smith and Andy Warhol. Here the filmmaker is either present as highly artificial performer (Smith) or absent from the text, though known as a self-consciously one-dimensional celebrity (Warhol). In other words, through various strategies, the idea of self-expression (and fragmentation) has given way to something like self-performance. Everything is superficial, playing lesbian/gay is presented as a particular way of carrying on.

Again, lesbian, women's, and gay liberation cinema always had another dimension to it aside from presenting affirmative images of who we are. The impulse to do the latter stemmed from an awareness of how 'we' were/are constructed in the media in general. Talking heads documentaries sought to provide alternative images to that dominant construction, but other films wanted to deconstruct mainstream media constructions. The process of doing so proved more perplexing than early gay liberation theory had anticipated, because it became clear, once you started dealing with those constructions, that they were not in any simple sense untrue. They might be distortions of the truth, but there was something in them, and even something we often found attractive. For instance, it might be inaccurate of straight movies and television to make out that all gay men are screaming queens and that that is something frightful to be, but plenty of gay men do enjoy a good scream. Lesbian/gay cinema had to take on board the fact that lesbian/gay cultures and identities are themselves impure, made against but nonetheless with available and dominant imagery.

Films that examined the imagery of lesbian/gay identity were thus not straight in any sense of the word. *Comedy in Six Unnatural Acts* (1975), *Madame X – eine absolute Herrscherin* (1977), and *Outrageous!* (1977), Lionel Soukaz's provocative examinations of pornography and pedophilia, and much of the new lesbian and gay film work all fit this description. Even apparently straightforward films like *Desert Hearts* (1985) and *Parting Glances* (1985) are surprisingly ironic and self-conscious about how to represent lesbians and gay men. They take imagery to bits without rejecting it, they work it without endorsing it. They are, I guess, postmodern, but a postmodernism rooted in a sub-cultural, and largely politicised, tradition which has always known, at least part of the time, the importance, nay inescapability, of performance.

Lesbian/gay culture has always had for the sake of political clarity to include assertions of clear images of lesbian/gay identity, but it has also always carried an awareness of the way that a shared and necessary public identity outstrips the particularity and messiness of actual lesbian/gay lives. We have felt a need to authorise our own images, to speak for ourselves, even while we have known that those images don't quite get what any one of us is or what all of us are. So too, whether as filmmakers or historians of film, we go on believing in those fairies, the author and the homosexual, *because* we know that they are only ('only'!) human inventions.

Acknowledgement

From Diana Fuss (ed.) *Inside/Out: Lesbian Theories Gay Theories*, London: Routledge, 1991.

Notes

I should like to thank Diana Fuss, Janice Radway, and especially Hilary Hinds and Jackie Stacey for their help in the preparation and writing of this essay.

1   For a bracing exposition of the distortions of (film) anti-authorship, see Perkins 1990.

2   See, respectively, Grahn 1984, Dyer 1986.

3   I have not dealt any further with the political importance of claiming authorship, a point discussed in relation to women and authorship in, among others, Battersby 1989 and Cook 1981. Gay/lesbian cultural history is not only concerned, like feminist and black work, with bringing to light those who have been actively neglected by tradition, but also with making visible the lesbian/gay sexuality of already familiar artists (in a sense, outing them) or

showing that their already known sexuality matters. On this last point, see the introduction in Lilly 1990.

References

Battersby, Christine (1989) *Gender and Genius*, London: The Women's Press.

Cook, Pam (1981) 'The Point of Self-Expression in Film', in Caughie, John (ed.) *Theories of Authorship*, London: Routledge and Kegan Paul, 271–281.

Dyer, Richard (1986) *Heavenly Bodies: Film Stars and Society*, London: Macmillan.

Dyer, Richard (1991) *Now You See It: Studies in Lesbian and Gay Film*, London: Routledge.

Gates, Henry Louis (ed.) (1984) *Black Literature and Literary Theory*, New York: Methuen.

Grahn, Judy (1984) *Another Mother Tongue: Gay Words, Gay Worlds*, Boston: Beacon Press.

Lilly, Mark (ed.) (1990) *Lesbian and Gay Writing*, London: Macmillan.

Miller, Nancy K. (1988) 'Changing the Subject: Authorship, Writing and the Reader', in De Lauretis, Teresa (ed.) *Feminist Studies/Critical Studies*, London: Macmillan, 102–121.

Perkins, V. F. (1990) 'Film Authorship: The Premature Burial', *CinemAction!* 21/22, 57–64.

Sartre, Jean-Paul (1968) *Search for a Method*, New York: Vintage.

Showalter, Elaine (1985) 'Feminist Criticism in the Wilderness', in Showalter, Elaine (ed.) *The New Feminist Criticism*, New York: Pantheon Books, 243–270.

Waugh, Thomas (1988) 'Lesbian and Gay Documentary: Minority Self-Imaging, Oppositional Film Practice and the Question of Image Ethics', in Gross, Larry, John Stuart Katz and Jay Ruby (eds) *Image Ethics: The Moral Rights of Subjects in Photography, Film and Television*, New York: Oxford University Press, 248–272.

Wolff, Janet (1981) *The Social Production of Art*, London: Macmillan.

Further reading

Doty, Alexander (1993) 'Whose Text Is It Anyway? Queer Cultures, Queer Auteurs and Queer Authorship', *Quarterly Review of Film and Video* 15: 1, 41–54.

Lewis, Reina (1992) 'The Death of the Author and the Resurrection of the Dyke', in Munt, Sally (ed.) *New Lesbian Criticism*, Hemel Hempstead: Harvester, 17–32.

Lippe, Richard (1990) 'Authorship and Cukor: A Reappraisal', *CineAction!* 21–22, 21–34.

Mayne, Judith (1991) 'A Parallax View of Lesbian Authorship', in Fuss, Diana (ed.) *Inside/Out: Lesbian Theories, Gay Theories*, New York: Routledge.

Medhurst, Andy (1991) 'That Special Thrill: *Brief Encounter*, Homosexuality and Authorship', *Screen* 32: 2, 197–208.

3

GAY MISOGYNY

Here are three myths about women and gay men. Like all myths, none is entirely untrue.

One: Queers can't stand women. This is the one I was brought up with. The idea was that queers turned to men because they were physically repelled by women, and since they were women's rivals for men, and bound to lose, they hated women even more. This always seemed daft – disliking women's bodies could hardly account for liking men's; it implied a kind of teeth-gritted turning to men rather than real desire for them. Yet in Germany earlier this century there were groups of queer men who thought the only way for men to be healthy and *über alles* clean was to bond together and eschew women; and there has always been a pursed lipped queer slang to describe women. Some queers can't stand women.

Two: Queers ADORE women. For starters, every single one of us *loves* his mother. There is *nothing we like more* than dishing with women friends. We *worship* Judy, Liza and Kylie. Now as a matter of fact I happen to know queers who don't get on with their mothers, can't gossip and don't have a single diva album. Yet a heterosexual woman I knew who was going through a marital break-up told me she'd been advised that the best thing for women in such circumstances is to befriend a gay man. And the fact is I was a better friend to her than a heterosexual man who found her in tears by herself at home, suggested she stay at his place and, when he got her there, threw her out because she wouldn't have sex with him. By contrast, some queers do like women very much.

Three: Gay men are just as bad as straight ones. This was the view of women in Gay Liberation. Like straight men, gay men didn't listen to women, were just as liable to use sexist terms. We couldn't believe it was true, that we were as bad as straights – after all, it wasn't us who raped, wife beat, offspring abused. And we just didn't notice that it was the women who were clearing up after meetings, making the tea, offering to be secretary . . . Nowadays, with queerness chic and everyone desperate not to be considered politically correct (how very effective *anti*-pc propaganda has been), you don't hear these criticisms so much. Or rather, as those who voice them have always said, we don't listen to them, proof of a kind that some gay men are just as bad as straight.

Gay misogyny is something we don't like to talk about – and that we're allowed to get away with. I wonder if Almodóvar were straight, there'd be quite so much enthusiasm for his rape fantasies and crazy ladies? We want to distance ourselves from the myths I've just outlined, from the nonsense of detestation, from the scorn poured on our enthusiasms, from the supposed sourness of pc sexual politics, and we've drifted back into thinking that we can't be misogynistic because we're queer. Well, we can – though in some ways differently.

Much gay male misogyny is the same as straight – we are brought up as men, after all. Many of us still don't do the washing up if there are women around, still don't take the care with other people that women have been socialised to, paying attention, listening. Lesbians have put extraordinary energies into supporting gay men with AIDS; would we have done the same if it had been the other way around? Gay men, like straight, have changed in the past twenty-five years, have done some unlearning of masculinity. But we're still mostly brought up to the habits of male privilege. We don't claim them, but we don't think about them either and so continue to enjoy and perpetuate them, at women's expense.

Yet there are differences. I have never heard a gay man express the hatred of women that I have overheard from straight men. Gay men don't have the same power investment in relations with women that straights do. In many ways, we do get on better with women. I can always tell which of my male students is gay – they're the ones talking with the women.

But we have our own misogyny. We often feel that the fact that we are not caught up in heterosexual arrangements lets us off the hook – isn't it within heterosexuality that men really harm women the most? Yes – but it is also where they love them most, with the special intensity that comes with sex. Our distance from that allows us to be personal and intimate with women in a way rare between straight men and women – but it is a distance. Being a gay man is not the same as being a straight woman, yet when we get together, we often talk as if it were – which means we often don't really listen to what women say and may even seduce them into casting their lives in our terms.

This distance informs what is, paradoxically, the most problematic aspect of gay misogyny – that *adoration* of women. I think it does suggest a warmer, more open attitude towards women to prefer Marlene or Madonna over Clint Eastwood or a tabloid pin-up, yet I am also troubled by how this adoration comes out. When a gay man tells me he loves Bette Davis, my heart sinks when he goes on to say, especially in *Baby Jane*, she's such a hag and a bitch in that. *Priscilla Queen of the Desert* may be a drag celebration of femininity, but the real women in the film are a detestable butch, a whining Philippina popping ping-pong balls from her vagina and a token 'good lesbian'. Our enthusiasms may reveal that for all our interest in femininity, we're often not really interested in women.

Acknowledgement

From *Attitude* July 1994.

Further reading

Maddison, Stephen (2001) *Fags, Hags and Queer Sisters: Gender Dissent and Heterosocial Bonding*, Basingstoke: Palgrave.

4

IT'S BEING SO CAMP AS
KEEPS US GOING

Arguments have lasted all night about what camp really is and what it means.[1] There are two different interpretations which connect at certain points: camping about, mincing and screaming; and a certain taste in art and entertainment, a certain sensibility.

Camping about has a lot to be said for it. First of all and above all, it's very us. It is a distinctive way of behaving and of relating to each other that we have evolved. To have a good camp together gives you a tremendous sense of identification and belonging. It is just about the only style, language and culture that is distinctively and unambiguously gay male. One of our greatest problems is that we are cut adrift for most of the time in a world drenched in straightness. All the images and words of the society express and confirm the rightness of heterosexuality. Camp is one thing that expresses and confirms being a gay man.

Then again camp is fun. It's quite easy to pick up the lingo and get into the style, and it makes even quite dull people witty. Fun and wit are their own justification, but camp fun has other merits too. It's a form of self-defence. Particularly in the past, the fact that gay men could so sharply and brightly make fun of themselves meant that the real awfulness of their situation could be kept at bay – they need not take things too seriously, need not let it get them down. Camp kept, and keeps, a lot of gay men going.

And camp is not masculine. By definition, camping about is not butch. So camp is a way of being human, witty and vital, without conforming to the drabness and rigidity of the hetero male role. You've only got to think of the impact of Quentin Crisp's high camp (as charted in *The Naked Civil Servant*[2]) on the straight world he came up against, to see that camp has a radical/progressive potential: scaring muggers who know that all this butch male bit is not really them but who feel they have to act as if it is (Quentin showed that he knew they were screamers underneath it all); running rings of logic and wit round the pedestrian ideas of psychiatrists, magistrates and the rest; and developing by living out a high camp life-style a serenity and a sense of being-at-one-with-yourself ('I am one of the stately homos of Britain').

Identity and togetherness, fun and wit, self-protection and thorns in the flesh of straight society – these are the pluses of camp. Unfortunately there are also minuses, and they are precisely the opposite side of those positive features.

The togetherness you get from camping about is fine, but not everybody actually feels able to camp about. A bunch of queens screaming together can be very exclusive for someone who isn't a queen or feels unable to camp. The very tight togetherness that makes it so good to be one of the queens is just the thing that makes a lot of other gay men feel left out. One of the sadder features of the gay movement is the down so many activists have on queens and camp, on the only heritage we've got. But it can work the other way around too: some queens despise the straight-looking (or otherwise non-queenly) gays around them, as if camping about is the only way of being gay. You have to let people be gay in the way that's best for them.

The fun, the wit, has its drawbacks too. It tends to lead to an attitude that you can't take anything seriously, everything has to be turned into a witticism or a joke. Camp finds CHE[3] too dull, GLF[4] too political, all the movement activities just not fun enough. It's a fair point, up to a point – CHE and GLF can be a bit glum and a bit heavy. But actually they've got quite a serious job to do. Life is not a bed of roses for gay men, still; sexism and our own male chauvinism are hard to understand, come to terms with, change. That does not always lend itself to fun and wit, but it needs to be done all the same.

Again, the self-mockery of self-protection can have a corrosive effect on us. We can keep mocking ourselves to the point where we really do think we're a rather pathetic, inferior lot. Phrases like 'silly Nelly', 'Chance'd be a fine thing' and 'It's too much for a white woman',[5] funny though they are, have a lot that is self-hating about them – behind them linger such ideas as 'How stupid I am', 'I'm too wretched and ugly to attract anyone', 'I'm too sexually hung-up to be able to give myself physically'. . . . Camp can help us from letting the social, cultural situation of gays getting us down: but it is the situation that's wrong, not ourselves. Camp sometimes stops us seeing that.

Camping about then is good and bad, progressive and reactionary. Often it's very hard to disentangle these two aspects. For instance, I am very much in the habit of calling men 'she': a man with a large cock is 'a big girl'; to a man showing off, I'll say 'Get her!'; I welcome friends with 'It's Miss Jones' (or whatever the man's name is). In one way, this is a good habit. After all, I'm glad to be gay and I prefer straight women (i.e. most women) to straight men (i.e. most men). Calling gay men 'she' means I don't think of them, or myself, as straight men (with all that that implies). But given the actual situation of women in society, and given that however hard I try, there's still plenty of male chauvinism about me, there is something rather suspect about this habit. Isn't it tantamount to saying gay men are inferior to straight men, just as women are? Isn't it really a put-down of gay men, and of women? It's hard to decide, and in the end I think I'll go on doing it because I'd rather gay men identified with straight women than with straight men, since most of the values associated with masculinity in this society (aggressiveness, competitiveness, being 'above' tenderness and emotion) I reject. Yet the whole practice, like so much of camp, is deeply ambiguous. So much depends on what you feel about men and women, about sex, about being gay.

The context of camp is important too. Camp means a lot at a gathering of queers, or used defiantly by queers against straightness: but it is very easily taken up by straight society and used against us. We know two things about camp that straights, at any rate as the media and everyday jokes show it, don't: that it is nice to be a queen (can be, should be), and that not all queers are queens. The straight media have taken up the queen image, which we have created, but use it against us. To a limited extent, they appreciate the wit, but they don't see why it was necessary. They pick up the undertow of self-oppression without ever latching on to the elements of criticism and defiance of straightness. And they just never seem to realise that camping is only one way of being gay. Camp queens are the inevitable image of gayness in art and the media. As I see it, this rather catches us in a cleft stick. We should defend camp, whether we're queens or not; at the same time, we've got to make it clear that we are not all camp all the same. That's a rather complicated argument for the straight media. It's also quite a complicated problem for us too – but ultimately I think we should be open about allowing each other to be queens or not as we feel, and should try to build on the anti-butch fun and wit of camp as a way of building gayness into a better society.

What of camp as a kind of taste or sensibility?

It is easy, and usual, to offer a list of camp things at the beginning of discussions of camp, so that we all know what we are talking about. Thus:

Nelson Eddy and Jeanette MacDonald
Aubrey Beardsley
Vienna waltzes
most classical ballet
Busby Berkeley
Marlene Dietrich
the Queen Mother
Ronald Firbank
Pakeezah
velvet and brocade curtains
Little Richard and Sylvester

Such lists are, however, a bit misleading, since camp is far more a question of how you respond to things rather than qualities actually inherent in those things. It's perfectly possible to take MacDonald and Eddy seriously as lovers in musicals, or the Queen Mother as an embodiment of Britannic royalty, or Beardsley as a draughtsman, and so on. Equally, you can find things camp which are, on the face of it, the very antithesis of camp: John Wayne, for instance, or Wagner. It's all a question of how you look at it.

How then to define the camp way of looking at things? Basically, it is a way of prising the form of something away from its content, of revelling in the style while dismissing the content as trivial. If you really believed in the emotions and stories of classical ballet, in the rightness and value of royalty, in the properness of supervirility and fascism, then you could not find *The Sleeping Beauty*, the Queen Mother, or John Wayne camp. What I value about camp is that it is precisely a weapon against the mystique surrounding art, royalty and masculinity: it cocks an irresistible snook, it demystifies by playing up the artifice by means of which such things as these retain their hold on the majority of the population.

It is interesting to speculate about why it is that camp should be the form that male gay culture has taken. Susan Sontag (1967) suggests that camp is the way homosexuals have sought to make some impression on the culture of the society they live in. Mastery of style and wit has been a way of declaiming that queens have something distinctive to offer society. This seems to me to be true. Gay men have made certain 'style professions' very much theirs (at any rate by association, even if not necessarily in terms of the numbers of gays actually employed in these professions): hairdressing, interior decoration, dress design, ballet, musicals, revue. These occupations have made the life of society as a whole more elegant and graceful, and the showbiz end has provided the world at large with many pleasant evenings. At the same time hairdressing, interior decoration and the rest are clearly marked with the camp sensibility: they are style for style's sake, they don't have 'serious' content (a hairstyle is not 'about' anything), they don't have a practical use (they're just nice), and the actual forms taken accentuate artifice, fun and occasionally outrageous – all that chi-chi and tat, those pinks and lace and sequins and tassels, curlicues and 'features' in the hair, satin drapes and chiffon scarves and fussy ornaments, all the paraphernalia of a camp sensibility that has provided gay men with a certain legitimacy in the world.

A certain legitimacy only. The very luxuriousness and 'uselessness' of these professions have also tended to reinforce the image of gay men as decadent, marginal, frivolous – above all, not involved in the real production of wealth (on the shopfloor or in the management offices) in society, just sterile parasites on the edges. And too the association of so much of the camp style professions with women is ambiguous. Although women in our society are involved in production, none the less their social role is seen as being adjuncts to men, not just to provide a man with a wife, servant and mother

Figure 4.1 The Queen Mother.

Figure 4.2 Marlene Dietrich.

Figure 4.3 Nelson Eddy and Jeanette MacDonald.

Figure 4.4 Little Richard.

Figure 4.5 John Wayne.

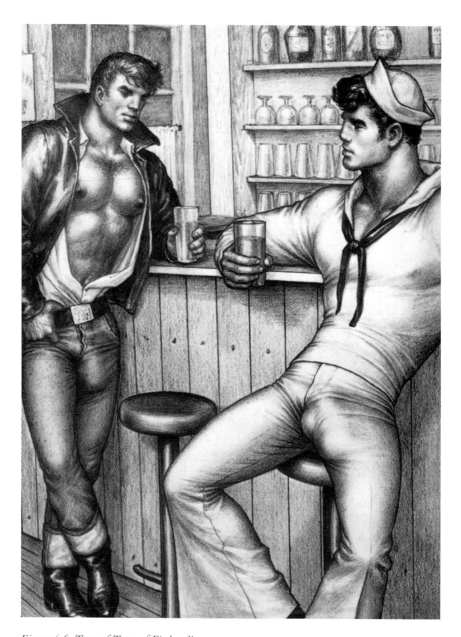

Figure 4.6 Two of Tom of Finland's men.

to 'his' kids, but also to display his wealth by her smartness, the frequency of her hair-dos, the number of her frocks. This applies above all to the wealthy of course, where the lady in her Paris fashions displays her husband's buying power and her access (by virtue of his position) to the canons of fashion and good taste. But in less spectacular forms it works further down the social scale. Most husbands expect their wives to 'look nice', to make an effort with their appearance when they take them out. It is only the poorest husband whose wife cannot afford a bouffant hair-do, some fake fur and a glass brooch for Saturday night out. And we gay men have been deeply involved in creating the styles and providing the services for the 'turn-out' of the women of the western world. This gives us legitimacy – but as parasites on women, who are themselves seen as subordinate to men and objects of luxury (however meagre). Moreover, the involvement of camp in objectifying women in this way (reaching its apotheosis in Busby Berkeley's production numbers (though I've never heard that he himself was gay)) makes it something that anyone who cares about everyone's liberation should be wary of.

But that's a digression. Let's get back to the point about camp evolving because gay men have staked out a claim on society at large by mastery of style and artifice. That seems true, but the question still remains: why style and artifice rather than anything else? A reason is suggested by a German survey of gay people, the results of which were published in an early *Gay News* (London). It found that gays were extremely 'adaptable'; that is, we tend to find it easy to fit in to any occupation, or set-up, or circle of people. Or rather, and this is the point, we find it easy to appear to fit in, we are good at picking up the rules, conventions, forms and appearances of different social circles. And why? Because we've had to be good at it, we've had to be good at disguise, at appearing to be one of the crowd, the same as everyone else. Because we had to hide what we really felt (gayness) for so much of the time, we had to master the façade of whatever social set-up we found ourselves in – we couldn't afford to stand out in any way, for it might give the game away about our gayness. So we have developed an eye and an ear for surfaces, appearances, forms: style. Small wonder then that when we came to develop our own culture, the habit of style should have remained so dominant in it.

Looked at in this way, the camp sensibility is very much a product of our oppression. And, inevitably, it is scarred by that oppression. Some of the minuses of camp as a sensibility I've already mentioned – the relegation of its practitioners to licensed decorators on the edges of society, its involvement with the objectification of women. Other minuses resemble the drawbacks of camp behaviour.

The emphasis on surface and style can become obsessive – nothing can be taken seriously, anything deep or problematic or heavy is shimmied away from in a flurry of chic. Camp seems often unable to discriminate between those things that need to be treated for laughs and style, and those that are genuinely serious and important.

Beside this, camp is so beguiling that it has been adopted by many straights of late. But something happens to camp when taken over by straights: it loses its cutting edge, its identification with the gay experience, its distance from the straight sexual world-view. Take the example of John Wayne. Gay camp can emphasise what a production number the Wayne image is – the lumbering gait, drawling voice and ever more craggy face are a deliberately constructed and manufactured image of virility. In this way, gay camp can stop us from treating John Wayne as an embodiment of what it 'really' means to be a man. Straight camp puts a different emphasis. The authority, power and roughness of the Wayne image are still dear to the straight imagination, but they have been criticised heavily enough in recent years (by gays and camp among others) for there to be embarrassment about directly accepting or endorsing such qualities. Camp allows straight audiences to reject the style of John Wayne; but because it is so pleasant to laugh, it also allows for a certain wistful affection for him to linger on. However, affection for John Wayne can only be in reality affection for that way of being a man. Straight camp allows images of butchness to retain their hold even while they are apparently being rejected.

Of course, this twisting of camp away from its radical/progressive/critical potential is only possible because of the ambiguity of camp even within gay circles. (For instance, the drawings of Tom of Finland are at one level over-the-top camp, but also clearly a turn-on too.) Not all gay camp is in fact progressive, but none the less it does have the potential of being so. What camp can do is to demystify the images and world-view of art and the media. We are encouraged by schooling to be very solemn in the presence of art; and we are tempted by film and television to be drawn into the worlds they present as if they were real. Camp can make us see that what art and the media give us are not the Truth or Reality but fabrications, particular ways of talking about the world, particular understandings and feelings of the way life is. Art and the media don't give us life as it really is – how could they ever? – but only life as artists and producers think it is. Camp, by drawing attention to the artifices employed by artists, can constantly remind us that what we are seeing is only a view of life. This doesn't stop us enjoying it, but it does stop us believing what we are shown too readily. It stops us thinking that those who create the landscape of culture know more about life than we do ourselves. A camp appreciation of art and the media can keep us on our guard against them – and considering their view of gayness, and sexuality in general, that's got to be a good thing.

In his introduction to the first *Playguy*[6] he edited, Roger Baker quoted Dennis Altman's lovely phrase, 'Camp is to gay what soul is to black'. That's right – but push at the resemblance a bit and you get to the ambiguities of both camp and soul. Soul is not unequivocally a good thing. Certainly, it provides blacks (some blacks) with a definitely black culture; with its roots in religion, it provides an openness to irrational experience that white culture tends to play down; and with its connections to dance and ritual, it allows for a physical freedom, a being-at-home-in-your-body, that repressed white culture shies away from. But soul also reinforces notions of black people as mindless, superstitious and sex-obsessed – it may at times hold them back from making claims on the equally human and useful attributes of rationality and restraint. There is the same equivocality about camp. It does give us (some of us) an identity, it does undercut sex roles and the dominant world-view, it is fun; but it can also trap us if we are not careful in the endless pursuit of enjoyment at any price, in a rejection of seriousness and depth of feeling. What we've got to do is to activate the positive attributes of camp – mince in the streets, send up Kojak and Burt Reynolds and Colt models, come together for a camp, keep our oppression at bay with a scream and a joke – without letting them trap us.

You know those clenched fists you get on political badges (including women's liberation and GLF)? Well, why shouldn't it be a clenched fist on a limp wrist? Divine.

Acknowledgement

From *Playguy* and was reprinted in 1977 in *The Body Politic* 36.

Notes

1   The most complete and scholarly account is Cleto 1999, which also includes most of the classic texts. I only give in the further reading below works not included in Cleto.
2   Autobiography Crisp 1968, TV movie Jack Gold/Thames Television 1975.
3   Campaign for Homosexual Equality.
4   Gay Liberation Front.
5   When this essay was written, I did not pause to consider the implications of this then quite common phrase among white queens for my account of camp. The relation of camp to whiteness is discussed in Robertson 1999. However, although the camp I discuss here is basically white, camp is certainly not an exclusively white phenomenon (cf. Riggs 1992, Varia 2000). I admit to adding *Pakeezah* (a fabulous Hindi movie with a big gay following), Little Richard and Sylvester to my list of camp things for this republication. My thanks to Kush Varia for correspondence on this matter.
6   The British softporn gay magazine which originally commissioned this article. This may also be the opportunity for acknowledging that the thing people always like most about this article, its title, was in fact supplied by *Playguy*'s editor, Roger Baker.

References

Cleto, Fabio (ed.) (1999) *Camp: Queer Aesthetics and the Performing Subject: A Reader*, Edinburgh: Edinburgh University Press.

Crisp, Quentin (1968) *The Naked Civil Servant*, London: Jonathan Cape.

Riggs, Marlon T. (1992) 'Unleash the Queen', in Dent, Gina (ed.) *Black Popular Culture*, Seattle: Bay Press, 99–105.

Sontag, Susan (1967) 'Notes on Camp', in *Against Interpretation*, London: Eyre and Spottiswoode, 275–292.

Robertson, Pamela (1999) 'Mae West's Maids: Race, "Authenticity" and the Discourse of Camp', in Cleto, 393–408.

Varia, Kush (2000) 'Bombay Exposé', *London Lesbian and Gay Film Festival Programme*.

Further reading

Bergman, David (ed.) (1993) *Camp Grounds: Style and Homosexuality*, Amherst: University of Massachusetts Press.

Boone, Bruce (1979) 'Gay Language as Political Praxis: the Poetry of Frank O'Hara', *Social Text* 1, 59–92.

Graham, Paula (1995) 'Girl's Camp? The Politics of Parody', in Wilton, Tamsin (ed.) *Immortal, Invisible: Lesbians and the Moving Image*, London: Routledge, 163–181.

Medhurst, Andy (1997) 'Camp', in Medhurst, Andy and Munt, Sally (eds) *Lesbian and Gay Studies: A Critical Introduction*, London: Cassell, 274–293.

Meyer, Moe (ed.) (1994) *The Politics and Poetics of Camp*, London: Routledge.

Russo, Vito (1979) 'Camp', in Levene, Martin P. (ed.) *Gay Men: The Sociology of Male Homosexuality*, New York: Harper & Row, 205–210.

5

DRESSING THE PART

Twenty years ago there was nothing in the world more hilarious, nothing more naff, than a man wearing baggy khaki shorts that reached to his knees. Seven or so years ago, it was a real head-turner. Now it's delightfully routine, and thus probably on the way out. I don't know for certain that it was a gay man who first saw the stylish potential of long shorts, but I'd be willing to bet on it and on the assumption that it was gay men as a group who turned them into a fashion item.

Gay men have always played a leading role in the male (as well as, of course, the female) fashion industry. If the vast majority of gay men have had nothing particular to do with it and may have dressed or decorated as ineptly as the next straight man, still enough of us were into such things visibly and triumphantly enough to constitute a distinctive and recognisable gay culture. There are various possible explanations for this. In practice, fashion was a form of employment that was relatively relaxed about us (though also one of the first places that blackmailers, police and yellow journalism would look for queer material). It was also a job that allowed us to pay physical attention to men, most of the time unemphatically and inexplicitly but occasionally blossoming into changing-room fumbling and more (I shall never forget that time in Harrods...)

Behind such explanations lies a broader one, to do with the nature of being gay in a homophobic society. Fashion and the other style trades gave us a space to exercise a skill we have had to be very good at, namely, presentation. Surviving as a queer meant mastering appearances, knowing how to manipulate clothes, mannerisms and lifestyle so as to be able to pass for straight and also to signal that we weren't. To stay alive and unharmed we had to handle the codes of heterosexuality with consummate skill; to have any erotic and sentimental life we had to find ways of conveying our otherwise invisible desires. As I say, not all gay men managed both, or felt happy with either; but enough have, making the stereotype of gay men's investment in style not so utterly wide of the mark.

It's an investment by no means confined to people professionally involved with clothes, décor, design and so on. It pervades our everyday life. I am conscious of trying to tread the thin line between passing and flaunting. I rarely have other than casual dealings with people who don't know I'm gay but I'm aware of wanting simultaneously to express the fact that I am and yet also to fit in. I recently had an interview for a good job and had a wonderful discussion with a friend about what I should wear. It had to be a suit, of course, one knows the rules; a plain black one makes a statement about conscious choice over attire that the indeterminate brown and grey mixes of most men's clothes disavow. More difficult to decide upon was the obligatory tie. How ironic should it be, how over the top should I go to signal that I know that ties are just a piece of manly frippery; how far back from over the top should I withdraw in order not to appear to be sending the panel up? On such precipices of decision is gay style lived.

The importance of gay men in setting male fashions has given the whole question of masculine style in most western cultures a particular ambiguity (though what I have to say is a lot less true of Black and Latin, and especially Italian, cultures, where being stylish and macho are not seen as so contradictory). Concern with appearance is so associated with gay men in this society that not to be concerned with it has often been taken as a badge of real/heterosexual masculinity.

Clothing is an issue for straight men, yet one they cannot be seen to have any expertise in. Much clothing for heterosexual men has been chosen by women (mothers and spouses), but the latter could not try the fashions out, could not themselves pioneer male styles. So, over the years, it is from gay men's interest that straight men and women have learnt, our soft white shirts, our suede shoes, our 501s, our baggy shorts. The trouble is that such stylishness has thus always been tainted by queerness. Straight men have often resisted the purchases of their womenfolk because they've thought they would make them look like pansies; and straight women used to be heard to say that they didn't like a man who took too much interest in his appearance.

Yet the styles have caught on all the same. Time and again straight men have adapted to the gay-led fashions. What is going on here? In part there has been nowhere else to look: gay men have tended, literally, to corner the market on male style innovation. But we may also underestimate the element of fascination with homosexuality which is the inevitable accompaniment of something so strenuously abominated. I mean this in two ways. First, homosexual men, because they are presumed not to be involved in heterosexual relations, embody a potentially enviable alternative to such relations, for both sexes. For straight men, we may represent the possibility of being free of the restrictions of domesticity and the responsibilities of breadwinning; for straight women, we are men who are not going to force ourselves upon them, we are not part of the coerciveness and power play of heterosexuality. Secondly our sexuality is a matter of enthralled, if also appalled, interest. Many straight men have had some gay experience and fondly wish for some more on the side. In short, for all the opprobrium cast on us, there is also a great deal of envy, fascination and desire. When straight men adopt our style it's not just to please women or because the fashion industry (like any other capitalist industry) has to have new products to sell, it's also because of the *frisson* of the association with gay sexuality.

All this has, if anything, become more explicit in recent years. While Levi ads or the Chippendales are resolutely heterosexual in their address and attendant publicity, their gay style resonances are too explicit to be dismissed as unconscious. In the world of pop, gay association (whether or not strictly 'true') has not only not done any harm to the appeal of, for instance, David Bowie, Freddie Mercury, Erasure, Marky Mark or George Michael, but seems to be very much part of their appeal. At the time of Jason Donovan's case (against the *Face* for reprinting a poster outing him), it was clear from interviews that many of his adolescent female fans not only didn't care if he was gay but felt that would all be part of what made him sexy. Similarly, Take That carried very clearly the signs of their earlier career, entertaining in gay clubs, into their mainstream success.

Gay style has then always been, indeed is, *the* influence on straight male style, in a fascinatingly ambivalent process. There has however been a profound shift in the nature of gay style. Up until some time in the 1970s, gay style was about feminising male attire; since then it has been about quoting mainstream masculinity.

Feminisation of male attire did not mean wearing women's clothes but a readiness to wear bright or pastel colours, to put extra flounce or decoration to an outfit, to do things, in short, that only women were supposed to do.

Oscar Wilde's descriptions of beautiful young men have recourse to flower smiles, speak of ruby lips and golden curls, and indeed of 'beauty', a term rather dodgy in relation to men until perhaps recently. In the novel *Teleny*, apparently written by Wilde and some other men around 1893, the descriptions of the attractive and homosexual men's attire always stress both their difference from the other men and those added notes of colour and swish. One character, for instance, has 'faultless' but 'a trifle eccentric' dress – he wears a white heliotrope in his lapel. Another, who has 'a most lovely neck and throat', stands out because 'when every gentleman was in black, he, on the contrary, wore a white flannel suit [with] a very open Bryon-like collar, and a red Lavallière cravat tied in a huge bow'.

Queens in Berlin in the 1920s pushed things further. Magnus Hirschfeld (a thorough cross-dresser himself) described one gay man who 'received his guests in an indeterminate garment made by himself, a cross between a ball gown and a dressing gown'. Another observer, Curt Moreck, wrote this description of the styles in the gay bars, which, though homophobic in intention, is, in its last sentence at least, utterly captivating:

In the more refined West [End of Berlin], resemblance to the opposite sex is achieved through powder puffs and lipstick. They are somewhat profligate with perfume and coquettish in their pretty coloured silks. They have plucked their eyebrows and have crimped, sleek, shiny hair in soft quiffs. They look at you yearningly, dreamily, out of Belladonna eyes.

The 'Belladonna' effect was described by another observer as 'the febrile sparkle of eyes darkened by kohl', a fashion associated with movie stars like Theda Bara – and Rudolph Valentino.

The attractive and outrageous young men of Greenwich Village, New York City, in the 1930s were no less fascinated by feminine grooming, if the 1933 novel, *The Young and the Evil* by Charles Ford and Parker Tyler is to be believed. Make-up, doing and discussing it, is a major preoccupation of the group of young queers at the novel's centre. One evening they are preparing for a party:

Julian wore a black shirt and light powder-green tie. His dark hair had been washed to a gold brown and fell over his forehead [this is a period when real men kept their hair well slicked back].

Karel, as he had promised, came by three hours before the others bringing his box of beauty that included eyelash curlers, mascara, various shades of powder, lip and eyebrow pencils, blue and brown eyeshadow and tweezers for the eyebrows.

[Karel's] eyebrows . . . could be pencilled into almost any expression: Clara Bow, Joan Crawford, Norma Shearer, etc. He thought he would choose something obvious for tonight. Purity.

Such goings-on were only possible, of course, for a screamingly courageous minority in a few metropolitan centres, but whether Victorian heliotropes, Weimar Belladonna eyes or Greenwich Village beauty boxes, gay male style involved incorporating markers of the feminine into male clothing. The history of straight adoption of such styles has yet to be written and will centre on such weighty matters as pomade (butched-up to Brylcreem), perfume (aka aftershave), floppy hair ('natural') and suede shoes (an absolute queer give-away in the 1950s that few new queers would be seen dead in today). It was not really until the 1960s that a gay-led male style emerged which crossed over so swiftly that, although at the time its queerness was evident to all, in the mythologisation of the period it has tended to be forgotten.

Carnaby Street and the swinging sixties were a turning point in sartorial history, the moment of men's rediscovery of the pleasures of unabashed dress and display – the 'rebirth of the peacock', as journalism of the day had it. Carnaby Street was originally a group of very queer little shops or 'boutiques', a word borrowed from female fashion marketing and only one of the many steps taken to incorporate the feminine into male clothing in what turned out to be a last, florid burst of this particular dynamic of male gay style. Carnaby Street went mad on colour, not only pinks and purples and powder blues and other sissy colours, and not only on ties but on shirts and, most shocking of all, jackets and trousers. Nor were garments just of one colour, as male clothes tend to be (when they are not a mix of sludge and drab); colours were thrown together in riots, most thrillingly in flower patterns. Shirts were waisted, fitting tight to the body; trousers were flared, creating a flowing line at odds with the military precision and control of straight legs (though no doubt revelling in the naval overtones). My most delirious memory of indubitably queer gear passing if not unnoticed then at any rate unmolested is strolling out of a Carnaby Street boutique and through London in a newly acquired pair of white lace trousers.

Such style lingered on in the 'radical drag' of the early gay liberation movement – unshaven men wearing frocks or men going to work wearing skimpy women's jumpers with flower motifs on them. Yet this happened at the very same time as the other gay style began to emerge which has now become dominant: the quoting of traditionally male styles. Indeed radical drag highlighted a terrible truth: that effeminacy was right-on but didn't get you men any more.

Macho men had of course always been objects of desire. Alongside the heliotropes, the kohl and the lace trousers, there had always been lads, rough trade, hunks. Yet there had always been an ambiguity about them – were they really queer? The preening and grooming involved were not in doubt and certainly raised question marks about their heterosexual masculinity, but it was doubts rather than indubitable queer association. What happened, alongside the last puff of effeminacy as a gay style in the sixties and seventies, was gay men's decision to start looking like these other objects of desire. Hence the turn to 501 Levis, bodybuilding, leather, short hair, boots, white jockey briefs, as well as the rediscovery of the suit and tie, worn with new panache, braces and matching socks and shirts (an almost feminine note), and later such things as the adoption of gym gear, and baggy shorts.

I call this quoting male styles because there is a self-consciousness about the way gay men adopt these styles. Much of the gay repertoire of the seventies and eighties drew upon two traditional arenas for the forging of (straight) masculine identity: work and sport. Jeans, short hair, boots are practical gear for men's work (by the same token, there was even for a crazed moment the wearing of construction workers' hard hats at discos); muscles are a product of both work and sport, something (real) men just have; leather has long been associated with 'hard' masculinity (perhaps because so directly evoking the slaughter that has made such adornment possible or more generally because of the association of masculinity with beastliness), while jockey briefs are seen to be manlily functional, right down to the rather dysfunctional front opening.

All these items are (or were) entirely normalised in everyday life, just what men wear in an unreflective, seemingly unchosen, nay, natural sort of way. Gay men on the other hand select them, and wear them in the context of fun and sex – and wear them with care, ironing 501s and leaving one button ostentatiously undone, making sure muscles obviously acquired by machine show, keeping briefs spankingly white, playing endless more and more self-conscious variations on short hair (shaved, tufted, dyed and so on). While the degree of grooming involved may suggest the feminine, the signs remain resolutely butch – no pastels, laces or lipsticks here, though the quoting effect is often enhanced by wearing a brooch or earring, drawing attention by its sudden effeminacy to the butch regime of the rest.

The result is gay in a number of different ways. First, these are acts of queering: they find or put in the homo-erotic at play in straight life, they bring out the gay while leaving enough reference to the straight to be at once exciting and disturbing. Second, they insist on clothes as performance: they give the lie to the notion that clothes really make the man, that clothes are in any sense natural or inevitable; they proclaim that the only things clothes are appropriate to is our fantasies of gender and sexuality. Third, they celebrate masculinity as erotic, they flaunt the pleasures of male exhibitionism and narcissism, they get off on the supposedly asexual signs of manliness. In this last way they are, in terms of sexual politics, unruly, for they are not just a statement about masculinity, they are also utterly absorbed and fascinated by it too: they may destabilise its supposed naturalness but not to the point of undercutting it altogether, and I sometimes find something remorselessly virile in the endless black clothes, scratchy heads and faces and clomping shoes. The feminine, above all the effeminate, has lost out in this development and we are the poorer for it.

When gay men out male fashion and when it eventually gets taken up by straight men, two processes are at work. One is the transformation of naff into style. No word is harder to define than naff (itself a term from queer slang taken up by straights). I often think of it as almost interchangeable with the word 'straight'; it's above all what happens when straight men make an inept lunge at being stylish. The magic of gay style is that it is capable of taking the very essence of naffness, to return to baggy shorts, and somehow make it seem stylish. It's a product of deciding to see something as stylish, to quote it with confidence, to wear it with irony: baggy shorts become stylish by the very act of them being taken up as stylish by gay men, as part of a way of relating to clothes and style that gay men are so skilled at. (Though again it's important to remember that not all, perhaps not even most, gay men are so skilled; but gay culture is.)

Second, the gay take-up of straight style makes it sexy. Much gay style has been sexual in the most obvious way: from groomed and adorned penises (shaved groins and cock rings) through bikinis and white, white jockeys to tight jeans worn with elaborate and gravity-defying genital arrangements to one or other side of the fly, and on to Lycra, gay men have seldom held back from making a spectacle of their sexual parts. Other styles have spectacularised other parts: the tight T-shirt, with sleeves rolled right up, or else the shortlived 'muscle shirt' with next to no sleeves at all; and most trousers, skilfully selected for the way they hang over the buttocks, involving years of practice in looking down over one's shoulder into a mirror. What is more extraordinary, even heroic, is gay men's ability to make clothes sexy that do not cling or reveal. Which takes us back to baggy shorts, and indeed very loose jeans and floppy shirts. Of course, they too look better on a better body (baggy jeans look best with cinched-in waists), but they are not exclusively about that: they are sexy without making direct sexual reference.

The dynamic of gay style is unpredictable. After baggy shorts, can floppy jumpers and sports jackets be far behind? Or are there still some new variations to play on denim and short hair? Could we even hope for a return to pastels and flow? It will be delightful to see and to behold the ripple of queerness as one or another gay style spreads back out into society.

Acknowledgement

From Healey, Emma and Mason, Angela (eds) *Stonewall 25: The Making of the Lesbian and Gay Community in Britain*, London: Virago, 1994.

Further reading

Cole, Shaun (2000) *'Don We Now Our Gay Apparel': Gay Men's Dress in the Twentieth Century*, London: Berg.

Higgins, Ross (1998) 'A la mode: Fashioning Gay Community in Montreal', in Brydon, Anne and Niessen, Sandra (eds) *Consuming Fashion: Adorning the Transnational Body*, London: Berg, 129–161.

Holland, David (1978) 'The Politics of Dress', in Jay, Karla and Young, Allen (eds) *Lavender Culture*, New York: Harcourt Brace Jovanovich, 396–402.

Wilson, Elizabeth (1994) 'Dyke Style or Lesbians Make an Appearance', in Healey, Emma and Mason, Angela (eds) *Stonewall 25: The Making of the Lesbian and Gay Community in Britain*, London: Virago, 167–177.

6

IT'S IN HIS KISS!

Vampirism as homosexuality, homosexuality as vampirism

One of the first avowedly homosexual stories ever published is a vampire story: 'Manor', written and published by Carl Heinrich Ulrichs in Leipzig in 1885.[1] Ulrichs was among the first people to write about and proclaim a homosexual identity, 'coming out', as we would say now, to his family in 1862 and thereafter publishing a series of mostly theoretical books on the nature and rights of homosexuals.[2] 'Manor' is set in the Faroe Islands and tells of the love between a youth, Har, and Manor, a seaman; when the latter is killed at sea in a storm, he returns as a spirit and sucks blood at Har's breast. The islanders realise what is happening and drive a stake through Manor's corpse, but Har is so alone without Manor that he wills himself to die; his last wish is that he be laid beside Manor in the grave and that the stake be removed from Manor's corpse – 'And they did what he asked'.

The date of 'Manor' is remarkable, but the choice of the vampire image is less so. The vampire returns time and again in popular homosexual writing. Nina Auerbach (1995: 13–18) suggests that the foundational texts of the modern vampire tale, Lord Byron's 'Fragment of a Tale' (1816) and John Polidori's 'The Vampyre' (1819), are based, and fairly evidently, on their authors' morbidly homo-erotic relationship. *Der Eigene*, a gay male magazine published in Berlin by Adolf Brand from 1896 to 1931, contained much vampire imagery in its fiction and at least one complete vampire story (cf. Hohmann 1981). The British 'bisexual' magazine of the early seventies, *Jeremy*, published in one of its first editions Count Stenbock's 'The True Story of a Vampire', a queer vampire tale first published in 1894. Although not written by a gay man, Anne Rice's vampire novels, beginning with *Interview with the Vampire* in 1976, became cult gay reading, not least because homosexual love is in them an inherent part of the ecstasies of vampirising (cf. Gelder 1994: 108–123).

Even when not specifically vampiric, homosexual writers have often been drawn more generally to the Gothic from early on in the genre's existence, with such notable examples as William Beckford's *Vathek* (1786), Matthew Lewis's *The Monk* (1796) and Mario Vacano's *Mysterien des Welt und Bühnen-lebens* (1861). At the other end of the time scale, one of the most successful early examples of the new gay pulp fiction was Vincent Varga's splendid parody, *Gaywick* (1980), inaugurating a wave of gay Gothic novels not yet abated.

From Manor and Har to Anne Rice's Louis, Armond and Lestat, or from *Vathek* to *Gaywick*, there is a line of vampire or Gothic writing that is predominantly queer/gay produced, or which at any rate forms part of a queer/gay male reading tradition. The situation in relation to lesbianism and vampirism is, as one should expect, different. There is certainly a tradition of lesbian vampires in literature – a listing would probably come up with more titles than with queer male vampires, and with some classier names, including Coleridge and Baudelaire. Yet the overwhelming majority of this lesbian vampire literature was produced by men, notably the influential story by Sheridan LeFanu, 'Carmilla' (1872).

However, as Paulina Palmer notes (1999: 101), although the 'vampire's reputation for transgressive sexuality explains ... the popularity that the motif is currently enjoying in lesbian and queer circles', lesbian produced lesbian vampires only appeared in the 1980s, beginning with Jewelle Gomez's short story 'No Day Too Long' (1981, the start of what would become *The Gilda Stories* 1991) and Jody Scott's science fiction novel *I, Vampire*. In both, the female vampire is the heroine and her vampirising and activity is celebrated. 'No Day Too Long' has the central vampire character Gilda resisting her attraction to the younger woman Effie until she discovers that Effie too is a vampire 'centuries older than she' (225) and thus that she has no reason to run away from her – Gilda is a vampire who lives off mortals' blood but does not kill them or seek to turn them into 'a creature of the night like herself' (224), so it is only when she meets another like herself that she can give her love. *I, Vampire* is about an affair between the main character, an androgynously named but definitely female vampire Sterling O'Blivion, and a genderless creature from outer space (lesbianism breaks down all gender barriers) who is in disguise as Virginia Woolf (lesbianism as a definite sexual identity and tradition). Since these two tales, 'texts centring on the motif have proliferated' (cf. Palmer 1999: 99–127).

There seems however to be no lesbian-produced lesbian vampire tradition behind this. Palmer gives no precedents. There is no reference to a lesbian vampire novel or story written by a lesbian in Jeannette Foster's exhaustive *Sex Variant Women in Literature* (1985) nor have I yet come up with anything from hours of scouring the shelves of lesbian/gay bookshops, such as Gay's the Word in London or Giovanni's Room in Philadelphia. Yet it is hard to believe that *I, Vampire*, *The Gilda Stories* and the rest emerged out of nothing whatsoever. If there are no lesbian lesbian-vampire fictions, there is certainly a tradition of lesbian Gothic, going back at least as far as Djuna Barnes' *Nightwood* (1937) (which has its vampiric overtones) and coming up to date with such enjoyably self-conscious novels as Victoria Ramstetter's *The Marquise and the Novice* (1981) and the wealth of material discussed in Palmer's

Lesbian Gothic. This in turn relates to the general status of Gothic as a 'female' genre, first developed by women, centring on female protagonists and exhibiting a strong sense of being addressed to women (Fleenor 1983; Modleski 1984: 59–84). The most famous illustration of the idea that there is something particularly female-centred about the Gothic is of course Jane Austen's *Northanger Abbey*, first published in 1818, which pokes fun at its heroine's naïve fascination with things Gothic as culled from her extensive reading.

It is perhaps worth pointing out the form of the argument in the previous paragraph, since it diverges so markedly from one that would be made about male Gothic literature. Essentially I argued – as a matter of course, when I first wrote it down – that you could argue for there being something 'lesbian' about vampire literature by pointing to the fact not only of lesbian Gothic but also to the tradition of female Gothic in general. In other words, I argued the lesbian potential of the genre from its relevance to women in general, and not just lesbian women. It would be trickier to make the same sort of case in relation to gay men. Whereas lesbian fiction and culture can often be seen as an extension of female literary and cultural traditions, the writing of queers is often at odds with male fiction and culture. Lesbian Gothic extends forms and feelings well developed within women's writing as a whole (Moers 1978: 90–110), whereas Gothic tends not to be like other men's writing – Gothic fiction, when it is not written by women, has been predominantly the product of homosexuals and/or men who otherwise, as David Punter puts it, 'display in their works and in their lives a tangential relation to socialised masculine norms...' (Punter 1980: 411).[3]

In addition to the suggestiveness of the lesbian/female Gothic tradition as a context for contemporary lesbian vampire fiction, there is also the possibility of a lesbian reading of the vampire images produced by men, as several lesbian essays on the lesbian vampire film suggest (Zimmerman 1981; Weiss 1992: 84–108; Krzywinska 1995). Such a reading may even find something rather progressive in the image:

> The myth of the lesbian vampire ... carries in it the potentiality for a feminist revision of meaning...sexual attraction between women can threaten the authority of a male-dominated society. The lesbian vampire [story] can lend itself to an even more extreme reading: that in turning to each other, women triumph over and destroy men themselves.
>
> (Zimmerman 1981: 23)

Short films like *The Mark of Lillith* (GB 1986) and *Because the Dawn* (USA 1988) explore some of these feminist possibilities.

Apart from specific traditions of gay and lesbian vampire fictions, there is also at a broader level a fit between the values and feelings explored and produced in vampire fiction and the values and feelings of emergent homo-sexual identities in the nineteenth and twentieth century. What has been imagined through the vampire image is of a piece with how people have thought and felt about homosexual women and men – how others have thought and felt about us, and how we have thought and felt about our-selves. Let me illustrate this here from a rather negative example.

Lillian Faderman in her book *Surpassing the Love of Men* (1981) suggests that there is a virtual sub-genre of lesbian vampire novels in the early part of the twentieth century, citing such examples as *Regiment of Women* (1915) by Winifred Ashton (under the pseudonym of Clemence Dane), *White Ladies* (1935) by Francis Brett Young and *Trio* (1943) by Dorothy Baker. These are not vampire novels in the strictest sense of the term – there is no blood-sucking, no notions of being 'un-dead', none of the paraphernalia of the popular vampire tales, but the imagery describing the lesbian relationships in these novels is drawn from vampirism. In *Regiment of Women*, the effect on Alwynne of her relationship with Clare (the headteacher of the school where she works) is noted by Elsbeth, Alwynne's aunt:

> So thin – she's growing so dreadfully thin. Her neck! You should see her neck – salt-cellars, literally! And she had such a beautiful neck! [. . .] And so white and listless!
>
> (Dane 1966: 204)

The effect of lesbianism is the same as the effect of vampirism in the classic vampire tales: loss of weight, blood, energy. Perhaps even more striking here is the effect on the victim's neck: no bite marks, yet still the focus of anxious attention. When Alwynne is 'saved' by taking a holiday away from Clare and meeting a young man, her symptoms disappear; on her return she has 'grown *rosy* and cheerful, affectionate and satisfyingly garrulous' (278, my emphasis). Even more devastatingly vampiric is the effect Clare has on one of her pupils, Louise, who kills herself, leaving behind in one of her school essays a chilling description of being 'pressed to death' by a slab of stone. Ostensibly an account of medieval torture, the writing swiftly becomes per-sonalised until she seems to be writing of her morbid fantasies of death:

> and all the time the stone is sinking – sinking – . . . And perhaps you go to sleep at last. . . . Perhaps you dream. You dream you are free and people love you, and you have done nothing wrong and you are frightfully happy, and the one you love most kisses your fore-head. But then the kiss grows so cold that you shrink away, only you cannot, and it presses you harder and harder, and you wake up and it is the stone. It is the sinking stone that is pressing you, press-ing you, pressing you to death . . .
>
> (196)

The kiss stolen in the victim's sleep, a kiss she desires until she realises it is literally the kiss of death – this is classic vampire imagery, and in the context it is clear that 'the one you love most' is, for Louise, Clare.

Even where the language of the writing does not so explicitly evoke vampirism, the nature of the relationships in the novels Faderman discusses is always one in which a stronger woman dominates and draws the life out of a weaker (and often younger) woman. Faderman's discussion is part of a wider account of a shift in the social definition of intense relationships between women. Where earlier periods had conceived of 'romantic friendships' between women (which might or might not have involved sexual relations), by the early twentieth century the medical and psychological profession had started to think of such relationships in terms of 'lesbianism', as, in other words, defined by the sexual element. Faderman sees this as springing from men's desire to prohibit the possibility of women forming important attachments to each other separate from and even over against their attachments to men. The notion of 'lesbianism', seen as a sickness, was used to discredit both romantic friendship between women and the growth of women's political and educational independence. Thus there is a fit between the general associations of the vampire tale and the way in which friendships between women were being pathologised in the period.

As I indicated, Faderman's examples are negative instances of the general point I wish to make about the fit between vampire imagery and lesbian/gay identities. Quite apart from misgivings one may have about Faderman's account of lesbian identities and her assumption that such identities are necessarily male imposed (cf. Moore 1992), I want here to discuss both the negative and the positive ways in which thinking and feeling about being homosexual have been expressed, by writers and readers, in vampire imagery.

There is clearly a tradition of queer vampire writing and reading. Why should this be?

It is possible to suggest historically specific reasons for given associations of homosexuality and vampirism:

* vampires are classically aristocrats and much of the development of a public face for homosexuality and/or decadent sexuality was at the hands of aristocrats – de Sade, Byron – or writers posing as aristocrats – Lautréamont, Wilde. Auerbach (1995: 102–104) discusses the presiding presence of the latter in the 1907 novel *The House of the Vampire* by George Sylvester Viereck, in which Reginald Clarke, a fascinating 'paragon of brilliance, wit and "world-embracing intellect"' ensnares two young men, Ernest and Jack, who 'breathe poetry at each other while "twitching with a strange ascetic passion"';
* the female character whose potential vampirism is most threatening in

Dracula, Mina, is associated with the emergent 'New Woman' in Victorian society, financially and maritally independent (Senf 1982), and from New Woman to lesbian is but a step in the ideology of the day, leading to the vampiric lesbianism discussed by Faderman;

• in German homosexual writings up to the 1930s, vampirism is the consummation of love with a dead young man, who may represent the lost perfect friendship extolled by the youth movements and/or the loved one lost in the slaughter of the First World War, common themes in the homosexual writing of the period.

Such historically precise connections certainly account for particular inflections of the image, but it is the wider metaphorical possibilities of the vampire that account for its longer hold in queer terms.

The vampire has been used to mean many things – such is the nature of popular cultural symbolism. Vampirism has represented the weight of the past as it lays on the present, or the way the rich live off the poor, or the threat of an unresolved and unpeaceful death, or the baneful influence of Europe on American culture, or an alternative lifestyle as it threatens the established order, or the way the listless white race leeches off the vigour of the black races. The vampire has been used to articulate all such meanings and more (cf. Frayling 1978; Gelder 1994), yet the sexual symbolism of the vampire does seem the most obvious, and many of the other meanings are articulated through the sexual meanings.

The sexuality of the vampire image is obvious if one compares the vampire to two of her/his close relations, as it were, the zombie and the werewolf. The zombie, like the vampire, is 'un-dead', a human being who has died but nonetheless still leads, unlike the vampire, a mindless existence, kept alive in some versions under the spell of voodoo, in others by a purely instinctive drive to savage and eat human flesh. The werewolf, like the vampire, operates only at night and, like the zombie, savages the humans whose flesh he[4] consumes. All three can articulate notions of sexuality. Robin Wood (1985), and a number of other writers on the horror film, have suggested, adapting Freudian ideas, that all 'monsters' in some measure represent the hideous and terrifying form that sexual energies take when they 'return' from being socially and culturally repressed. Yet the vampire seems especially to represent sexuality, for his/her interest in humans is not purely instinctual, and s/he does not characteristically savage them – s/he bites them, with a bite just as often described as a kiss.

The vampire characteristically sinks his/her teeth into the neck of his/her victim and sucks the blood out. You don't have to read this as a sexual image, but an awful lot suggests that you should. Even when the writing does not seem to emphasise the sexual, the act itself is so like a sexual act that it seems almost perverse not to see it as one. Biting itself is, after all, part of the repertoire of sexual acts; call it a kiss, and, when it is as deep a kiss as this, it is a sexual act; it is then by extension obviously analogous to other forms of oral sex acts, all of which (fellatio, cunnilingus, rimming) importantly involve contact not only with orifices but with body fluids as well. Moreover, it is not just what the vampire does that makes vampirism so readable in sexual terms but the social space that it occupies. The act of vampirism takes place in private, at night, most archetypally in a bedroom, that is, the same space as our society accords the sex act.

That vampirism has been thought of in sexual terms is evident when one starts to look at how it is in fact described. *Dracula* (1897) contains passages that are pretty well pornographic in their detailing of the experience of being vampirised:

> The fair girl went on her knees and bent over me, fairly gloating. There was a deliberate voluptuousness which was both thrilling and repulsive, and as she arched her neck she actually licked her lips like an animal, till I could see in the moonlight the moisture shining on the scarlet lips and on the red tongue as it lapped the white sharp teeth. ... Then ... I could feel the soft, shivering touch of the lips on the supersensitive skin of my throat, and the hard dents of two sharp teeth, just touching and pausing there. I closed my eyes in a languorous ecstasy and waited – waited with beating heart.
>
> (Stoker 1985: 52)

Compare this ecstasy with that evoked eighty years later by Anne Rice in *Interview with the Vampire*, where it is possible to make more explicit genital reference but which is in other respects only building on the delicious perversity of the voluptuousness already evoked so clearly in Stoker. Here the vampire is the narrator and, like his 'victim', male:

> Never had I felt this, never had I experienced it, this yielding of a conscious mortal. But before I could push him away for his own sake, I saw the bluish bruise on his tender neck. He was offering it to me. He was pressing the length of his body against me now, and I felt the hard strength of his sex beneath his clothes pressing against my leg. A wretched gasp escaped my lips, but he bent close, his lips on what must have been so cold, so lifeless for him; and I sank my teeth into his skin, my body rigid, that hard sex driving against me, and I lifted him in passion off the floor. Wave after wave of his beating heart passed into me as, weightless, I rocked with him, devouring him, his ecstasy, his conscious pleasure.
>
> (Rice 1976: 248)

The vampire idea lends itself to a sexual reading and is even, in Rosemary Jackson's words, 'perhaps the highest symbolic representation of eroticism'

(1981: 120). It has articulated particular conceptions of sexuality (in Jackson, psycho-analytic ones) and it is some of these that I want to go through now, indicating both how they relate to general ideas about sexuality and how they are particularly amenable to queer interpretations. I shall be making reference to explicitly queer vampire fictions, and also to heterosexual fictions where, nonetheless, much of the form of the vampirism/ sexuality is homologous with the social construction of queerness.

To begin with, the physical space where the act of vampirism/sex takes place is also a symbolic, psychological space, namely the realm of the private. It is at night when we are alone in our beds that the vampire classically comes to call, when we are by ourselves and, as we commonly think, when we are most ourselves. Equally, it is one of the contentions of the history of sexuality, inspired by the work of Michel Foucault, that we live in an age which considers the sexual to be both the most private of things and the realm of life in which we are most ourselves.

The privacy of the sexual is embodied in one of the set-pieces of the vampire tale: the heroine left by herself at night, the vampire at the window tapping to come in. Yet as so often with popular genre conventions, this set-piece is also endlessly being reversed, departed from. Very often, it is not the privatised experience of the act of vampirism that is given us, but those thrilling moments when the privacy is violated. Voyeurism, the act of seeing without being seen, is a central narrative device in the vampire story; it is the means by which the hero discovers the vampirism of the vampire, and the sensation lies not only in the lurid description of fangs dripping with blood and swooning victims, their clothes all awry, but also in that sense of violating a moment of private physical consummation, violating its privacy by looking at it.

Voyeurism is one of the vampire tale's perverse disruptions of the construction of the sexual as private and is central to the genre. Characteristically, it is Anne Rice who further twists the pleasures of perversity by introducing exhibitionism, actively displaying sexuality to the view. In *Interview with the Vampire*, she depicts a Théâtre des Vampires in nineteenth-century Paris. Louis, the narrator of the book (and the interviewee of the title), visits the show and sees performed a strange, ritualistic play in which a young woman is sucked to death by a band of vampires. The sensuality of the scene is emphasised by the language and by the emphasis on the way the audience leans forward to see the moment of ravishment. They are relishing the enactment of the decadent idea of vampirism; but Louis, and therefore the reader, knows these vampires are no actors and the woman's sacrifice no mere performance. So not only do we pick up on the frisson of the jaded Paris audience, but we have the extra thrill of knowing that we, through Louis, are really seeing a fatal act of vampirism.

There is nothing inherently gay or lesbian about ideas of privacy, voyeurism and exhibitionism. Yet homosexual desire, like other forbidden sexual desires, may well find expression, as a matter of necessity rather than exquisite choice, in privacy and voyeurism. The sense that being a queer is something one must keep to oneself certainly accords with an idea of the authenticity of private sexuality, but it is also something one had better keep private if one is not to lose job, family, friends and so on. Furtive looking may be the most one dare do. In this context, exhibitionism may take on a special voluptuousness, emerging from the privacy of the closet in the most extravagant act of going public.

Vampirism is not merely, like all our sexuality, private, it is also secret. It is something to be hidden, to be done without anyone knowing. The narrative structure of the vampire tale frequently consists of two parts, the first leading up to the discovery of the vampire's hidden nature, the second concerned with his/her destruction. It is this first part that I want to consider here.

In most vampire tales, the fact that a character is a vampire is only gradually discovered – it is a secret that has to be found out. The analogy with homosexuality as a secret erotic practice works in two contradictory ways. On the one hand, the point about sexual orientation is that it doesn't 'show', you can't tell who is and who isn't just by looking; but on the other hand, there is also a widespread discourse that there are tell-tale signs that someone 'is'. The vampire myth reproduces this double view in its very structures of suspense.

Much of the suspense of the story is about finding out. There are strange goings-on, people dying of a mysterious plague, characters feeling unaccountably weak after a deep night's sleep, noticing odd scratches or a pair of little holes at their neck – what can it all mean? The nature of this suspense may vary for the reader. It may be a genuine mystery to us, so that the discovery of what has caused all this – vampirism – and/or who (which already-known character) has caused it, comes as a satisfying moment of revelation akin to the pleasures of the whodunnit. However, it is probably the case that one seldom reads a vampire story without knowing that that is what it is. This is especially true since the publication of *Dracula* and even more so when you are reading any of the numerous collections of vampire tales. The first readers of 'Carmilla' may have had the shock of discovery that Carmilla is a vampire (compounded by the fact that she is lesbian), but few people reading it today are likely to be unforearmed. Rather, what we enjoy is knowing that plagues, fatigues, scratches and holes spell vampire and the suspense that that affords us: when will s/he find out what we already know and will it be in time (before being vampirised, or else dying)? A special inflection here occurs with the use of first person narrators, so that all we get is the narrator's perceptions and yet we know, as old hands at the genre, what those perceptions mean. So the sense of menace, as the narrator rubs shoulders with the person we know is a vampire, is greater for us than her/him – we know better.

Such reader–text relations offer specific pleasures to homosexual readers. Much of the suspense of a life lived in the closet is precisely, 'will they find out?' An obvious way to read a vampire story is self-oppressively, in the sense of siding with the narrator (whether s/he is the main character or not) and investing energy in the hope that s/he will be saved from the knowledge of vampirism (homosexuality). Maybe that is how queers have often read it. But there are other ways. One is to identify with the vampire in some sort, despite the narrative position, and to enjoy the ignorance of the main character(s). What fools these mortals be. The structure whereby we the reader know more than the protagonist (heightened in first person narration) is delicious, and turns what is perilous in a closeted queer life (knowing something dreadful about oneself that they don't) into something flattering, for it makes one superior. Another enjoyable way of positioning oneself in this text–reader relation is in thrilling to the extraordinary power credited to the vampire, transcendent powers of seduction, they can have anyone they want it seems. Most queers experienced exactly the opposite, certainly outside of the gay scene, certainly up until very recently. Even though the vampire is invariably killed off at the end (except in recent examples), how splendid to know what a threat our secret is to them!

The structure of the narration reinforces the idea that you can't tell who is and isn't, but the descriptive language often suggests the opposing discourse, that you can indeed spot a queer. It is not that they often come on with all the accoutrements of the screen vampires of Lugosi, Lee *et al.*; perhaps only Dracula and a few very close to him are described like that. What there are instead are give-away aspects of character. Count Vardalek, for instance, in 'The True Story of a Vampire' is tall and fair with an attractive smile. Nothing very vampiric about this, as the narrator herself notes. But along with it he is also 'refined', with an 'intense sadness of the expression of the eyes'; he looks 'worn and wearied'; above all, he is 'very pale' (Stenbock 1970: 22). There is even less of the vampire about Carmilla, except that – and it is the give-away to alert readers – 'her movements were languid – very languid – indeed' (LeFanu n.d.: 387).

Not only has it been common to try to indicate that you can always tell a queer/lessie if you know how (indeed, this is one of the functions of homosexual stereotypes), but very often the vocabulary of queer spotting has been the languid, worn, sad, refined paleness of vampire imagery. This is what makes the lesbianism of the books discussed by Faderman vampiric; it is what used to tell me in the fifties and sixties that a book had a gay theme – if it was called *Women in the Shadows*, *Twilight Men*, *Desire in the Shadows*, then it had to be about queers. This imagery derives in part from the idea of decadence, people who do not go out into public life, whose complexions are not weathered, who are always indoors or in the shade. It may also relate to the idea that lesbians and gay men are not 'real' women and men, we have not got the blood (with its very different gender associations) of normal human beings.

The ideas of privacy and secrecy also suggest the idea of a double life: s/he looks normal, but underneath s/he's a vampire/queer. This simple structure is often given complex inflections. At the end of 'Carmilla' the narrator, Laura, recalls the two faces of the vampire Carmilla: 'sometimes the playful, languid, beautiful, girl; sometimes the writhing fiend I saw in the ruined church' (LeFanu n.d.: 471). Part of the fascination of the story, however, lies in the way these two aspects of Carmilla's personality alternate, merge and interact throughout, less separate than perhaps Laura, ten years later, likes to think, for perhaps her adolescent crush on Carmilla was not only because of the latter's languidness ... In Théophile Gautier's 'La Morte amoureuse' (first published in *Chronique de Paris*, June 23–26, 1836), the priest hero Romuald has succumbed to the vampiric caresses of Clarimonde who visits him and

> [from] that night onward my nature was in some way doubled; there was within me two men, neither of whom knew the other. Sometimes I thought I was a priest who dreamed every night he was a nobleman, sometimes I was a nobleman who dreamed that he was a priest.
>
> (Gautier 1962: 118)

Not only does the act of vampirism release the character's sexuality, and not only is the latter equated with the nobility and chastity with the priesthood, but a fascinating ambivalence remains, since both the sexual and chaste sides of himself dream of being the other.

The classic metaphoric Gothic statement of the idea of the gay male double life is Wilde's *The Picture of Dorian Gray* (1891), which has fixed an image of the gay man as a sparkling, agreeable surface masking a hidden depravity, brilliant charm concealing a corrupt and sordid sexuality. Dorian Gray in Wilde's novel is not a vampire, but in 'The Amplified Journal of D.G.' (serialised anonymously in the gay softporn magazine *Mandate*) he is. In the second diary entry (October 1986), the narrator explains that he has given himself the name Dorian Gray, because that is the name Wilde gave the character for which the narrator was the original inspiration. Thus 'D.G.' suggests that Dorian Gray, an archetype of queer existence, is a fundamentally vampiric creation.

Vampirism is private and secret, and may therefore be the terrible reality of the inner self, but in another sense it is beyond the self because it is beyond the individual's will and control. This is true for vampire and victim alike. Vampires are driven on by the absolute necessity for blood to stay 'alive', they can't help themselves; victims are either asleep or mesmerised by the vampire's power or charm, so that they have no responsibility for surrendering to the latter's kiss.

The queer resonances are even stronger here. One of the most important –

and, it must be said, effective – ways in which homosexuality has been justified and defended in the twentieth century is through the argument that 'we/they can't help it'. Much of the feel of apologia for homosexuality, whether written by queers themselves or by others, has been a mix of distaste for homosexuality with a recognition that it cannot be resisted: 'I don't know why I want to do these disgusting things, but I do and can't stop myself and there's no real harm in it.'

But the point about uncontrollability is more interesting than that. There is, as indicated above, an active (vampire) and a passive (victim) form to this lack of control, but it is not necessarily correlated with active = male and passive = female. Even *Dracula*, while it gives us the typical lady-asleep-with-vampire-at-her-neck set pieces, also gives us the delirium of the pleasures of male passivity:

> I could feel the soft, shivering touch of the lips on the supersensitive skin of my throat, and the hard dents of two sharp teeth, just touching and pausing there. I closed my eyes in a languorous ecstasy and waited – waited with beating heart.
>
> (52)

Alas, the Count interrupts the fulfilment of Jonathan Harker's languor, and his own no doubt even more deliciously soft-yet-hard treatment of Jonathan's recumbent person is concealed in the gap between two chapters.[5] Equally enthralled by the pleasures of passivity is Romuald in 'La Morte amoureuse' and here the language of male sexuality is applied to what the woman does, first at the moment of seduction:

> the coolness of Clarimonde's hand *penetrated* mine, and I felt voluptuous shivers run all over my body.
>
> (Gautier 1962: 115, my emphasis)

Later, when she holds sway over him, the phallic imagery (the needle, the prick, the man lying back and enjoying it) is clear enough for the most unconvinced Freudian:

> When she felt sure that I was asleep, she bared my arm and drew a golden pin from her hair; then she began to murmur in a low voice: 'One drop, just one little red drop, a ruby on the point of my needle! [...] Ah! poor love! your beautiful blood, such a vivid crimson, I am going to drink it! Sleep, my only treasure; sleep, my god, my child. [...] Ah! what a lovely arm! how round it is! how white it is! I shall never dare to prick that pretty blue vein'.
>
> (ibid.: 121)

But of course she does dare, to everyone's (her, his, our) satisfaction. Indeed her threat not to dare to prick him can be seen as a classic foreplay tease of the passive lover, and her love language evokes her as both adoringly sub-servient woman ('my god') and warmly encompassing mother ('my child') even while in fact being a deliciously phallic woman.

The pleasures of passivity for men are then frequently evoked in vampire fiction; the pleasures of activity for women less so. We have images of sex-ually/vampirically active women, and no doubt these can be identified with, but the point-of-view is nearly always the man's. This is partly because, as discussed below, until recently very few vampire stories are told from the point of view of the vampire anyway, but only from that of the victim or onlooker. So although we have images of an active female sexuality, this is more often seen in terms of its threat/treat for the man. It is not until Jody Scott's *I, Vampire*, that we get the pleasures of active female desire, and then with a vengeance:

> And then the thrill of victory forever new, the ritualized ecstasy as I master the unconscious victim and at long last that slow, marvel-lous caress on the tongue as the Ruby slips down my throat . . .
>
> (5)

Again, male passivity and female activity, and slipping between the two, does not have to be an expression of queer sexuality, but there is no doubt that the felt inevitability, or propriety, of the usual equation in heterosexual relations goes to the wall in homosexual ones. It is not very profitable to talk in terms of active and passive in relation to oral sex, which is, after mutual masturbation, the commonest form of lesbian and gay sexual practice and is also the most obvious sexual reference point of vampirism. Though there is often much gender role-playing, even to the point of exaggeration, in queer relationships, this correlates unpredictably with who does what in bed, who is really strongest in the relationship. The play of gender role, sexual posi-tion, active/passive is part of the structure of vampirism and lesbian/gay sex-uality alike – unlike heterosexuality (at least at the level of representation), such play is the rule, not the exception.

The ideas in vampire fiction of what sexuality is like – privacy, secrecy, uncontrollability, active/passive – have a complex relationship to the place of sexuality within the social order. Until the 1960s, sexuality was approved only within marriage. Vampirism takes place outside of marriage. Marriage is the social institution of the privacy of sexuality – the vampire violates it, tapping at the window to get in, providing sexual scenes for the narrator to witness. Marriage contains female sexuality – hence the horror of the female vampire, walking the streets at night in search of sex. Men are allowed to walk those streets for that purpose, hence the ambivalence of the male vampire, the fulfilment of the importunate nature of male sexuality, dangerous, horrible, but also taken to be what men, alas, are. Finally, marriage restricts sexuality to heterosexuality – vampirism is the alternative, dreaded and desired in equal measure.

I have so far been trying to indicate why vampirism is so easy to read as an image of queer sexuality and experience. What interests me finally is the way this potential for queer meaning also articulates evaluations of homosexuality. In all vampire fiction, vampirism can be taken to evoke the thrill of a forbidden sexuality, but whereas earlier examples also express horror and revulsion at it, later examples turn this on its head and celebrate it.

One way we might note this shift in emphasis is in the narrator. In most vampire tales up to the 1970s, the narrator is not her or himself a vampire. Either we have the convention of the omniscient narrator telling what befell a group of people; or we have personal testimony (multiple in the case of *Dracula*) about being involved in a case of vampirism as victim, observer or rescuer. But in no case does the vampire tell his/her own story. Although there may be earlier examples, the most striking example of a shift to the vampire as narrator of his/her own tale is *Interview with the Vampire*, and the very remarkableness of this shift is signalled by the use of the rather elaborate device of having the vampire interviewed. The book starts with an omniscient narrator describing the scene of 'the boy', a magazine reporter, and the vampire together in a room in New Orleans and with the boy eliciting the vampire's story from him. Most of the book consists of the vampire, Louis's, first person narration of his life, but every paragraph opens with double inverted commas to remind us of the interview situation and there are occasional interruptions from the boy, putting questions, asking Louis to stop while he changes the cassette. This device constantly reminds us of the fact that a vampire is speaking for himself. By the time of the sequel, *The Vampire Lestat* (1985), there was no need for such signalling and we get a straightforward first-person vampire's account of his life. Likewise *I, Vampire*, as its title announces, launches straight into first person vampire narrative. Interestingly some later chapters deal with non-vampire characters in a third person narration. It is not clear whether this is meant to be the hero, Sterling O'Blivion's, words, but in any case it is striking that whereas the vampire speaks for herself, 'normals' are left to be described in the third person from without.

This shift in the position of the narrator *vis-à-vis* vampirism is surely analogous with the shift, and insistence upon the shift, from homosexuals as persons who are spoken about to persons who speak for themselves. It is also a shift from disgust to delight. Compare the two 'pornographic' quotations above, from *Dracula* and *Interview with the Vampire*. In *Dracula* the act is revolting: thrilling but 'repulsive', animalistic, with 'churning' sounds and flesh tingling. When, later, Jonathan discovers the Count, his vampiric lust satisfied, he describes him 'gorged with blood' laying 'like a filthy leech, exhausted with his repletion'. Louis and his 'victim', on the other hand, are both clearly transported by their quite explicitly sexual vampiric union – they experience 'passion', 'ecstasy', 'pleasure'; repeated references to hardness and rigidity indicate male sexual response; and there is even an aestheticising of the experience in the way 'the boy' 'offers' Louis 'the bluish bruise on his tender neck'.

The earlier vampire fictions are not written in the first person, but of course this does not mean that queers may not have identified with the negative image of a disgusting, uncontrollable, forbidden vampire lust. In his fine 1984 novel, *Why We Never Danced the Charleston*, Harlan Greene describes the lives of a group of young men in Charleston in the 1920s. He returns repeatedly to vampire imagery to express how they felt about themselves:

> I was condemned like a vampire . . . to eternal darkness. I was nauseatingly white and sluglike; I was a repulsive moonlit thing that crawled out from under a rock and in to the evening. In a word, I was queer.
>
> (26)

Early homosexual vampire fiction does not in fact express quite such self-loathing as this. In 'Vampir' by Julius Neuss (published in *Der Eigene* in 1922), the vampire Morsa, dark, cadaverous and 'feminine', represents the threat/promise of adventure and pleasure for Adolf, fair, youthful and muscular. In the end Morsa overcomes Adolf's resistance, the feminine overcoming the muscular to the point of death, in a sequence of intense moral ambiguity but erotic certainty.

> Never had the magic of his [Adolf's] face had a more powerful effect on Morsa than now, as the struggle with death played across it.
>
> Never had his sacrifice seemed more enchantingly beautiful to him . . . than now, as he clasped Adolf in his arms, the bitter taste of blood on his tongue and, in a paroxysm of despair, sobbing endlessly like one insane: 'Your soul! Your soul!'.
>
> (Hohmann 1981: 199)

Other early tales express a sorrowful sympathy for the 'curse' of being a vampire/queer. 'The True Story of a Vampire' is suffused with melancholy. Count Vardalek wishes he did not have to vampirise the boy Gabriel; he says to him:

> 'My darling, I fain would spare thee: but thy life is my life, and I must live, I who would rather die. Will God not have any mercy on me? Oh! oh! life; oh, the torture of life!'
>
> (Stenbock 1970: 24)

Vardalek's tragedy is that he wants to die but cannot. Elsewhere vampirism represents the promise of death as a release from the confines of normal society and the very form of the consummation of gay love. Har's death in 'Manor' provides a gay happy ending to the story, becoming 'un-dead' is to become one's true sexual nature.

There is a potential contradiction in a 'positive' use of the vampire in gay/lesbian fiction. Classically vampires do not vampirise each other. What will Har and Manor 'do' now they are both un-dead? The transcendent reunion that ends the tale leaves this question unasked and, besides, transcendent friendship was the ostensible goal of much German gay culture of the period. For later writers it has been an interesting problem. Vampirism can now be celebrated as the most exquisite form of sexual pleasuring, yet it remains outside of ideal sexual relationships. The different ways of handling this in contemporary lesbian and gay vampire fiction relate to different conceptions of what it is to be homosexual within both the lesbian and gay communities.

One approach is to play down the erotic overtones of vampirising. In Gomez's 'No Day Too Long', vampirism is a sign of Gilda's difference, an intensification of her lesbianism. She was a runaway slave who killed a white man who'd tracked her down and was made into a vampire by a woman who found her; her vampirism relates to an heroic, Amazonian past and separates her from the mortal lesbians with whom she works as a nightclub singer. Vampirism here is a metaphor for lesbianism as something more than a sexual preference, a different way of grasping the essence of womanhood, with the resonance of the black feminist concept of 'womanism' (Walker 1983). The act of vampirising in 'No Day Too Long' is merely the way Gilda survives; and yet being a vampire does give her character a powerful erotic charge. The point of the narrative is Gilda's happiness at finding someone else like herself. Gilda and Effie, both vampires, end up in each other's arms but not at each other's throats.

Other examples retain the eroticism of vampirism and yet distinguish it from love. In *I, Vampire*, Sterling's sexy vampirising is kept distinct from her feeling for her loved one, Benaroya:

> Sterling was deeply, sincerely in love for the first time in her life. But she couldn't even extol her loved one's eyes, lips, hair, and so on; because it was not a body she loved, but a person.
>
> (178)

This body:person split is explicable within the narrative, because Benaroya is an alien who has merely assumed the body of Virginia Woolf for its visit to Earth – but the very choice of this device permits a traditional moral dualism for which the relish with which vampirising is described in the book does not prepare you. Anne Rice's vampire novels dwell at length on the eroticism of vampirism, but they too distinguish it from relationships. In *Interview with the Vampire* there is a pervading sense of loneliness, the endless pursuit of sexual/vampiric ecstasy without romantic fulfilment. Louis hates the other main vampire character in the book, Lestat, the man who made him a vampire. The sequel is Lestat's own story and contains more than one fulfilling gay love affair, but these are always implicitly sexual but not vampiric. Both partners go on vampirising. The genre requires this, of course, it is how vampires 'live', but, as it retains its erotic charge, it also corresponds to the widespread model of gay male coupledom where a stable central relationship and continued cruising and promiscuity are not held to be incompatible.

AIDS of course has appeared to challenge that model and it might seem too that it spelt the end of 'positive' gay vampire fiction, with body fluids and blood so central to both vampirism and the passing on of AIDS. Ellis Hanson (1991) discusses the ways that the vampire tradition feeds into the homophobic imagery of AIDS hysteria, 'the irrational fear of PWAs and gay men who "bite"' (325). Yet *The Amplified Journal of D.G.* suggests a different way of feeling the relationship between AIDS and sexuality. Dorian, the vampire narrator/hero, cruises New York, a city that is dying:

> They are renouncing it, they who have kept me company since my reawakening from the Long Sleep. Something beautiful is dying, and only I will mourn it. Others weep for those who pass. I alone weep for what is passing.
>
> (October 1986: 60)

The reference is clearly to the decline of gay night life with the coming of AIDS – but the importance is that the writer continues to affirm that life, to mourn its passing more than the deaths it has supposedly caused. He rejects too the antiseptic notions of sexuality with which ideas of safe sex may resonate:

> at the notion of 'safe sex' I am bound to laugh. Sex – all sex – is dangerous. Between strangers, friends, lovers; between husband and wife; in groups, alone. Sex is exquisitely dangerous – to the soul, always; to the body, sometimes, if your blood should be invaded, or if you and your partner should choose to play medieval games before first mastering the rules, or if dark misfortune should put you in the arms of the wrong alluring stranger.
>
> (ibid.: 88)

This is a familiar gay voice: it is the voice of that part of the gay liberation movement which set itself against respectability and fitting in, against monogamy and passing for straight; it is the voice many hear in Genet, and others of the *poètes maudits*, where depravity and degradation are validated; it is the voice that prizes gayness as outlawry and living on the edge. Through the vampire image it pushes at the boundaries of sexual ecstasy. Even sadomasochism, often presented as the very frontier of sexual outlawry, is seen by Dorian as mere theatre, without the true ecstasy of vampirism. When Dorian, in the first entry, picks up a man who fancies an S&M scene, the man loses his nerve when Dorian gets into real (vampiric) sadism. As elsewhere in the writing, Dorian addresses the reader as the ideal lover he is looking for; here he compares the reader with the man he has picked up:

> He trembles against me. He sobs on my shoulder. He is not wearing his fear well. There is not a tatter of doubt left in me: He is not you. You would be afraid, yes; but your fear would be thrilling. And you would know how to ride it.
>
> (June 1986: 71–72)

Thus the writer enlists the reader in the fantasy of homosexual outlawry; defiantly he asks us to feel still the thrill of the dangers of sex just at the point when the danger of those thrills seems to have become too great.

The variations in the use of vampirism as homosexuality in contemporary lesbian and gay fiction do not exhaust the range of ways in which lesbians and gay men inhabit their sexuality, but they do indicate that there is life in the metaphor yet. Or rather that it remains un-dead. In all cases vampirism represents something about homosexual desire that remains stubbornly marginal, unruly, fascinating and indispensable – the blood remains, as it was for Dracula, 'the life'. But also, in all cases, homosexuality is the basis for the most intense, even transcendent romantic relationships. The difference lies in whether this is constructed as something distinct from (blood) lust (Gomez, Scott, Rice) or is to be plucked from the very heart of lust ('D.G.').

Acknowledgement

From (revised) Susannah Radstone (ed.) *Sweet Dreams: Sexuality, Gender and Popular Fiction*, London: Lawrence and Wishart, 1988.

Notes

1 Reprinted many times thereafter and available in Hohmann 1983: 271–278.
2 His works were known collectively as *Forschungen über das Räthsel der mann-männlichen Liebe* (Researches on the Riddle of Love between Men). See Steakley 1975: 3–9 and Baumgardt 1984: 13–16.
3 Vampirism can express a notion of the outsiderdom of male heterosexuality, seen as inherently violent, insistent and unruly, as unsocialised, uncivilised and above all undomesticated. There is certainly room for consideration of the differences (cf. Dyer 1993) but also similarities between this construction of sexuality

– at once dominant and marginal – and a queer one. Auerbach 1995: 83–84 suggests a starting point, arguing that the model for Dracula was Oscar Wilde (the book appearing two years after Wilde's trial).

4   I do not know of a story of a female werewolf, and the majority of werewolf stories are in part about the notion of the beast that dwells in the breast of the apparently civilised man – in other words, the werewolf image seems to articulate part of our culture's concept of masculinity.

5   For an analysis of male passivity, suppressed homo-eroticism and the male desire to be penetrated in *Dracula*, see Craft 1984.

References

Anon (1986–7) *The Amplified Journal of D.G.*, *Mandate*, July 1986: 5–6, 60, 66, 70–72; October 1986: 50, 60, 88–94; November 1986: 50–53, 71–72; January 1987: 7–9, 75–76, 90–92.

Auerbach, Nina (1995) *Our Vampires, Ourselves*, Chicago: University of Chicago.

Barnes, Djuna (1937) *Nightwood*, New York: Harcourt, Brace & Co.

Baumgardt, Manfred (1984) 'Berlin, ein Zentrum der entstehenden Sexualwissenchaft und die Vorläufer der Homosexuellen-Bewegung', in Bollé, Michael (ed.) *Eldorado. Homosexuelle Frauen und Männer in Berlin 1850–1950. Geschichte, Alltag und Kultur*, Berlin: Frölich and Kaufmann.

Craft, Christopher (1984) ' "Kiss Me With Those Red Lips": Gender and Inversion in Bram Stoker's *Dracula*', *Representations* 8: 107–133.

Dane, Clemence (1966) *Regiment of Women*, London: Heinemann (first published 1917).

Dyer, Richard (1993) 'Dracula and Desire', *Sight and Sound* NS 3: 1, 8–11.

Faderman, Lillian (1981) *Surpassing the Love of Men*, New York: Morrow.

Fleenor, Juliann E. (ed.) (1983) *The Female Gothic*, Montreal: Eden Press.

Foster, Jeanette (1985) *Sex Variant Women in Literature*, Tallahassee: Naiad (first published 1956).

Frayling, Christopher (1978) *The Vampyre*, London: Gollancz.

Gautier, Théophile (1962), *Contes fantastiques*, Paris: José Corti.

Gelder, Ken (1994) *Reading the Vampire*, London: Routledge.

Gomez, Jewelle (1981) 'No Day Too Long', in Bulkin, Elly (ed.) *Lesbian Fiction*, Watertown, MA: Persephone.

Gomez, Jewelle (1991) *The Gilda Stories*, London: Sheba.

Greene, Harlan (1984) *Why We Never Danced the Charleston*, New York: St. Martin's Press.

Hanson, Ellis (1991) 'Undead', in Fuss, Diana (ed.) *Inside/Out: Lesbian Theories, Gay Theories*, New York: Routledge, 324–340.

Hohmann, Joachim S. (ed.) (1981) *Der Eigene. Ein Querschnitt durch die erste Homosexuellenzeitschrift der Welt*, Frankfurt am Main/Berlin: Foerster.

Hohmann, Joachim S. (ed.) (1983) *Entstellte Engel: Homosexuelle Schreiben*, Frankfurt am Main: Fisher.

Jackson, Rosemary (1981) *Fantasy, the Literature of Subversion*, London: Methuen.

Keesey, Pam (ed.) (1995) *Dark Angels: Lesbian Vampire Stories*, Pittsburgh: Cleis.

Krzywinska, Tanya (1995) 'La Belle Dame Sans Merci?', in Burston, Paul and Richardson, Colin (eds) *A Queer Romance: Lesbians, Gay Men and Popular Culture*, London: Routledge, 99–110.

LeFanu, Sheridan (n.d.) *In a Glass Darkly*, London: Eveleigh Nash & Grayson (first published 1872).

Modleski, Tania (1984) *Loving with a Vengeance*, New York: Methuen.

Moers, Ellen (1978) *Literary Women*, London: The Women's Press.

Moore, Lisa (1992) '"Something More Tender Still than Friendship": Romantic Friendship in Early Nineteenth Century England', *Feminist Studies* 18 (3): 499–520.

Palmer, Paulina (1999) *Lesbian Gothic: Transgressive Fictions*, London: Cassell.

Punter, David (1980) *The Literature of Terror*, London: Longman.

Ramstetter, Victoria (1981) *The Marquise and the Novice*, Tallahassee: Naiad.

Rice, Anne (1976) *Interview with the Vampire*, New York: Knopf.

Scott, Jody (1984) *I, Vampire*, New York: Ace Science Fiction.

Senf, Carol A. (1982) '*Dracula*: Stoker's Response to the New Woman', *Victorian Studies* 26: 33–39.

Steakley, James D. (1975) *The Homosexual Emancipation Movement in Germany*, New York: Arno Press.

Stenbock, Count (1970) 'The True Story of a Vampire', *Jeremy* 2: 20–24. (First published 1894; reprinted in Dickie, James (ed.) *The Undead: Vampire Masterpieces*, London: Pan, 169–70.)

Stoker, Bram (1985) *Dracula*, Harmondsworth: Penguin. (First published 1897.)

Varga, Vincent (1980) *Gaywick*, New York: Avon Books.

Walker, Alice (1983) *In Search of Our Mother's Gardens*, London: The Women's Press.

Weiss, Andrea (1992) *Vampires and Violets: Lesbians in the Cinema*, London: Cape.

Wood, Robin (1985) 'An Introduction to the American Horror Film', in Nichols, Bill (ed.) *Movies and Methods II*, Berkeley: University of California Press, 195–220.

Zimmerman, Bonnie (1981) 'Lesbian Vampires', *Jump Cut* 24/25, 23–24.

Further reading

Benshoff, Harry M. (1997) *Monsters in the Closet: Homosexuality and the Horror Film*, Manchester: Manchester University Press.

Case, Sue-Ellen (1991) 'Tracking the Vampire', *Differences* 3: 2, 1–20.

7

QUEER NOIR

What are you doing in a neighbourhood like this?
(Johnny to Ballin in *Gilda*)

They'll be looking for us in every closet.
(Fante to Mingo in *The Big Combo*)

It is widely known that male homosexuals[1] figure significantly in film noir.[2] By no means all noir films have queers in them, yet many of the most celebrated do or may (*The Big Sleep, Gilda, Laura, The Maltese Falcon, Strangers on a Train*) and they stand out in a period (the 1940s and early 1950s) when there was little other such representation. However, when one looks at the films again, it's not always so clear why we think there are queers in them: in noir, some of the most obvious queens are married, some straight guy friendships could just be that while other nominations are hard to swallow. I've had students at each other's throats over whether the relationship of Johnny and Ballin in *Gilda* is really homosexual and I have myself been taken aback by some proposed examples, such as Jack Marlowe in *Phantom Lady* and Walter Neff and Keyes in *Double Indemnity*. One may feel strongly that so-and-so is a queer and he may well be, but it is seldom certain.

In this chapter I want to suggest that such uncertainty is not just the perennial difficulty of reading homosexuality back into past culture, but very much part of the mood, the noirness, of these films. One can explain the uncertainty in part by reference to censorship (one is not going to find explicit physical contact or verbal declaration in the period), but it is also of a piece with noir's general uncertainty about how to decipher the world.

Uncertainty is built into noir's central narrative organisation. These are films about finding out. In most cases, what is to be found out is eventually found out, but in the process a world profoundly deceptive and disorienting is revealed: you can't rely on how things look or what people say (not even the innocent); the process of unravelling the mystery is confusing, full of deceptions, detours, blind alleys; the telling involves complicated, sometimes contradictory flash-backs, voice-overs and dream sequences; the geography of the films can confuse, with rambling residences, mirrors that double the world or turn out to be windows, even literal mazes; and noir's famed chiaroscuro and skewed angles unsettle perception.

As a result, you cannot be sure that the co-ordinates of the film's implicit social world are securely in place. The classic detective story assumes that if you just sort out the crime at hand, that is, this particular disruption of the social order, then the pieces of that order will fall back into place; it assumes that the underlying fabric of society and the means for comprehending it are sound. This is not the case with noir. Here crime and respectability are bedfellows, Anglo-Saxon supremacy is being nudged out by Latin and other (though not yet black) pretenders, women have added money and independence to the power of sexual allure that they always had, and there seem to be all these queers, marginal yet insidiously present.

I begin exploring the latter – all these queers – with the question of reading, of why certain characters might be thought to be queers. I look in detail at two contentious examples (*Kiss of Death* and *The Big Sleep*) before considering other examples even less clear than these. I then look at three aspects of queer noir uncertainty – stereotypes, noir queers' devotion to women, male–male relationships – before situating these representations in relation to noir more generally, considering what it was about noir that facilitated the re-emergence of queers in Hollywood cinema and the role of queers in noir: villainy, uncertainty, unmasculinity.

In *Kiss of Death* (1947), Nick Bianco (Victor Mature), a convict on parole, is persuaded by the police to pick up an acquaintance with psychotic hoodlum Tommy Udo (Richard Widmark) in order to get evidence against him and those he works for. Nick bumps into Tommy accidentally on purpose at a boxing match; they go drinking together at a flash nightclub and Tommy sends his girlfriend away so he can be with Nick alone. There is then a cut from the noisy nightclub to a high-angled shot looking down on a quite spacious, rather old-fashioned, drab and utterly silent entrance hall; a man goes to the door and lets in Tommy and Nick; they walk across the hall into the back, Nick asking, 'What's that smell?' and Tommy replying, 'Perfume'; end of shot.

There is no doubt that this last shot is entirely understandable in terms of heterosexuality: two guys out on the town go to a brothel together. The strangeness of the treatment (the silence, the dowdy *mise-en-scène*, the high-angle shot and single take) can be plausibly accounted for in terms of censorship (you could not make it too clear it was a brothel) or possibly class (it might be an up-market brothel, quiet, unflashy). Yet it is also very easy, inspired by that odd opacity of treatment (what *is* going on here?), to make the case for this as a queer moment.

Tommy, like many noir queers, dresses at once smoothly and showily (very neatly slicked back hair, off-white coat and tie against black shirt and jacket) (Figure 7.1). At the boxing match (with its male flesh display), reaction shots show Tommy slavering as one guy lays into another in the ring. He gets rid of the girl, who could be a fig leaf or beard, a trophy to mask his queerness, and throughout the film he calls Nick 'big man'. Finally, when he says 'Perfume', he evokes something with which, as I shall discuss, queers are often associated in noir film. In short, Tommy takes Nick to a male brothel (even less representable than a female one, which in fact could be somewhat more clearly suggested in the period). This might explain why, in a cut straight from the brothel to the police station, Nick's first line is that it was an evening he 'wouldn't want to go through again': surely, by the conventions of the day, hanging out with a dreary guy who hero-worships you, having a few drinks and going to a (female) brothel is not such a ghastly way of spending an evening for a normal guy – but if the hero-worship is lustful and the brothel queer, not far off a fate worse than death.

None of this is decisive. Bad guys often dress well in noir, straight guys get worked up at boxing matches, getting rid of a clinging female is par for the course for a laddish night on the town, perfume is what women wear (and strong perfume characterises brothels) and Nick is established as a highly moral character who loathes Tommy and wants family life above all else. But it is precisely the undecidability of the example, the fact that it might be queer, that makes it also so noir.

Figure 7.1 Kiss of Death 1947: Tommy Udo (Richard Widmark) (centre) (BFI Stills, Posters and Designs).

92

If *Kiss of Death* is overall relatively straightforward, *The Big Sleep* (1946) is a by-word for uncertainty, some would say incomprehensibility. The basic enigmas are solved: at the start of the film General Sternwood asks private eye Philip Marlowe directly to find out what his younger daughter, Carmen, is up to and, indirectly, what has become of his valet, Sean Regan; by the end we know that Carmen was being blackmailed because she got herself mixed up in pornography and drugs and that Sean Regan has been killed by the very same Carmen, because he didn't return her love. If some of this and a lot of incidental material is elusive, it is partly because much information is delivered fast and only once, people lie or are misinformed and some elements (e.g. pornography) are cryptically signalled. It is also because we are encouraged to put quite a lot of our narrative curiosity into the wrong question about a character who never appears: from the beginning of the film we ought to be asking 'Who killed Sean Regan?' but instead the characters ask on our behalf where he has gotten to; moreover he himself never appears (of course, being dead – but we don't know that till the end). The question 'Where is he?' displaces 'Who killed him?', and there is also a third question that is never quite clearly asked or answered and yet which drives much of the narrative: 'Who was he?'.

We know that he worked for General Sternwood and that Marlowe remembers him from his time on the force, but everything else remains enigmatic. Marlowe says to General Sternwood that he'd heard that Sean had been taken on 'as your . . . whatever he was', thus sort of asking the question, but quite what he was remains unclear: employee, friend, son, lover? The first three are explicitly named as possibilities by General Sternwood while other formulations could suggest the fourth, the lover (General Sternwood: 'He left me', 'I was only his employer but I had hoped he'd come to regard me as something more than that'; Mrs Rutledge, General Sternwood's older daughter: 'It broke dad's heart, his going off like that'). It is also obvious to Mrs Rutledge that Sean not Carmen is the real object of her father's concern in calling on Marlowe's services (she assumes it in her first conversation with Marlowe after he's seen the General and she's even surprised that Carmen has been mentioned at all) and the same thing is obvious to the District Attorney, a Mr Wilde, who feels that Marlowe should carry on looking for Sean to reassure the General that his 'whatever he was' was not mixed up in the pornography and drugs racket that Marlowe has just uncovered.

General Sternwood is himself portrayed as a man who married late (after a no doubt stimulating life among men) but now is not only confined to a wheelchair but has developed a morbid sensitivity. He is thus, in common with other rich queers in noir (and beyond), at once sexless and exquisitely sensitive, metaphorically a hot-house plant but also actually living out his days in a conservatory hot enough to grow orchids. The last detail is interesting. Though orchids are rare and precious, signs of extravagant love during heterosexual courtship, they are also suspect, over-elaborate blooms with a sickly sweet smell, the product of unnatural cultivation. All of this, especially the scent, is consonant with the representation of queers as decadent.[3] General Sternwood refers to the orchids' scent and how much he loathes it – yet he chooses to live in the midst of it (he could after all have the orchids removed). What conundrum of wallowing in sickliness is at play here?

As with Tommy Udo and the brothel in *Kiss of Death*, none of this is certain, but it's uncertain either way, it's just as plausibly queer as not. The same could be said of Sean, though here we know even less. He is said to have been having an affair with a Mrs Mars and that's why Carmen killed him; but Mrs Mars says there was no affair, they were just friends. In a film peopled with such chronic liars, who knows what is true? Mrs Mars could have good reason to deny the affair, married as she is to the wealthy and menacing Mr Mars; on the other hand, women bonding with queers is also a feature of film noir, as we shall see, in which case Carmen's fury at being rebuffed by Sean might come from his being queer (or, of course, bisexual but, either, as Marlowe notes, a good guy, not wishing to betray General Sternwood with his own daughter, or else, simply not fancying her). We simply don't know.

Tommy Udo, General Sternwood and Sean Regan are at the very least plausibly read as queers, but other proposed instances might raise eyebrows. Mike Lagana in *The Big Heat* (1953) dresses well, with a carnation in his buttonhole; he has a portrait of his late mother over his fireplace, a good-looking manservant wakes him in the night to answer the phone wearing a dressing gown but no pyjamas, and he does not engage with his henchman in their talk about women.[4] Does all of this make him 'a homosexual type' (Naremore 1998: 222)? One might see Jack Marlowe (Franchot Tone), the killer in *Phantom Lady* (1944), as a queer (ibid.: 99): he's unmarried, a sculptor (artists are often suspect), with a superiority complex (like Waldo Lydeker in *Laura*) and a sense of paranoia (people 'hate me because I'm different'). However he's a modernist sculptor (his work has none of the feminine fussiness of Waldo's tastes), his sense of superiority is as much Ayn Rand as wounded aesthete and, although paranoia is one of Freud's signs of homosexuality,[5] not every paranoiac – or every unmarried man – has to be read as queer. Besides, Jack's motive for killing the woman he kills, Marcella, is that she'd said she'd go away with him and then laughed at him and said she wouldn't, which doesn't really sound all that queer a motive. However, while it would never have occurred to me to think of him as a queer, it's also true that he could be: perhaps she laughed at him for his presumption (do you really think I'd run off with a queer?), and despite his oh so straight name, Jack Marlowe, there is something epicene about Franchot Tone's performance of him. Other examples seem to me even more tenuous and yet are perhaps touched by noir's endemic uncertainty. What reason has one for thinking that the heavy-featured, lugubrious police detective Ed Cornell in

Hot Spot/I Wake Up Screaming (1941) (McGillivray 1997: 173) is queer except the counter-intuitive one that he was obsessed with the murdered woman to the point of making a shrine of her portrait in his dowdy flat? It's true that some noir queers do similar things, but it's not this alone that suggests their queerness.[6]

There is a different kind of reading uncertainty in two films adapted from sources in which the homosexuality is explicit even if it has ostensibly been expunged from the adaptation: *The Lost Weekend* (1945), where homosexuality is not offered as one of the causes of Don Birnam's (Ray Milland) alcoholism, and *Crossfire* (1947), where the motive for murder becomes anti-Semitism not homophobia. Both were based on best selling novels (*The Lost Weekend* 1944 and *The Brick Foxhole* 1945). As Chon Noriega (1990) points out, audiences could bring a knowledge of the source to the reading of a film, and critics sometimes drew attention to what was missing. Even without such extra-filmic possibilities, the films may still leave room for queer doubt. Vito Russo (1981: 96–97) notes some of the ways *The Lost Weekend* hints that Don Birnam's 'whispered problem might be rooted in greater psychological depths than the typewriter he keeps in his closet would indicate', such as his becoming 'coyly and cruelly entertaining when drunk' and feyly proposing marriage to a bartender, and the knowing treatment of him by a 'lewdly homosexual' male nurse in the sanatorium for alcoholics. And what, in *Crossfire*, is this man doing befriending soldiers in bars?[7]

To these two examples we may add a third where in the source, too, there is no homosexuality and yet which, like the source, it seems almost impossible not to read as queer: *Christmas Holiday* (1944), based on (part of) Somerset Maugham's 1939 novel. Here a young woman, Abigail Martin (Deanna Durbin), falls in love with a young man, Robert Manette (Gene Kelly); he hints that he has another side he can't talk about but anyway she must meet his mother; the latter welcomes her, hoping that her love may be able to overcome 'certain traits in Robert'; in voice-over Abigail tells us that the formidable Mrs Manette believed her to be 'her last chance to ... save Robert' (pause as in film), adding 'I've often wondered what would have happened if she'd told me all she knew of Robert that first afternoon'; after they marry, Robert takes to staying out late at night, coming back in the early morning looking pretty rough, refusing to say where's he's been. Certain unmentionable 'traits', a dominating mother, inexplicable nocturnal absences – but it turns out that Robert is a compulsive gambler which leads him into bad company and eventually murder. It is of course easy to forget that gambling was a crime and a sin, and to underestimate the havoc caused by compulsive gambling, yet the whole structure of the films seems to build towards the revelation of something more utterly unspeakable and it is perhaps only the introduction of murder that stops the revelation being bathetic.

All the films discussed above make sense if read in terms of given characters being queer but also if read straight. Uncertainty is the point. These representations appear in chronically uncertain films, but they also emerge at a moment of intensified uncertainty in representing sexuality between men. Homosexuality was at once ever more present in discourse and experience and, for that very reason, ever more unclear and contradictory. On the one hand, despite their extreme marginalisation in the output of Hollywood, the idea of queers was becoming more familiar, from at least a half century of science, scandal, literary treatments, louche humour in popular entertainment and expanding urban queenery. On the other hand World War Two had facilitated a widespread encounter with homosexuality, in one's self and in others, temporarily, *faute de mieux* or decisively (Bérubé 1990), developments made concrete by official military policies and then in 1948 by the Kinsey report on male sexuality, which showed that homosexuality was a far more widespread practice than that involving a few obvious fags. All the elements – of science, making visible through scandal, the evidence of experience, political and erotic self-production – promise knowledge of homosexuality but at the same time taken together produce a confusing and contradictory knowledge: queers were that type of man, that 'everyone' knew about but mainstream media didn't mention, and yet queerness was also in all types of men, everywhere, maybe.

In noir, this uncertainty is both assuaged and produced by one of the means by which certain knowledge of homosexuality was supposedly conveyed: stereotyping. This is how the characters in noir most readily recognised as queers are so identified. The males are fastidiously and just a little over-elaborately dressed, coiffed, manicured and perfumed, their speech is over-refined and their wit bitchy, and they love art, antiques, jewellery and cuisine: Joel Cairo (*The Maltese Falcon* 1941), Waldo Lydeker (*Laura* 1944), Lindsay Marriott (*Farewell My Lovely* 1945[8]), Hardy Cathcart (*The Dark Corner* 1946), Ballin Mundsen (*Gilda* 1946), Captain Munsey (*Brute Force* 1947), 'Grandy' Grandison (*The Unsuspected* 1947), Brandon and Philip (*Rope* 1948) and Bruno (*Strangers on a Train* 1951), together with, as already discussed, Tommy Udo, General Sternwood, Mike Lagana and Jack Marlowe; females[9] are large, big boned or fat, have cropped or tightly drawn back hair, wear shapeless or else highly tailored clothes and generally work for a living: Rose (*Cry of the City* 1948) and Martha (*In a Lonely Place* 1950), both masseuses, housekeeper Mrs Danvers (*Rebecca* 1940), cosmetics tycoon Mrs Redi (*The Seventh Victim* 1943), a Chicano leather girl in *Touch of Evil* (1958) and, softer versions of the type, rich girl Amy (*Young Man with a Horn*) and sanatorium director Miss Holloway (*The Uninvited* 1944); later examples include brothel keepers Jo (*A Walk on the Wild Side* 1962) and Frances Amthor (*Farewell My Lovely* 1976).

Both male and female queer stereotypes assume that homosexuals are a particular kind of person. They also draw upon the notions of homosexuality as gender in-betweenism, inversion and androgyny, notions found not only in homophobic (religious, psychiatric, sociological) discourses but in subcultural practices, sympathetic sexology and such homosexual rights activism as there was. In this understanding, queer has something to do with not being properly masculine or feminine. That 'properly' is grounded in heterosexuality, but it is held together with the assumption that if a person does not have the sexual responses appropriate to his or her sex (to wit, heterosexual ones), then he or she will not have fully the other attributes of his or her sex. This is how signs of effeminacy and mannishness, that have nothing directly to do with sexual preference but with gender, nonetheless come to indicate homosexuality. Moreover, they are a visible indicator of homosexuality, something which, short of showing acts, can't otherwise be seen.

The queers in the penultimate paragraph are all constructed through such gender stereotypification and it would not require immense sophistication to spot them. Yet few are as obvious as the earliest, Joel Cairo (signalled by the look given Sam Spade by his secretary Effie when she announces him), and many could be missed. In other words, for all the use of stereotyping, even these representations are not as assuaging of uncertainty as all that; indeed, to some degree, it is actually because of the use of stereotypes, and the peculiarity of homosexual typification, that they end up producing uncertainty.

All stereotyping has the function of fixing our perception of, in the words of the term's coiner, 'the great blooming, buzzing confusion of reality' (Lippman 1956: 96) into recognisable categories in order to gain a measure of control over it. However, queer stereotyping has a particularly odd logic. Stereotypes of, say, blacks or the disabled tell us that people who look like that are like this in character; stereotypes of queers seem to work in the same way (men and women who dress like that are like this), but they are founded on the opposite need, to say people who are like that (queer), even though you can't see that, look like this. Queer stereotypes are posited on the assumption that there is a grounding, an essential being which is queer, but since this is not immediately available to perception, they have to work all the harder to demonstrate that queers can be perceived. In other words, the problem with queers is you can't tell who is and who isn't – except that, maybe, if you know the tell-tale signs, you can. However, given that the whole thing is founded on a far from universally accepted or understood assumption (there are such things as queers), that it is telling us you can tell in the context of fearing you can't and that it does so by referencing gender misfit rather than sexual practice, given all this, it's not surprising that these stereotypes generate uncertainty even as they attempt to produce certainty – which is why one can have such, according to view, enjoyable or fruitless discussions about whether so-and-so is or isn't a queer. It may also be why they are so relatively widespread in noir, since they suit so well its general sense of uncertainty.

If it was not universally agreed that queers were a type of person, this might be for reasons of morality (homosexuality is a widespread temptation everyone should fight against or, in some bohemian discourse, give a go), experience (notably that made possible through single-sex schooling, prisons, the armed services and the temporary 'widowhood' caused by overseas military engagement), or even sexological stumbling over such cognitively dissonant categories as lesbian femmes, regular guy homos, effeminate straight men and the many gradations of bisexuality. All of these in turn produce that other construal of the uncertainty of homosexuality, namely that it may be fluid, potential or temporary. This too is glimpsed in film noir, in two forms. One – that some queer males are married or otherwise devoted to women – generally winds up reinforcing the stereotype discussed above. The other, and rarer – that straight looking guys may be doing it with each other – doesn't.

Hardy Cathcart (*The Dark Corner*) and Ballin Mundsen (*Gilda*) are married, General Sternwood (*The Big Sleep*) is a widower, Waldo Lydeker (*Laura*) adores the eponymous heroine, Jack Marlowe (*Phantom Lady*) wants to run off with Marcella, a friend's wife, Mike Lagana (*The Big Heat*) has a daughter, Ed Cornell (*Hot Spot/I Wake Up Screaming*) has a shrine to the murdered woman in his bedroom. Of the other obvious noir queers, Lindsay Marriott (*Farewell My Lovely*) is very much a woman's best friend, as perhaps was General Sternwood's Sean Regan, while Bruno (*Strangers on a Train*) is at once devoted to and disparaging of his mother. Yet these women loving men[10] are also, apart from Ed Cornell, all pretty queeny.

Whilst one could read many of these characters as either bisexual or effeminate straight men, they do seem really rather little driven by sexual desire in their nonetheless intense relations with women. Rather they 'adore' women, aestheticising them and treating them as beautiful creatures. They are refined connoisseurs of women. The two portrayals by the virtually out Clifton Webb,[11] Waldo and Hardy, are definitive.

Waldo is a classically waspish, fussily dressed queen, with rococo and Orientalist tastes in the decorative arts, established in a bravura opening tracking shot through his apartment ('it's lavish, but I feel at home'). His by-play with detective McPherson in the opening sequence is suggestive: standing up out of the bath naked before him, or saying 'I've always liked a detective . . . with a silver shinbone' and pausing as indicated to give a slight innuendo to this appreciation of McPherson's prowess (he was shot in the leg in a raid). All very regal. Yet he also mocks McPherson throughout the film, shows only contempt for other men and is obsessed with Laura, even saying (in voice over) that he is the only man who really knew her, while ducking McPherson's question as to whether he was in love with her. He moulded Laura into the ideal woman, elegant, gracious, cultivated and above all beautiful. Much of his flashback is his account to McPherson of the process by which he effected the transformation of a rather ordinary, if pushy, young woman into the epitome of high class glamour, a woman worthy to be seen on his arm and to sit among his antiques, so much so that she became, as he says, 'as well known as Waldo Lydecker's walking stick and his white carnation'.

Hardy in *The Dark Corner* is in many ways a re-run of Waldo, an art dealer apparently most relaxed in the company of old women (whom he patronises) and a blond gigolo, Tony Jardine (Figure 7.2). The first scene in which he appears establishes his character in a series of bons mots at a party he is throwing: he greets one woman with 'Guten Abend, Frau Keller', then whispers to Jardine in explanation that she is the 'wife of the Austrian critic – she always looks like she's been out in the rain, feeding poultry', a queer cocktail of snobbery, misogyny and unkindness masquerading as wit; his remark, 'I never confuse business with sentiment – unless it's extremely profitable of course', is Wildean in its pacing, while, 'As long as I'm amusing you'll forgive me' is surely the queer's credo. Yet Hardy keeps a female portrait by Raphael in his vault, recounting to a group of visitors (Figure 7.3) how he worshipped it until one day he met Mary, its living embodiment, whom he promptly married. He tells the latter that he never wants her to grow old, a sort of transferral on to her of the crypto-queer desire to fix beauty recounted in *The Portrait of Dorian Gray*.

Figure 7.2 The Dark Corner 1946: Hardy Cathcart (Clifton Webb, left) shows Tony Jardine (Kurt Kreuger) his etchings in a rococo setting (BFI Stills, Posters and Designs).

Figure 7.3 The Dark Corner: Hardy's 'Raphael', Mary (Cathy Downs), its modern reincarnation, Hardy, Tony and guests (BFI Stills, Posters and Designs).

Mary tells her lover Jardine that, though Hardy gives her 'everything a man can give a woman', yet 'still it isn't enough' – a fascinatingly ambiguous pronouncement that surely strongly suggests that Hardy does not give her the one thing that it is most commonly assumed men give women within marriage: sex. For Hardy, Mary is a work of art, adored to the point of sickness, providing a grim undertow to his quip to a party guest that 'the enjoyment of art is the only remaining ecstasy that is neither illegal nor immoral'.

Both Waldo and Hardy kill their beautiful women, Laura and Mary, ostensibly because they are showing an interest in other men (hunks that one might speculate would interest Waldo and Hardy) (Figure 7.4), but really because they don't want their works of art to be robbed. This syndrome – queer adoration of women – provides the template explaining the relationship of Ballin (previously so attached to Johnny) to Gilda and even yoking in Jack Marlowe and Ed Cornell.

More broadly, queers share, and sometimes bond with women over, an interest in the artier arts and feminine adornment (though there are no queenly noir hairdressers or couturiers). Lindsay Marriott's queerness, for instance, is established through his dealing in jewellery, the ring on his

Figure 7.4 Who desires whom?: Waldo (Clifton Webb), Laura (Gene Tierney), Shelby (Vincent Price) and Ann (Judith Anderson) in *Laura* 1944: (BFI Stills, Posters and Designs).

little finger, the softness of his large overcoat, the almost blowsy quality of his white cravat which he primps up during his conversation with Marlowe and, especially, his perfume, the very fact of being perfumed. A gag is made out of this: the lift man tells Marlowe he has a visitor and Marlowe assumes it's his hulking client, Moose Malloy; he asks if he's sober and the lift man says yes, adding in a sardonic voice, 'he smells real nice'; when Marlowe reaches his office, he discovers Marriott, reeking of perfume. The whole thing is laid on with a trowel in the re-make, with Marlowe remarking repeatedly to Marriott on the smell, and a character later commenting that all the fatale Mrs Grayle's male friends are 'like that'. Perfume links Marriott (in the 1944 version) to another queer, Jules Amthor, when Marlowe takes a carnation from Amthor's corpse and sniffs it,[12] and also to Joel Cairo in *The Maltese Falcon*, whom, like Marriott, we are first introduced to via his perfume ('Gardenia,' says Effie archly, handing Sam Cairo's calling card) and, as we've seen, to Tommy Udo and General Sternwood. Perfume is not only feminine, it is insidious: it gets in everywhere, can't be seen or touched or, therefore, controlled, it's a typically female piece of indirection, of a piece with seduction, manipulation, deceit and the other strategies of fatality.

So, while marriage and adoration generate uncertainty ('But he's a queer!') round the figure of many noir queens, in the end, through notions of sexless adoration and shared, perfumed femininity, noir queens reinforce the in-betweenist stereotype of male queers. If there is uncertainty, it is much more because of noir's general construction of the treacherous and fatale uncertainty of femininity in general than because we can't be sure (though we can't absolutely) whether Waldo, Cairo or Lindsay really are queers.[13]

Noir also sometimes features a male couple where neither man is stereotypically suspect, leave alone homosexually obvious. Let me start consideration of this by giving accounts of two such instances.

The narrative of *Dead Reckoning* (1947) is driven by the efforts of Rip to investigate the disappearance of his army buddy, Johnny. The first scene (before Johnny disappears) has them sharing a railway sleeping compartment, with Johnny changing his clothes in front of him; at the end of the film Rip tells Coral, the woman of the film, unequivocally that he 'loved him [Johnny] more' than her. At one point, he describes Johnny, beautifully and hauntingly, as 'tough, laughing and lonesome': why was Johnny lonesome? and what did Rip do to comfort him?

In *The Big Combo* (1955), the two henchmen of the master criminal Mr Brown are called Fante and Mingo. They share a bedroom together (twin beds, but that was common in representing straight couples too); in one scene, Fante is naked to the waist in the bed next to Mingo's; in another they both receive an unexpected visitor wearing dressing gowns (Figure 7.5).[14] Towards the end of the film, they are holed up in a disused airfield; at one point, Mingo puts his hand on Fante's arm and says, 'When we get out, let's never come back'; Fante looks down at Mingo's hand but does not remove it as he says how worried he is that when they get out 'the cops'll be looking for us in every closet';[15] Mingo drops his hand away, slightly caressing Fante's arm with his thumb first. Mr Brown plants a bomb in their bunker, which kills Fante straight off but leaves Mingo still just alive; when he realises what has happened, he agrees to tell Leonard, the film's police detective hero, all he knows:

He [Mr Brown] shouldna done it. Fante was my friend. OK, I'll tell you. But not for you.

In both these films the relationship with another man is the main thing in a character's life; both involve declarations of love ('I loved him more than you', 'Fante was my friend') and scenes between the two of semi-nakedness in an intimate, bedroom space. There are however two important differences between them. First, Rip has a girlfriend Coral, as did Johnny before him.

Figure 7.5 The Big Combo 1955: Fante (Lee Van Cleef) (centre) and Mingo (Earl Holiman) (right) receive Joe (Brian Donlevy) at home (BFI Stills, Posters and Designs).

Secondly, Rip is the main character played by a star (Humphrey Bogart), whereas Fante and Mingo are minor characters played (rather well) by jobbing actors. *The Big Combo* is a B-picture that can allow itself pretty well unequivocally queer characters in minor roles, but *Dead Reckoning* must supply heterosexuality, not out of any homophobic consciousness, but because main male characters played by stars have to have a woman (its part of their heterosexual appeal) and because a noir femme fatale is never going to be ignored by a hero. *Dead Reckoning* might raise questions about Rip's relationship with Johnny, opening out on to a perception of homosexuality as something that a man might in certain circumstances experience, and experience as intense and profound, without that meaning that he is a queer. And if it does, it leaves it in the past.

One of the exceptional things about the relationship of Fante and Mingo is that, although they do the dirty work for Mr Brown, they show no particular pleasure in cruelty (unlike most of the noir queers and notably Jeff in *The Glass Key* 1942[16] and Captain Munsey in *Brute Force* 1947) and Mingo's conversion to the right side of the law is entirely motivated by his love for Fante (this is what he means when he says he'll tell Leonard all, 'But not for you'). Within its limits, it's a positive image. The other striking thing is the emphasis on their sameness. Perhaps Fante is slightly older, more worldly, less demonstrative than Mingo, but there's not much in it, certainly not as much as Brandon's dominance of Philip in *Rope* or Jeff's pitiful subordination to Johnny in *Johnny Eager* (1941).[17] Fante and Mingo's similarity is underlined by their identical clothes (except for their ties): very light coloured suits where all the other hoodlums where dark. This emphasis on sameness, and the same masculinity, is much less clear in the most notorious case of queer noir, *Gilda*'s Ballin and Johnny.

In the first scene of *Gilda*, after Ballin has intervened to rescue him from muggers in a dockland district, Johnny asks him, 'What are you doing in a neighbourhood like this?' What indeed? Maybe Ballin has some assignation to do with tungsten (which we later learn he traffics in), but Johnny's question surely raises a much greater likelihood: Ballin's been cruising and has picked Johnny up. This is only one of a number of small remarks and details that suggest the relationship between them is a queer one. Consider this dialogue, prompted by Ballin's description of his cane with a knife in its tip (Figure 7.6):

Figure 7.6 Gilda 1946: Ballin (George Macready) with cane, Johnny (Glenn Ford) and Gilda (Rita Hayworth) (BFI Stills, Posters and Designs).

BALLIN: It is a most faithful and obedient friend. It is silent when I wish
    to be silent, it talks when I wish to talk.
JOHNNY: That's your idea of a friend?
BALLIN: That is my idea of a friend.
JOHNNY: You must lead a gay life.
BALLIN: I lead the life I like to lead.

The term 'gay' was certainly well established in queer sub-cultural (and
therefore certainly Hollywood) circles by the 1930s (Chauncey 1994:
16–20); Vito Russo (1981: 47) notes its use in *Bringing Up Baby* (1938),
when Cary Grant, dressed in a fluffy woman's night-gown, explains that he's
'just gone gay all of a sudden'. Its use here in *Gilda* to mean homosexually
queer (itself a much better known term in the period) makes sense, allowing
Johnny to seem to pick up on the emphasis on sameness and identity in
Ballin's evocation of friendship (man and stick/friend are as one) and to
allow Ballin to assert implicitly his defiance of morals and convention. The
exchange also hints at the sado-masochistic edge to the relationship: a
suggestive cane,[18] 'faithful and obedient'. Johnny uses the latter terms later,
when asking Ballin to take him on in his casino: 'You've no idea how

Figure 7.7 *The Maltese Falcon* 1941: Joel Cairo (Peter Lorre) with cane, Brigid
    O'Shaughnessy (Mary Astor) and Sam Spade (Humphrey Bogart) (BFI
    Stills, Posters and Designs).

faithful and obedient I can be ... for a nice salary'. Glenn Ford as Johnny flashes his eyes and smiles suggestively here, implying some of the ambiguity of the relationship: employment, personal devotion, masochistic obedience, paid consort. Ballin then seems to underline what's at stake:

BALLIN: This I must be sure of – that there's no woman anywhere.
JOHNNY: There's no woman anywhere.
BALLIN: Gambling and women do not mix.
JOHNNY: Those are the very words I use myself.

As in *Christmas Holiday*, gambling seems to be a metaphor for homosexuality – except that in *Gilda*, gambling and women are mixed. Ballin marries Gilda and it turns out that Johnny has had a relationship with her and by the end of the film does again. In the most obvious sense, the arrival of Gilda seems to confirm that 'gambling' and women don't mix: she breaks up the Ballin–Johnny relationship, signalled by Johnny's returning the key to Ballin's house:

BALLIN: What's this?
JOHNNY: Tact.

Yet structurally Gilda also illuminates the Ballin–Johnny relationship. I've already suggested above that Ballin can be thought of alongside Waldo and Hardy as an adorer of beautiful women. He is much less of a queen than them, more commanding in the masculine world, considerably less witty and brilliant (George Macready is no Clifton Webb), yet he is, like them, fastidiously dressed and mockingly perverse. There is never any sign of any marital intimacy between him and Gilda, none of the touching and glances, the closeness in the frame and intense, unspeaking shot/reverse shot patterns, the musical surges and chromaticism, that construct physical 'chemistry' in Hollywood cinema of the period. Like Waldo and Hardy, he parades Gilda for all to see, a sign of his wealth and taste as much as his libido – as Parker Tyler puts it, 'he "owns" rather than "loves"' her (1972: 167).

Simultaneously, Gilda also brings out the femininity of Johnny's position, comparing it to her own. Her mocking looks and teasing remarks to him can be explained as the anger of an ex-lover but might also be because she knows about him and Ballin.

JOHNNY: I was down and out – he put me on my feet.
GILDA: What a coincidence.

Johnny himself recognises the parallel in a bad tempered exchange with Ballin after his first meeting (in the film) with Gilda. He comments to Ballin on the speed with which he has married her:

106

BALLIN: You should know Johnny that when I want something...
JOHNNY: ...You buy it quick.

Ballin has bought Gilda just as earlier he bought Johnny. There may be a perverse symmetry here: Johnny was definitely paid to be an employee and was probably a lover: Gilda was definitely acquired to be a wife but may not actually be used much as a lover.

The film underscores the similarity between them as covetable items. One hardly needs to go into Rita Hayworth's screen goddess glamour in this, her most famous role, but this is complemented by a glamorisation of Glenn Ford as Johnny. Where his previous appearances (mainly in Westerns and action films) used harsh lighting, close-cropped hair and rough costuming, here he is softly lit (with his weakly sensual mouth in particular highlighted), his hair is crimped and oiled and he is attractively dressed (Figure 7.8). His desirability is intensified by the fact that he is the object of her reciprocal gaze on their first meeting (in the film). From the moment we first see her, cut in on a movement tossing her hair back and looking straight to where Johnny is standing, each shot of her looking at him is complemented by a shot of him looking at her. Each shot is of equal length; a shot over his shoulder matches a shot over hers, and so on; the sensuous

Figure 7.8 Gilda: Glenn Ford looking cute as Johnny (BFI Stills, Posters and Designs).

play of light is identical. Her heterosexual gaze licenses a perception of his desirability that could not be given to us so unequivocally through Ballin's eyes. When a bit later she remarks, more than once, on how 'pretty' he is (Figure 7.9), she mocks her own desire and his role as Ballin's kept boy.

Gilda scrambles some of the period's and noir's frameworks for understanding (homo)sexuality in a way that I, at any rate, find psychologically convincing rather than incoherent. Ballin is a bit of a queen who nonetheless probably has sex with women and men and, in either case, has the masculine power position. Johnny has regular guy good looks, but can swing either way sexually and is in the feminine position in his relationship with Ballin. In short, both Ballin and Johnny are touched by ideas of gender dissonance (Ballin's bit of queenliness, Johnny's pretty boy status) and by notions of regular guys doing it with each other sometimes, for a time.

Noir was one of the first places in Hollywood cinema to produce images of homosexuals on a scale that makes their presence one of its defining characteristics. One may account for this partly by the fact that queers are so ineluctably tied to villainy in the films – if there was going to be a space, it was going to be a negative one. Thus noir queers are accessories to crime (*Farewell My Lovely*, Cairo in *The Maltese Falcon*), bullies (*Brute Force*), henchmen (*The Big Combo*, *The Glass Key*, *Kiss of Death*), murderers (*The Dark*

Figure 7.9 Gilda: Gilda looks at pomaded Johnny (BFI Stills, Posters and Designs).

Corner, *Laura*, *Phantom Lady*, *Rope*, *Strangers on a Train*, *The Unsuspected*) or masterminds (*The Big Heat*, Ballin in *Gilda*, Nick Varna in *The Glass Key*, Gutman in *The Maltese Falcon*).

However, noir had no need of queers in order to have villains. We need to look further at what it was about noir that made the complex mid-century construction of homosexuality so serviceable to it.

For the most part, noir was a feature of B-movie production in Hollywood, a stratum of production at once more impoverished and routine than high budget, high profile production, but also less surveilled and controlled. Hollywood invested less both economically and culturally in B-movies, which also meant that B-movie production was for the most part left alone. The result was most often dreary banality, with perfunctory scripts and lacklustre *mise-en-scène*, but B-movie production could also be a space for greater exploitation (of sexual and other sensations) and, on occasion, experimentation. Noir displays both these possibilities.

Noir is sleazy, taking pleasure in sex and violence, in perverse sexualities and decadent lifestyles. Intimations of homosexuality suited this perfectly (alongside sado-masochism, kept men and femmes fatales). Homosexuality was something most adults knew something about, but it was not represented in popular public media; to do so was intrinsically shocking. Mainstream Hollywood would not cater to the taste for sexual sensation, which left a space for B-movies, including noir. This was not a conscious marketing strategy; rather, in a period of massive film output, an awful lot of things could happen that no-one took much notice of – indeed, most B-movies, and therefore much noir, barely figure in contemporary public discourse at all. Nor probably was the exploitation of homosexuality aimed at a homosexual audience (though one should not assume this did not occur to anyone involved); rather homosexuality, strange and shocking, was part of a wider appeal to sexual sensation aimed at a heterosexual and, if you like, Queer audience.

Noir was also experimental,[19] not just in its visual and narrational daring, but in its un-American pessimism. Central to this is the problem of knowledge – the images and stories are confusing because the world is hard to know. I have already indicated the uncertainty of both noir and the representation of homosexuality within it. At the most general level, homosexuality is simply one more trope in the performance of uncertainty. However, homosexuality is also central to the structure of narrative confusion in many of the films; nor is it any old trope of uncertainty.

Homosexuality, and the doubt over it, often contributes to the confusion of the narrative both in terms of being able to follow it and in terms of explaining what has happened. *The Big Sleep* would be much easier to follow if we knew from the start what was at stake in the investigation that General Sternwood employs Marlowe to undertake; all the fuss and anxiety in *Christmas Holiday* would be easier to make sense of if Robert were brought out of the closet. Lindsay Marriott puts Marlowe off the scent (by means of scent) in *Farewell My Lovely*, while Tommy Udo's ambiguities are one of the difficulties facing Nick in coming to terms with life after prison. The peculiarity of Waldo's and Hardy's attachment to women make them seem sideshows to the central drama of *Laura* and *The Dark Corner* respectively, when they are in fact the heart of it. The endemic confusions of *The Maltese Falcon* stem entirely from the lies and manipulations of the women and queers – we never know where we are because of the shifting webs of truth and untruth spun by women (who have always practised the wiles of deception) and queers (whose being is constituted in passing, a *ne plus ultra* of deceit).

Many films imply that homosexuality would explain why characters have done what they have done – this is why Johnny is so jealous and cruel in *Gilda*, why Bruno wants to kill his father in *Strangers on a Train*, why Captain Munsey takes such pleasure in inflicting pain in *Brute Force*, why Waldo and Hardy kill women they want to possess but are incapable of having, why Don in *The Lost Weekend* is an alcoholic, why Montgomery (*Crossfire*) kills the man who befriended him, why Johnny Eager is so elusive in his relations with Jeff.

In a much more complex argument, first published in 1947, Parker Tyler (1971: 169–178) suggests that homosexuality may also explain the actions of Neff and Keyes in *Double Indemnity* (1944). Insurance salesman Walter Neff schemes with Phyllis Dietrichson to kill her husband as part of an insurance scam – but why does he turn on her in the end and why does he pour the whole story out to claims adjuster Keyes? Tyler suggests that Neff is a sexual salesman, selling insurance policies by selling his sexual charm; Keyes, unmarried and Neff's mentor, sees through this, through Neff's excessive talk about his success with women; Neff, unable to deliver on the sexual promise to Phyllis after the murder, turns to confess to the one man who has understood him all along. Tyler is careful not to suggest that Neff and Keyes are having an affair, or want to (even unconsciously), though he does make this claim in his later book on homosexuality in the movies (Tyler 1972: 166).[20] Rather the force of his argument is the uncertainty for the characters themselves of their sexual motivations, with murderous consequences.

Making clear the homosexuality of the characters would sort out a lot of mysteries, but there'd be no film then – both in the sense of less mystery but also, more importantly, less evocation of the feeling of not knowing. If homosexuality were definite, then much of the uncertainty – about what is going on, about why people do things – would evaporate. Noir needs homosexuals not as villains but as part of its endemic epistemological uncertainty.

Noir queers constitute a disturbance in knowledge; they unsettle the process of knowing that drives the narrative and contribute to the experience of not knowing that is such a characteristic flavour of noir. They are a gender

disturbance: they are like women and often bond with them in a shared femininity, but they also lurk in the foundational institutions of heterosexuality,
marriage and buddiness. In so far as one of the comforts of normal masculinity is to be in possession of knowledge, including and perhaps especially the
knowledge of gender, queers are discomforting.

In the opening bedroom scene in *Laura*, detective McPherson plays with
a bagatelle game in his hand, whose board depicts a baseball game (Figure
7.10). He concentrates on this while Waldo prattles on; at one point, there
is even a close-up of the game in McPherson's hand, to emphasise that he is
looking at it not Waldo, as the latter preens in front of the mirror. Is this
because he is too embarrassed, confused and even disturbed to look Waldo
in the face and, indeed, in the body? Maybe, just as the haunted, twitchy
quality of Brad (*The Dark Corner*) and the washed out, defeated demeanour
of Scott (*Phantom Lady*) might be attributed to their dealing with queers
with whom they were professionally but also perhaps erotically involved in
their past, and Nick in *Kiss of Death* perhaps protests too much about his
awful, never to be repeated night out with Tommy Udo.

Queers may sometimes disturb the central male characters in
these oblique ways, just as queerness may disturb our perception of such

Figure 7.10 Laura: Detective McPherson (Dana Andrews) plays bagatelle while
Waldo gets dressed (BFI Stills, Posters and Designs).

characters as Johnny in *Gilda* and Neff and Keyes in *Double Indemnity*. More generally, they constitute part of a world whose uncertainty noir heroes fail to master and, because they are often more vivid and more fun, they take attention away from the hero, decentring him. However, it is also the case that often, at any rate, the protagonists don't act like they're disturbed. McPherson does not seem ruffled by the decadent world he has fallen among and any tensions in the encounters of Leonard Diamond with Mingo and Fante (*The Big Combo*) and Dave Bannion with Mike Lagana (*The Big Heat*) seem fully accounted for by the role of the villains in relation to the hero's loved one, that is, respectively, acting as bodyguards to the man whose possession she has become and ordering the murder of his wife. Moreover, the noir protagonist par excellence, Humphrey Bogart, seems unfazed in his encounters with queers, including his own attachment to Johnny in *Dead Reckoning* and even to Sean in *The Big Sleep*. Indeed, perhaps the secret of noir as entertainment is that, even as it presents the audience with the discomfort of a queerly uncertain world, it also offers the reassurance of a hero who takes it all in his stride, maybe a little cynical, maybe a little crumpled, but not really, as it were, put out. This is perhaps the most significant reason of all why noir could permit such at times brilliant (Waldo) and touching (Mingo and Fante) epistemological disturbances, namely, that they didn't really seem to dislodge straight masculinity from the centre of knowing. Whether they in fact gave a decisive nudge in that direction must remain an imponderable of cultural history.

Notes

1 So does female homosexuality. Though I touch on it at various points here, I focus on male queers in line with the general emphasis in this book. For some more discussion of noir lesbians see Dyer 1993, 1998b.

2 On the definition of film noir see Naremore 1998. In my usage, 'noir' is a characteristic of films, wholly or in part, rather than a category. I stick here to films within the classic period of the 1940s and 50s, though noir can be found in later examples, even in genres less associated with it and notably to represent homosexuality (e.g. *Advise and Consent* 1962, *The Killing of Sister George* 1968).

3 They are used as a metaphor for queerness and its decadence by the Baron de Charlus in Proust's *A la recherche du temps perdu*.

4 I'm grateful to Malcolm Gibb for this last observation. Interestingly, I was watching *The Big Heat* casually with him one afternoon and he wondered at the end whether Lagana was supposed to be gay, whereas this had never occurred to me when I first saw it. See also McArthur 1992: 51.

5 Of course one hardly needs a theory of the unconscious to work out why people liable to be ridiculed, beaten up and dismissed from employment if known to be queer might feel the world is against them.

6 Other characters tentatively proposed as queer include Jeff (*The Glass Key* 1942) (McGillivray 1997: 173, Naremore 1998: 63), Bart (*Gun Crazy* 1947) (ibid.:

151), Niles (*Cry of the City* 1948) (Walker 1992: 137) and the Paul Henreid character in *Rope of Sand* (1949) (Durgnat 1996: 97).

7 See also Naremore's discussion of how the film 'enables us to "see" . . . many of the things that censorship was trying to repress' (1998: 118).

8 The original US title of this is *Murder My Sweet*; the British title is also the title of the source novel and the 1976 remake.

9 See Note 1. To draw up this list, I've had to stray further from what is usually considered film noir, though all these films have noirish elements. On *Caged*, *Rebecca*, *The Seventh Victim*, *Touch of Evil* and *The Uninvited*, see White (1999) passim; note also her discussion (188–9) of *Dark Passage* (1947).

10 The only noir queens who seem at all hostile to women are Joel Cairo (*The Maltese Falcon*) and perhaps Brandon (*Rope*). Cairo's sneering politeness to Brigid O'Shaughnessy could just be because she is a rival for the falcon, but it does seem informed by queer misogyny. There is also, in a cryptic exchange, the implication that they have been rivals for men. Cairo refers to the problem of a boy watching the apartment from the street outside; Brigid: 'I'm sure you could get round him, as you did the one in Istanbul – what was his name?', Cairo: 'You mean the one you couldn't get to come . . . ?', at which point she slaps his face.

11 On Webb, see Tyler 1972: 328–330.

12 See Buchsbaum 1992: 96.

13 The consequences of this argument for the representation of women are discussed in Dyer 1998b.

14 Tom Milne considers their visitor, Joe, the boss's henchman, to be perhaps in love with the boss until the humiliation the latter heaps on him turns love into hatred (1980: 80).

15 Although this phrase is too suggestive not to quote, George Chauncey's researches suggest that the term 'closet' in a specifically gay sense was not in circulation before the 1960s (1994: 6, 374–375).

16 I'm not sure if I do see Jeff as queer (pace McGillivray 1997: 173 and Naremore 1998: 63), but he is unmarried, enjoys torturing the hero but later becomes drunkenly maudlin with him, and his boss Nick Varna takes him and his other henchman Rusty upstairs with him when he announces to a party of guests that it's time for bed.

17 In this fascinating film, more old fashioned gangster movie than noir, Van Heflin plays Jeff, long-term room-mate to the glamorous mobster Johnny Eager, clearly in love with him and becoming alcoholic through lack of reciprocity (though perhaps Johnny gives him reason to hope once in a while?). Heflin won a best supporting Oscar for the role.

18 Joel Cairo (*The Maltese Falcon*) also has a suggestive cane (Figure 7.7), which he caresses to his lips during his first interview with Sam Spade.

19 The intertwining of experimental and sexual sensation also characterised the underground cinema emerging in the US in the same period (cf. Dyer 1990: 111–134).

20 Claire Johnston, writing in 1978 from within a Lacanian perspective, is even less cautious: 'the repressed homosexual desire of Neff for the idealised father [Keyes]', 'the repressed, homosexual desire between the two men' (1998: 91).

References

Bérubé, Allan (1990) *Coming Out Under Fire: The History of Gay Men and Women in World War Two*, New York: Free Press.

Buchsbaum, Jonathan (1992) 'Tame Wolves and Phoney Claims: Paranoia and Film Noir', in Cameron 1992: 88–97.

Cameron, Ian (ed.) *The Movie Book of Film Noir*, London: Studio Vista.

Chauncey, George (1994) *Gay New York: Gender, Urban Culture and the Making of the Gay Male World, 1890–1940*, New York: Basic Books.

Corber, Robert J. (1997) 'Resisting the Lure of the Commodity: *Laura* and the Spectacle of the Gay Male Body', in *Homosexuality in Cold War America: Resistance and the Crisis of Masculinity*, Durham NC: Duke University Press, 55–78.

D'Emilio, John (1983) *Sexual Politics, Sexual Communities: The Making of a Homosexual Minority in the United States 1940–1970*, Chicago: University of Chicago Press.

Durgnat, Raymond (1996) 'Paint It Black: The Family Tree of Film Noir', in Palmer, R. Barton (ed.) *Perspectives on Film Noir*, New York: G. K. Hall, 83–98. (First published 1970.)

Dyer, Richard (1990) *Now You See It*, London: Routledge.

Dyer, Richard (1993) 'Homosexuality and Film Noir', in *The Matter of Images: Essays on Representations*, London: Routledge, 52–72.

Dyer, Richard (1998a) 'Resistance through Charisma: Rita Hayworth and *Gilda*', in Kaplan: 115–122.

Dyer, Richard (1998b) 'Postscript: Queers and Women in Film Noir', in Kaplan 1998: 123–129.

Edelman, Lee (1994) 'Imagining the Homosexual: *Laura* and the Other Face of Gender', in *Homographesis: Essays in Gay Literary and Cultural Theory*, New York: Routledge, 192–241.

Johnstone, Claire (1998) '*Double Indemnity*', in Kaplan, 89–97.

Kaplan, E. Ann (ed.) (1998)*Women in Film Noir* (new edition), London: British Film Institute.

Lippman, Walter (1956) *Public Opinion*, New York: Macmillan. (First published 1922.)

McArthur, Colin (1992) *The Big Heat*, London: British Film Institute.

McGillivray, David (1997) 'Homosexuality', in Hardy, Phil (ed.) *The BFI Companion to Crime*, London: Cassell, 173–175.

Milne, Tom (1980) '*The Big Combo*', *Monthly Film Bulletin* 47: 555, 80.

Naremore, James (1998) *More than Night: Film Noir in its Contexts*, Berkeley: University of California Press.

Noriego, Chon (1990) '"Something's Missing Here!": Homosexuality and Film Reviews during the Production Code Era, 1934–1962', *Cinema Journal* 30: 1, 20–41.

Russo, Vito (1981) *The Celluloid Closet: Homosexuality in the Movies*, New York: Harper and Row.

Tyler, Parker (1971) *Magic and Myth of the Movies*, London: Secker and Warburg. (First published 1947.)

Tyler, Parker (1972) *Screening the Sexes: Homosexuality in the Movies*, New York: Holt, Rinehart and Winston.

Walker, Michael (1992) 'Robert Siodmak', in Cameron 1992: 110–151.

White, Patricia (1999) *Uninvited: Classical Hollywood Cinema and Lesbian Representability*, Bloomington: Indiana University Press.

8

COMING OUT AS GOING IN

The image of the homosexual as a sad young man

No-one he knew was beset with the melancholia, emotional
frigidity, or feminine symbolisms he found in himself.

(*Maybe – Tomorrow*)

When I was growing up in the 1950s and 1960s, I assented that the lot of
queers like myself was a melancholy one. I don't remember now exactly
where I first picked up this idea, but I do remember recognising my mood
in lines like the above, or seeing myself in the characters of Geoff in *A Taste
of Honey* and both Reggie and Pete in *The Leather Boys*, or knowing that
books with covers showing pairs of young men looking mournfully down-
wards yet towards each other were for me.

I related to this stereotype of gay men as sad young men selectively. Like
them I loved cookery, clothes and the arts and chose to ignore their taste for
sewing and interior decoration, which I didn't share at all; like them, I had a
penchant for dark-eyed, well-built chaps and just took no notice of their
incomprehensible passion for the school football hero. I had different sorts of
feeling about them too. I thought I virtually was Geoff in *A Taste of Honey*
and David in *Giovanni's Room* (even though I was neither working class nor
American), but it was more longing I felt towards Gaylord Le Claire in
Maybe – Tomorrow, a wish that I could both be him and have him with his
'earnest face and handsome physique'. And I took on board the two main
messages of the type – that to be homosexual was both irremediably sad and
overwhelmingly desirable.

I don't claim that my relation to this stereotype is that of all other
gay men of my generation, but I start with it, partly because I want to
use myself in evidence of the fact that stereotypes can be both a complex
and a formative mode of representation. We are accustomed to thinking
of them as simple, repetitive, boring and prejudiced group images
which, should they supposedly be about ourselves, we angrily reject. We

116

mistake their simplicity of formal means (a few broadly drawn, instantly identifiable signs endlessly repeated) and evident ideological purpose (to keep/put out-groups in their place) for a simplicity of connotation and actual ideological effect. What interests me in looking here at the gay man as sad young man is the way a stereotype can be complex, varied, intense and contradictory, an image of otherness in which it is still possible to find oneself.

> On a stage, empty but for some impressionistic, Noguchi-like set pieces, a young man . . . stabs the air with his arms in what seems like a futile attempt to break free from his past, and then doubles up in a foetal position while a flock of black-draped furies hover near. [. . .] He wants to go back to the days when he kissed a little girl among the hollyhocks, but this innocence is irretrievable and he turns to a young man for comfort. For this, the boy is taunted and gang-raped by a pack of schoolchums. With insult heaped upon injury, the boy kills himself . . .
>
> (*Monument for a Dead Boy*)[1]

The stereotype of the sad young man is found in probably all representational media, from novels and 'non-fiction' accounts (e.g. *Man on a Pendulum*, 'a case history of an invert presented by a religious counselor', told in a style broadly indistinguishable from novels like *The Divided Path* or *All the Sad Young Men*) to plays, films, even dance (e.g. *Monument for a Dead Boy*) and song ('Ballad of the Sad Young Men' recorded by Petula Clark and Roberta Flack). It is equally present in high and low culture, from critically acclaimed fiction (James Baldwin's *Giovanni's Room*) to soft-core pornography (Joe Leon Houston's *Desire in the Shadows* aka *The Gay Flesh*), and from avant-garde cinema (*Fragment of Seeking*, *Twice a Man*) via porn again (*Pink Narcissus*, *Passing Strangers*) to entertainment movies with 'serious themes' (*Rebel without a Cause*, *Tea and Sympathy*, *Victim*), though it seems to have remained doggedly middle-brow in the theatre (*The Green Bay Tree*, *The Immoralist*, *The Boys in the Band*). It is an important element in highly public star images such as Montgomery Clift, Sal Mineo (Figure 8.1), James Dean, Farley Granger (Figure 8.2) and Dirk Bogarde (Figure 8.3) just as in the more restrictedly circulated paintings of Christopher Wood or Cedric Morris (Figure 8.4) (cf. Cooper 1986).

The examples I have taken throughout this discussion are all Anglo-American. There certainly are equivalents throughout northern European culture (and perhaps in southern), but this is not something I have explored further. Something of the stereotype's rhetoric is also evident in lesbian titles like *Women in the Shadows* and *We Walk Alone*, not to mention *The Well of Loneliness*, but the similarities and differences between such images of lesbians and the sad young man need exploring rather than assuming. The

Figure 8.1. Sal Mineo.

centrality of the stereotype is most marked in the 1940s, 1950s and 1960s, although examples can be found before and after this.

> The hero ... is haunted by dream images of youths in muscular poses, dashes his worn-out mother's lovingly proffered breakfast-egg to the floor, and rushes out through grimy New York streets, until in the cemetery, he identifies his mother with the Virgin and his own suffering with Christ's, wallowing in the snow, between the graves, as if life were burial alive in some numb cold pain.
>
> (*Images in the Snow*)[2]

Like all stereotypes, the sad young man is a combination and condensation of many traditions of representation. This intensifies the image (so much history of significance caught by such spare formal means), gives it rich

118

Figure 8.2 Farley Granger.

possibilities of connotation and use and enables it to be read in a multiplicity of ways. The lineage of the sad young man includes:

Christianity, that is, the adoration of a naked, suffering young man, either Jesus or one of the martyrs, notably St Sebastian (Figures 8.5 and 8.6), something discussed by de Becker as 'the latent homosexual structure of Christianity' (1967: 94) and by Castello as 'le plaisir de mourir';[3]

the Romantic poets, ostensibly biographically heterosexual, but feminised in their long-haired, ultra-pale looks and hyper-emotional personalities, thus representing correlations between physical appearance, emotional capacity and gender identity, while also yielding more imagery of the cadaverously beautiful young man, notably in Wallis's painting of the death of Chatterton (Figure 8.7);

the Bildungsroman, and other traditions of the male coming of age novel, notably the Horatio Alger series, currently being re-read in terms of homoeroticism (cf. Moon 1987);

the third sex (or 'congenital inversion'), the notion of a distinct bodily

Figure 8.3 Dirk Bogarde.

type, the homosexual, placed on the cusp of male and female. Though only adhered to in the strictest biological sense by Magnus Hirschfeld, Havelock Ellis and others for a relatively short period,[4] versions of it (especially in terms of notions of a feminine personality within a male body) strongly persisted, often tricked out with

Freudianism, the popular perception of psychoanalytic ideas, including

Figure 8.4 Cedric Morris: *Self Portrait* 1930 (Trustees of the National Portrait Gallery, London).

especially the notion of the dangers of narcissism and/or excessive closeness between mothers and boy children and the designation of homosexuality as a phase through which boys will pass (and in which they may get stuck). This in turn relates to

the invention of adolescence, the social construction of a distinct phase of individual development with its own attendant rituals and forms. Though there is disagreement about whether conceiving of such a phase is specific to western society, and if so when it emerged as a concept (Springhall 1983–4), its peculiar salience in twentieth-century western culture is widely attested, especially as the focus of both moral panics and, until the 1980s, of moral, especially sexual, progress;

urbanism as 'alienation', the tradition of perceiving the city as a world of loneliness, loosened moral order, fleeting, impermanent contact and love for sale.

121

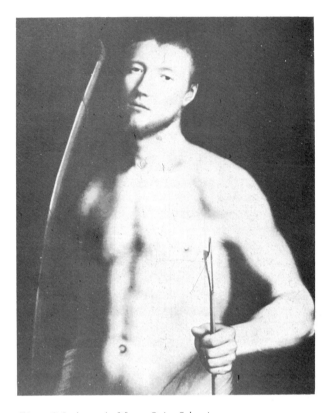

Figure 8.5 Antonio Moro: *Saint Sebastian.*

Theirs had been the laughter and the mocking pleasure – his the rounded shoulders, the sad eyes, the downturned mouth, the dismal apartment, the foggy windows...

(*The Gay Year*)

The image of the sad young man is distilled on the covers of the books and novels centred on him (Figures 8.8–8.18).

Most often, the people depicted are male. Women occasionally figure as on *Strange Brother* (Figure 8.8) and *Tea and Sympathy* (Figure 8.12). As in many of the narratives, she represents the sexual alternative to the sexuality troubling the sad young fellow. She offers herself sexually, in a pose which suggests at once the titillation of the sexually initiating women, the lot of characters like Laura (*Tea and Sympathy*) of saving the boy by showing him he is capable of heterosexual sex and, most interestingly, the strong sense of the sad young man's desirability to heterosexual women, a theme often strongly marked in the books and presumably not irrelevant to the appeal of Clift *et al*.

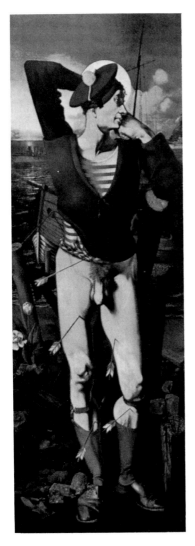

Figure 8.6 Alfred Courmes: *Saint Sebastian* 1934 (Centre Georges Pompidou, Paris).

The men on the covers are invariably white. There are examples of sad young black men as minor characters in the narratives, notably Johnny in *The L-Shaped Room*, yearning for the same straight boy as the heroine but with less success. However, I don't know of examples of main characters. Gay African-American writers have usually been distant or equivocal in their writings here, even James Baldwin making his sad young hero David in *Giovanni's Room* white. Though this may have been a self-protecting

123

Figure 8.7 Henry Wallis: *The Death of Chatterton* 1856 (Trustees of the Tate Gallery, London).

strategy on his part, it may also be because there is something specifically white about the stereotype. Black characters are often important in the narrative: Mark in *Strange Brother* is first discovered at a Harlem nightclub ('his face and hair stood out so extraordinarily fair, as he sat between two negro companions'); the white protagonists of both *All the Sad Young Men* and *Man on a Pendulum* have encounters with a young gay mulatto, the ultimate figure of in-between-ness, who is represented as happy with his lot in a manner that is not really possible for a white boy. In these examples, the sad young man's difference from black gay men is stressed and this perhaps has to do with the stereotype's roots in Christianity and the Romantic poets. The former, at the level of dominant representation a white (and gentile) tradition, focuses on the suffering male body, the moral worth and erotic beauty of white male flesh always seen at the point of agony; the Romantic poet promotes the association of paleness with emotionality and femininity, from which it is but a short step to queer masculinity as white sensitivity. The sad young man becomes part of much wider constructions of white identity in terms of suffering (the burden which becomes the badge of our superiority).

Figure 8.8 Strange Brother, cover (1949).

Figure 8.9 The Gay Year, cover (1949).

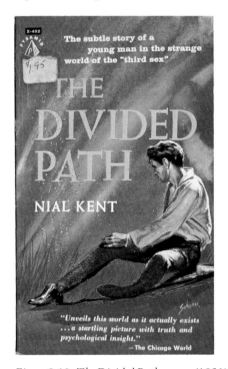

Figure 8.10 The Divided Path, cover (1951).

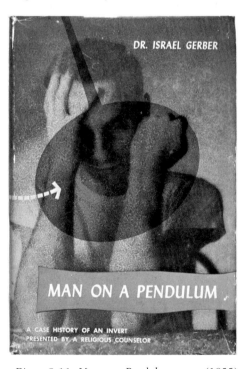

Figure 8.11 Man on a Pendulum, cover (1955).

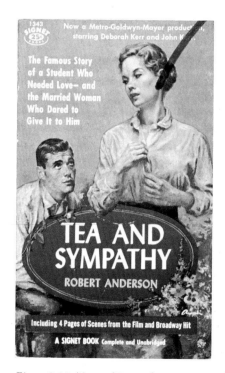

Figure 8.12 Tea and Sympathy, cover (1956). *Figure 8.13 Twilight Men*, cover (1957).

Figure 8.14 The Heart in Exile, cover (1961).

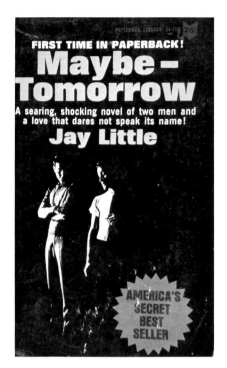

Figure 8.15 Maybe – Tomorrow, cover (1965).

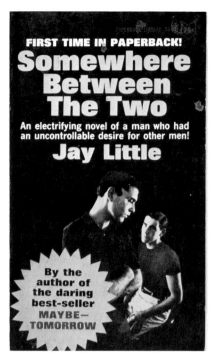

Figure 8.16 Somewhere Between the Two, cover (1965).

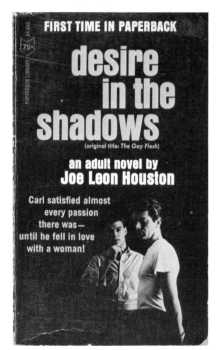

Figure 8.17 Desire in the Shadows, cover (1966).

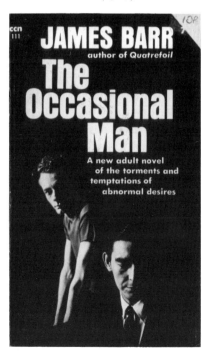

Figure 8.18 The Occasional Man, cover (1966).

The men depicted are young. Their youth is important in at least three respects. First of all, it provides a narrative tension to the image. Youth is a period of transition, of uncertain narrative outcome. In this context, outcome has to do not only with whether or not the young hero will have homosexual experience (that is more or less guaranteed) but whether he will turn out to be/become queer. Second, their youth is often part of their beauty. On the covers this seldom runs to the glowing descriptions inside but the use of averagely good-looking men (drawn or photographed) and the sometimes sensual use of light both indicate that the heroes of these books are to be found attractive. This attractiveness makes them figures for both identification (the better self often seen by fans in their chosen stars) and desire. In other words, as much as the image may be trumpeted as being about others, it is available to be taken as being about oneself, and as much as it is about a terrible, miserable way of being it also sets it up as an erotically desirable one. Third, the peaking of this mode of gay representation in the 1940s, 1950s and 1960s must be read through the cultural energy invested in the period in the notion of youth, a key aspect of which was the successful transition to responsible adulthood. In principle this applied to women as much as men, but men were constructed as the main focus of anxiety. The worry was about whether boys would become successful, mature adult males; the possibility that they might turn out queer was one of the dangers along the way.

There are usually two men on the covers, sometimes touching, more often yearning towards each other. The feeling is pornographic in that it stresses the longing for physical consummation, but also romantic in its isolation of the couple. This catches exactly the emotional tone in which the sad young man has his being: romantic–pornographic.

The young men on the covers generally have a downcast gaze, the sign of melancholy. Unlike other young men of the 1950s, they are not 'angry'. The sadness in store for them has many dimensions – among others, the 'inevitable' short-lived nature of gay relationships, the lack of children, social opprobrium. An image of what the gay world is like is held up as the appalling prospect for the young chap. When he has his first contact with the gay scene he is generally repulsed (Figure 8.19) and the image of the neurotic, hysterical, bitchy gay man as what the young man will become if he turns out to be/become queer haunts the image. Coming out – accepting that one is gay – thus takes the form of going in to another world ('cross[ing] over the border into the half-world of homosexuality' – *All the Sad Young Men*). This is striking in *Pink Narcissus*, which centres on a young man's sexual fantasies. He mooches about his apartment in various states of highly revealing dress, has various soft porn fantasies and towards the end invites a client into his room. The client, a pathetic old man, turns out to be himself, the terrible prospect of what he will become. The sad young man image is frozen on the moment before 'becoming' or knowing that one 'is' a

Armand felt ill-at-ease with these men about him displaying the sides of their natures that were usually so defended against the gaze of others.

Figure 8.19 Illustration from *Twilight Men* (1957 edition).

queer, and the narrative usually either stresses the inevitable hatefulness of this destiny (from which one may be rescued by a good woman or death) or else allows the fantasy that after all one might meet an ordinary fellow like oneself and maybe, just maybe, live with him in bliss for the rest of one's life.

The settings on the covers are generally implicitly urban. The city is where homosexual encounters occur and many of the negative associations of urbanism with alienation are present. In the US examples the young man comes from outside the city, discovers the queer world there but generally still yearns for the unqueer homo-eroticism of encounters with the loved one by a secluded pool.

Finally, the lighting and/or colouring generally suggests evening, twilight, shadows. This may have sinister resonances, drawing as it does (at many removes) on expressionist Angst and Surrealist dreamscapes; it may also suggest traditions of chiaroscuro erotica or the dimmed lights of the Hollywood *mise-en-scène* for making a pass. The wording anchors these fluid feeling tones in the symbolic possibilities of twilight. This connotes sadness, the dying of the light and so on; it is also a period of transition, which here is not so much that of childhood to adulthood as between straight and gay worlds. The idea of a 'half-world' suggests both being in between the sexes and also not being a self-sufficient world, one without the connectives that make normal society so rich and satisfying.

HANDSOME TERRY WALLACE LIVED IN THE TWILIGHT OF SEX BETWEEN THE DAYLIGHT OF NORMAL LOVE AND THE NIGHT OF FORBIDDEN DESIRE!
(Somewhere between the Two (back cover))

He had known infatuation, but this ... this was different! Bigger than anything he'd ever felt before. And it did not seem 'unnatural'.
(The Divided Path (back cover))

We don't really know what the relation is between a book and its cover, beyond the saw that we shouldn't use the latter as a basis for judgement. The cover sets up a tone, a promise of what we will find inside; it can be the reason why we buy the book and may be the filter of expectations through which, at least initially, we read it. Our desire that the book be like the cover may mean that we make it so as we read it, or are disappointed or pleasantly surprised to find it at variance to the cover. Particularly striking with the sad young man is the negative impression of the covers and the often far more upbeat and positive text inside, where the ecstasy of homosexual love, the unfairness of social attitudes and the fun of camp culture are all to varying degrees suggested.

The explanation of the gap between cover and text is to be found not only in the habit of lying that necessarily defines advertising, nor even in the widespread pull between meeting a readership pleasure in the romantic/erotic and a moral guardian pressure group demand for rectitude. Equally important is the ambiguity over whom these books are for. One imagines that most, especially those with more salacious blurbs, are intended for a queer readership, but to be clear about that automatically grants queers a legitimacy as a reading constituency, which is tantamount to giving them/us the subject position of a full citizen. So the books have to come on as if addressing a straight readership informing them about 'them'. Thus *Maybe – Tomorrow* announces that *The Navy News Review* considered it 'a book adults should read if they truly want to know more about one of the little known segments of the human race', which implies that no one who actually belongs to that segment is being addressed. Interestingly *Somewhere between the Two* on its inside cover acknowledges that there may be more than one audience. Though it says the book 'will be an eye-opening revelation of the world of homosexuality that is all around *us*' (my italics), it also says that 'the search for physical love and emotional security' of the two main characters 'will be instantly understood by the countless other men who secretly live in the shadows of the twilight world of sex'.

> 'I wish I'd been born a cripple. They wouldn't set such store by my body then.'
>
> (*Twilight Men*)

Homi Bhabha (1983) has argued in the context of racial stereotyping that the fixity and stability of stereotypes is only apparent. Stereotypes are a function of the desire to control through knowledge; the stereotype, its fixed contours and endless repetition, constantly reassures 'us' that such-and-such a group is known – *this* is what slags or niggers or queers are like and every time we look, 'they' are still the same as 'we' always knew they were. Yet the *stereo*-typicality of the stereotype, the endless need to repeat it, betrays, suggests Bhabha, the underlying knowledge that in actuality no social group is fixed, really under the grasp of knowledge, and in particular, that relations of power are not static, that they have to be endlessly remade and reasserted, that the frozen, forever, already known quality of the way out-groups are seen is really a mask for realities that are disturbingly fluid, impermanent and never really known.

The need for stereotypes to represent social groups as if they are fixedly known should not be taken to mean that stereotypes are always images of stasis. Many stereotypes do indeed assert the static, unchanging, settled nature of the designated group – perhaps the black mammy is one of the clearest instances. But stereotypes can also represent a state of impermanence or transience, and all age-based stereotypes must implicity do so, since no one remains the same age for ever. The sad young man is especially strongly marked in terms of transition, not only by virtue of age but also by virtue of the notion of moving between normal and queer worlds, always caught at the moment of exploration and discovery.

Other stereotypes that are mobilised in the context of the sad young man – especially that of the outrageous but miserable queen – do suggest a static personality, a known type whose main reassurance is his recognisability, his lack of the invisibility that in fact characterises gay people. But the sad young man is not so fixed. Indeed, in relation to visibility, he both is and is not knowable from appearance. Sometimes sad young men are definitely effeminate, sissy, even, in *The Gay Year*, incipiently hermaphroditic (though when he eventually starts to turn straight, the hero observes that his shoulders have broadened and his chest has flattened), but much of the time it is not clear. The *Twilight Men* cover (Figure 8.13) catches the middle point between *The Gay Year*'s over-neat, over-slim men and *Desire in the Shadows*' utterly ordinary-looking youths. *Twilight Men*'s men are square jawed, with casual male haircuts, yet with lips perhaps rather too full, shirts rather too open and collars rather too generously 'set'; as is most usual with sad young men, you can't tell one (queer) from the other (normal) and yet there are always tell-tale signs – the fear over our invisibility is stated simultaneously with the reassurance that we are not invisible.

Both physically and narratively the sad young man is a stereotype of impermanence and transience. Returning to Bhabha's argument, what reassuring knowledge is there in this stereotype? What is the fluidity and ungraspability at issue in this image which is itself of an unresolved, uncertain identity?

What the sad young man stereotype delivers is the reassurance that there *will be* resolution and certainty. The world before the sad young man offers four resolutions: death, normality, becoming a dreadful old queen or, especially in the later texts, finding 'someone like oneself' with whom one can settle down. What this asserts is that the situation in which options are open, in which sexual identity is not fixed, will not last. In other words, the mutability of sexual desire and identity, its unruly unsettledness, need not trouble the social order after all because it is only a function of youth when of course things are uncertain and up for grabs. Policing and controlling the body through the proliferation of sexual categories requires that there is always going to be a fixing into category; the sad young man allows for an expression of the experience of libidinal fluidity while offering the reassurance that it will not last.

There is another dimension of reassurance, concerning heterosexual masculinity. All anxiety about adolescent males has to do with the contradictory definitions of real manliness, on the one hand asserted and reproduced through compulsory heterosexuality but on the other hand most intensely expressed in the women-excluding buddy system, in a profound inculcation of woman-hating and in the celebration of tearaway, freewheeling, undomesticated adventuring. The reconciliation of responsible heterosexual masculinity with buddy–buddy thrills and spills is a hard act and forms the tedious basis of many tales of heterosexuality.

The sad young man relates to this in contradictory ways. On the one hand, the yearning for sexual closeness could, worryingly, be part of a continuum with asexual buddiness (and has often been so interpreted, most famously by Fiedler (1960)). The sad young man is a reassurance that this is not so, that sexual love is not buddy love, that queers are not real men and, what a relief, real men are not queers. (Even when the hero wins the high school jock, as in *The Divided Path* or *Maybe – Tomorrow*, still it is made clear that their relationship is not just buddiness carried on by other means but is different, more like man–woman 'love'.) On the other hand, very often the masculine ideal is held up by the texts as in fact unpleasant and undesirable. This is most explicitly worked through in *Tea and Sympathy*, where the hero is not homosexual though he is sad and sensitive; both play and film reassure him (us?) that one can be sensitive and hetero, that machismo is boring and often based on repressing homosexual feelings. ('This was the weakness you cried out for me to save you from', says Laura to her determinedly homophobic husband at the climax of the play.) The unequivocality of an anti-machismo message could perhaps be made only in the context of denying that sensitivity in men goes hand in hand with homosexuality, but the message remains implicit in many of the other texts, where it is clear that normal masculinity is a far from attractive prospect. All of which suggests that for all the impulse in the stereotype to put us off being queer, the very worries that give rise to it – libidinal fluidity, the contradiction of masculinity – also betray the fact that it might be rather nice to be gay.

> There is probably no more sensitive individual anywhere than the homosexual, and yet, as a rule, he wouldn't be anything but a homosexual. He talks of being a member of an ill-treated minority, but he wouldn't sign up with the majority tomorrow.
>
> (*The Sixth Man*)

Stereotypes mean differently for different groups, and especially for those who are members of the stereotyped group as compared to those who are not. It is partly a matter of how you see it. Tessa Perkins (1979) uses the example of the stereotype of the scatterbrained housewife to make this point. This may be read as an indication of women's essentially irrational psyche but may also be understood as an acknowledgement that housewifery demands and develops a capacity to think of many things at once, to keep on the go from one to another. The title of one of the first gay liberationist films, *It is not the Homosexual who is Perverse, but the Situation in which He Finds Himself* says it all, and the film in part takes the form of the sexual political education of a sad young man who comes to realise that if he is unhappy it is not because of himself but because of social oppression. The possibility of reading queer unhappiness in these terms is glimpsed even in the most homophobic of sad young man texts ('Don't be dejected, John. If only society were set up differently...' – *Man on a Pendulum*) and it must have been an available reading strategy in the years of emergent gay militancy and eventual law reform.

Equally the sad young man is a figure of romance/pornography. The image of handsome men nearly touching one another in sensual half-light is clearly titillating as are descriptions of a man 'endowed with a magnificent body and stunning good looks' (*Somewhere Between the Two*) or the casting of full-lipped Sal Mineo in *Rebel without a Cause* and fresh-faced John Kerr in *Tea and Sympathy*. A characteristic feature of gay/lesbian fantasy is the possibility of oscillation between wanting to be and wanting to have the object of desire. In heterosexual fantasy, the (always female) nurse is not supposed to want to be the (always male) doctor, the female reader is not supposed to lust after the heirs of Jane Eyre nor the male reader to fancy his out-of-focus substitute in porn magazines. Actual reading practices are always more complicated and insecure than this, but desiring both to be the object of desire and to want the subject of desire structures the text of lesbian/gay fantasy. The sad young man is the subject of desire of these texts; he longs for handsome guys that we are encouraged to fancy too; but writing or imaging also encourages us to fancy the sad young man himself. This could amount to a celebration of homosexual love. If we are turned on by the men he is turned on by, that means we share and, if only during the reading/viewing, endorse his desire; and if we think he is desirable because handsome and admirable because sensitive, then we also endorse being him. For all the bad feelings he has about himself, we could feel pretty good about him.

I don't want to overstate the scope of putative positive gay readings. The delicious melancholia in the presentation of the type was generally allied to social passivity, a sense that nothing could be done about social unfairness, that we had always been persecuted. Because it was about the sad *young* man, the pleasures of identifying with him were themselves wistful, for the sadness was that one could not go on being him and that wanting him when you'd stopped being him would be a pathetic business. The image could seldom really shake free from all this, yet it did construct a sense of feeling good about queer desire. If at one extreme it represented a warning of misery, which a gay man could have laid at the door of his ineradicable per-vertedness, at the other it offered an image of holy sensitivity, stunning good looks, overwhelming erotic experience and escape from the dreariness of real manliness, for all of which a gay man may have felt that some unrea-sonable, socially induced suffering was a small price to pay.

> Julian was incapable of changing, perhaps because inversion was a deeply ingrained habit with him, but largely because he found love for a man a beautiful and exciting mystery.
>
> (*The Heart in Exile*)

Acknowledgement

From Dyer, Richard: *The Matter of Images*, London: Routledge, 1993.

Notes

1 Ballet choreographed by Rudi van Dantzig and first performed by the Dutch National Ballet in Amsterdam in 1965; description from Jackson 1978: 38.
2 Film by Willard Maas made in 1948; description from Durgnat 1972: 252.
3 'Ce corps d'athlète gracieusement déhanché, percé de flèches, comme abandon-nés dans une agonie délicieuse et lascive, je conçois sans peine que des généra-tions de jeunes homme épris, dans le secret de leur coeur, de leurs semblables, l'aient caressé du regard, palpant chacun des ses muscles.' Castello 1983: 13–15.
4 See Steakley 1975 and Weeks 1977.

References

Becker, Raymond de (1967) *The Other Face of Love*, London: Neville Spearman & Rodney Books.

Bhabha, Homi (1983) 'The Other Question – the Stereotype and Colonial Discourse', *Screen* 24 (6): 18–36.

Castello, Michel del (1983) 'Le Plaisir de mourir', in *Saint Sébastien: Adonis et Martyr*, Paris: Persona.

Cooper, Emmanuel (1986) *The Sexual Perspective*, London: Routledge & Kegan Paul.

Durgnat, Raymond (1972) *Sexual Alienation in the Cinema*, London: Studio Vista.

Fiedler, Leslie (1960) *Love and Death in the American Novel*, New York: Criterion.

Jackson, Graham (1978) *Dance as Dance*, Ontario: Catalyst.

Moon, Michael (1987) '"The Gentle Boy from the Dangerous Classes": Pederasty, Domesticity, and Capitalism in Horatio Alger', *Representations* 19: 87–110.

Perkins, T. E. (1979) 'Rethinking Stereotypes', in Michèle Barrett, Philip Corrigan, Annette Kuhn and Janet Wolff (eds) *Ideology and Cultural Production*, London: Croom Health, 135–60.

Springhall, John (1983–4) 'The Origins of Adolescence', *Youth and Policy* 2 (3): 20–35.

Steakley, James (1975) *The Homosexual Emancipation Movement in Germany*, New York: Arno.

Weeks, Jeffrey (1977) *Coming Out*, London: Quartet.

Sad young men texts

Books

The reference given is for first publication which may be different from the edition of which the cover is discussed and illustrated.

Anderson, Robert, *Tea and Sympathy*, New York: Random House (1953).

Anon. *All the Sad Young Men*, New York: Wisdom House (1962).

Baldwin, James, *Giovanni's Room*, New York: Dial (1956).

De F., M., *The Gay Year*, New York: Castle Books (1949).

Garland, Rodney, *The Heart in Exile*, London: W. H. Allen (1953).

Gerber, Israel, *Man on a Pendulum*, New York: The American Press (1955).

Kent, Nial, *The Divided Path*, New York: Greenberg (1949).

Little, Jay, *Maybe – Tomorrow*, New York: Pageant Press (1952).

Little, Jay, *Somewhere Between the Two*, New York: Pageant Press (1956).

Niles, Blair, *Strange Brother*, New York: Liveright (1931).

Stearn, Jess, *The Sixth Man*, New York: Doubleday (1961).

Tellier, André, *Twilight Men*, New York: Greenberg (1931).

Vidal, Gore, *The City and the Pillar*, New York: E. P. Dutton (1948).

Films

Advise and Consent (USA 1962); d. Otto Preminger.
Boys in the Band, The (USA 1969–70); d. William Friedkin.
Fragment of Seeking (USA 1946–7); d. Curtis Harrington.
Images in the Snow (USA 1948); d. Willard Maas.
Leather Boys, The (GB 1964); d. Sidney Furie.
Lot in Sodom (USA 1930); d. Melville Webber and James Sibley Watson.
L-Shaped Room, The (GB 1962); d. Bryan Forbes.
Passing Strangers (USA 1974); d. Arthur Bressan.
Pink Narcissus (USA 1971); d. Anon.
Rebel without a Cause (GB 1955); d. Nicholas Ray.
Strange One, The (USA 1957); d. Jack Garfein.
Taste of Honey, A (GB 1961); d. Tony Richardson.
Tea and Sympathy (USA 1956); d. Vincente Minnelli.
Twice a Man (USA 1962–3); d. Gregory Markopoulos.
Victim (GB 1961); d. Basil Dearden.
Voices, The (USA 1953); d. John Smitz.

Further reading

Austen, Roger (1977) *Playing the Game: the Homosexual Novel in America*, New York: Bobbs-Merrill.

Curtin, Kaier (1987) *'We Can Always Call Them Bulgarians': the Emergence of Lesbians and Gay Men on the American Stage*, Boston: Alyson.

Dyer, Richard (1977) *Now You See It: Studies in Lesbian and Gay Film*, London: Routledge.

Russo, Vito (1981) *The Celluloid Closet: Homosexuality in the Movies*, New York: Harper & Row.

Sarotte, Georges-Michel (1978) *Like a Brother, Like a Lover*, Garden City, NY: Doubleday.

9

L'AIR DE PARIS

No place for homosexuality

The 1954 French film *L'Air de Paris*,[1] with major stars (Jean Gabin, Arletty) and a distinguished director (Marcel Carné), features a love story between men and much homo-erotic display (Figure 9.1). It stands out as a neglected early example of an explicitly homosexual mainstream feature film. Yet, as André Bazin suggested at the time, it is also a film that feels 'out of kilter, disoriented, and somehow untrue to itself'.[2] I want to explore here what made such a relatively daring film possible but also the way that the terms in which it was possible also produce the uneasy feeling identified by Bazin.

The film's story concerns a boxing trainer, Victor (Gabin), who takes on a young man, André (Roland Lesaffre), whom he believes he can make into a champion. Victor's wife, Blanche (Arletty), understands better than he does himself what is going on. She tells a friend that when Victor gets as serious as this about one of his 'poulains' (trainees), she'd rather it was for 'une poule' (a girl). When she says to Victor that André is 'the only thing that interests you – it's disgusting', he tells her she's jealous and she says, yes and why not? Meanwhile, André meets and has an affair with a woman, Corinne (Marie Daems), much to Victor's annoyance. However, Corinne realises the harm she's doing André (to his training and to his relationship with Victor) and leaves town. Outside her flat, Victor comforts André, throws a bracelet charm, symbol of Victor and Corinne's relationship, into the river, and the two men walk off together into the dawn.

The film displays Roland Lesaffre's athletic body to a very unusual degree: in singlet and short boxing shorts, in the shower, in pyjama bottoms only and, for a massage scene with Gabin, bikini briefs. By contrast, it hardly displays Marie Daems's body at all. Lesaffre is also the focus of glamorising lighting and of the explicitly libidinal looks in the film (not only from Corinne, but from a neighbourhood girl, Maria (Maria-Pia Casilio), and a camp couturier, Jean-Marc (Jean Parédès)).

Presented thus in terms of story and display, *L'Air de Paris* sounds like an obviously gay film; yet almost no-one at the time commented on it in these terms.[3] The reasons why, which I shall discuss first, are partly production

Figure 9.1 L'Air de Paris 1954: Victor (Jean Gabin) and André (Roland Lesaffre) (BFI Stills, Posters and Designs).

circumstances, partly the strategies of the closet. They are also, though, to do with the deployment of an impossible conception of desire between men. One of the consequences of this is that this film about place has no place for its two main protagonists, or in other words that it cannot imagine a social location for such desire.

1954 was not a propitious year in which to produce a homosexual film. This might at first sight seem surprising. In the 1940s Jean Cocteau and Jean Marais were a publicly famous couple, Jean Genet's film *Un Chant d'amour* was made in 1950, and there had been a line of remarkable gay representations in French cinema in the thirties (*Le Sang d'un poète* (*Blood of a Poet* 1931), *Paris-Béguin* (1931), *Zéro de conduite* (1933), *La Kermesse héroïque* (*Carnival in Flanders* 1935), *Hôtel du Nord* (1938), *La Règle du jeu* (*Rules of the Game* 1938–9)) and of lesbian representation not only then (*Club de femmes* 1936, *Hélène* 1936) but also through and beyond the 1950s itself (*Quai des Orfèvres* 1947, *Au Royaume des cieux* 1949, *Olivia* 1950, *Huis clos* 1954, *Les Collégiennes* 1956, *La Garçonne* 1957, *La Fille aux yeux d'or* (*The Girl with Golden Eyes* 1961), *Thérèse* 1962). However, anything approaching the latter grouping for gay male representation would have to wait until 1964 for *Olivia*'s equivalent, *Les Amitiés particulières* (*Special Friendships*), even though the source novel had been published in 1943. The only gay filmic representations in the period are *Un Chant d'amour*, virtually unknown, Cocteau's extremely indirect films, Michel Auclair's magnetic queer Nazi criminal in *Les Maudits* (*The Cursed* 1947) and a sprinkling of marginal, comic queens (to whom I shall return).

The apparent isolation[4] of *L'Air de Paris* in terms of gay representation should not really surprise. The post-war period was markedly homophobic. The anti-gay legislation introduced under Vichy in 1942[5] was maintained and the Paris police began cracking down on homosexuality from 1949 on; anti-gay laws were to be strengthened under De Gaulle (Girard 1981, Copley 1989, Martel 1996). With the Occupation fresh in the memory, male homosexuality might be seen as a product of Nazism (*Les Maudits*) or a form of collaborationism (as one may read Daniel in Jean-Paul Sartre's *Les Chemins de la liberté* (*Roads to Freedom* 1945–49))[6] and either way excoriated: it was not about to be openly celebrated in a mainstream film.

Aspects of the production also had the effect of hiding *L'Air*'s homoeroticism. One of the backers, Cino del Duca, published photo romances and insisted on the inclusion of 'a real love story' (i.e. that of André and Corinne) (Billard 1995: 557). The casting of Gabin also took away any queer taint. According to the film's openly gay director, Marcel Carné, Gabin was 'terribly frightened' of what people might think:

> When at the end of [the film] he meets up with the young boxer, I
> told him to put his hand on the back of his neck and lead him off:

'No way, I don't want to look like a queer'. He wasn't happy at all.
Gabin a queer, come off it, for goodness sake!

(Grant and Joecker 1982–3: 14)

Yet the very incompatibility of Gabin's image as 'the decent bloke' ('l'hon-nête homme' (Vincendeau 1993: 146)) with queerness may well have been what made *L'Air*'s audacity possible, whilst also simultaneously making a more overt gay representation impossible. As Victor is Gabin, he can't pos-sibly be a queer, which lets the film get away with suggesting just that in the relationship between him and André, but makes it hard for it to go too far beyond suggestion.

Carné's position is fascinatingly unclear. At the time (cf. Marrot 1962: 4) and in his autobiography, *La Vie à belles dents* (1979: 331), he maintained that what he wanted to do with *L'Air* was to make a film about boxing, of which he was, like Jean Cocteau, a fan. In a later interview (Grant and Joecker 1982–3: 14), he says that it is 'obvious' that Corinne and Chantal (see below) 'sleep together', but he is equivocal about Victor and André, evoking the suggestiveness of the massage scene ('there's no point him [Gabin] denying it') while also saying that all the same he hasn't ever really made a film centred on a male love story.

I will return to the exact terms in which he says this in a moment. First though I want to begin considering *L'Air* and homosexuality in relation to Carné's work more widely. Edward Baron Turk (1989) shows, with a scrupulous refusal to over-interpret, the persistence of gay themes and images throughout Carné's work, and even Pierre Billard, who is warier of Turk's gay readings, agrees that *L'Air* is about 'a profound affective relation-ship between two men' (1995: 615). Billard however feels that, given Carné's age and his roots in popular culture, he wasn't in 1954 'up for the slightest public display of his sexual life' (ibid.). Perhaps so, but in *Hôtel du Nord* he already had at any rate portrayed a gay man, Adrien (François Perrier), who is not only sympathetic and apparently integrated into the community of the hotel, but who also, as we might say now, comes out in the course of the film. This occurs when he is out walking with Renée (Annabella) one evening. A soldier passes by, glancing at Adrien. When Adrien calls him by name, Fernand, saying 'Didn't you recognise me?', Fernand replies, 'I didn't even look at you when I saw you with Mademoi-selle'. But he had (looked at him): Adrien insists on their acknowledging each other in public and they then go off together (presumably to Adrien's room which he had earlier told the hotel owner, Mme Lecouvreur, he had been getting ready for a visit from his 'mate'). 'Never again', as Turk puts it, 'would Carné be so direct and unmannered in his treatment of homosexual-ity' (1989: 140). This may have much to do with the increasingly homopho-bic climate in which he found himself, but it may also be more deeply rooted in his conceptualisation of homosexuality.

If production circumstances (legality, the need for a heterosexual love story, the presence of Gabin, Carné's apprehensiveness) closeted *L'Air de Paris*, it also bears two of the hallmarks of closet expression. First, the in some ways astonishing treatment of Lesaffre's body is nonetheless within the codes of the 'alibis' Thomas Waugh (1996) discusses in his history of gay erotic photography and film: showers, heterosexuality, massage as sports therapy. In *Thérèse Raquin* a year earlier, Carné's treatment of Lesaffre, in an important but secondary role invented for the film, is less body baring but, in one telling sequence, much more gay iconographic, with a striped sailor top torn to reveal a nipple and a bicep flexed to hold a hand mirror, imagery that could come straight from Cocteau's *Le Livre blanc* (*The White Book*, republished with said imagery in 1949) or much 1950s gay pornography. *L'Air de Paris*, though centrally homo-erotic, places its potentially homosexual imagery firmly within less declarative bounds.

A second, but paradoxical, strategy of the closet is the presence in the film of a very obviously gay character and (pace Carné) a less obviously lesbian one, Jean-Marc and Chantal (Simone Paris). The former, whose first words on greeting Corinne are 'J'ai passé une nuit complètement folle',[7] is virtually identical not only to the same actor's captain in *Fanfan la Tulipe* (1951) but also to Alain, one of quintuplets played by Fernandel in *Le Mouton à cinq pattes* (*The Sheep Has Five Legs* 1954): large men with rather small, manicured moustaches (rather like Proust's M. Charlus), walking with short steps and hands held out the side, given to too many fussy gestures and a shriek in the voice (Figure 9.2). Parédès' versions are livelier, warmer and wittier than Fernandel's, and more unequivocally gay,[8] but there is not a lot in it. Chantal fits the less sharply defined stereotype of the rich lesbian in the world of fashion and antiques (cf. *Club de femmes*, *Quai des*

Figure 9.2 Complètement folle: Jean-Marc (Jean Parédès) regales Corinne (Marie Daëms) (left) and Chantal (Simone Paris), *L'Air de Paris* (frame enlargement).

141

Orfèvres, *Olivia*, *La Garçonne*, *La Fille aux yeux d'or*, *Les Biches* (1967), *La Fiancée du pirate* (1969), to name only French examples): single, elegant, cold, with a large, ornately furnished dwelling. Corinne tells André that Chantal, the older woman, 'formed' her (itself a trope of lesbian representation (Dyer 1977: 33–34)); Daëms's pause before telling André that Chantal is 'a friend' is virtually a wink to the audience that there is more to it.

Jean-Marc and Chantal represent the world of smart high style to which Corinne, a model from the provinces, aspires. Though André and Corinne have seen each other before, it is Jean-Marc who brings them together for an impromptu photo shoot (they are eating in a restaurant in les Halles and notice André who is working there); Chantal prevents André and Corinne from making love the first time by arriving back too early (to the flat where she and Corinne live) and it is she who tells André with undisguised contempt that Corinne has left him (and her). In short, these queer characters' function is to take André from Victor and then also to break up André and Corinne. They represent a negative view of homosexuality in the film, but also its only explicit representation. By in effect attacking queers, *L'Air* may hope to ensure its central vision of homosexuality remains in the closet.

Production circumstances and the closet account for how *L'Air* got away with as much as it did, using strategies that readily allowed audiences to miss what it was dealing with. However, this is complicated by the film's conceptualisation of the latter, with its representation of . . . And here we have a problem. I have used a variety of terms above to characterise the central relationship in this and other films, but in many ways there is no term for it. *L'Air de Paris* aspires to represent something without naming or indeed really representing it.

One senses the problem in Carné's brief discussion of the film alluded to above. He has been asked why he has 'never shot a male love story'. First he replies that he has perhaps indeed never shot an 'histoire d'amour entre hommes', but, after talking about the homosexual elements in *Hôtel du Nord*, *Les Enfants du paradis* (Lacenaire and Avril) and *L'Air de Paris*, he affirms, 'Mais histoires entre homos, non' (Grant and Joecker 1982–3: 14). The slippage from 'hommes' to 'homos' is crucial. Though he then acknowledges that he may simply not have had the nerve, it does also seem that he wants to say that the 'evocative' relationship in *L'Air* is, all the same, not gay because it is about men, not queers. But how then is this relationship to be conceptualised?

In Carné's last feature film, *La Merveilleuse visite* (*The Wonderful Visit* 1974), the main character, the angel Jean (Gilles Kohler), tells Delia (Deborah Berger), the young woman who befriends him, that love can take many forms, that it 'can take thousands and thousands of colours'. 'What colour is yours?,' asks Delia, to which the angel replies, 'Transparency'. The homo-erotic tones of *La Merveilleuse visite* are even stronger than those of *L'Air de Paris* and validation of the many forms of love is standard pro-gay rhetoric. It is very hard not to hear in this exchange a message about homo-sexuality – but the really symptomatic element is the representation of the angel's love as transparency. Later Delia tries to explain the feelings between herself and the angel to her jealous boyfriend, François (Jean-Pierre Castaldi); it's not sex nor even really like sibling closeness, she says, 'I really don't know what it's called – there must be a word for it, but not in our lan-guage – you'd have to look elsewhere.' Transparency and namelessness – this is the ideal of love proposed by *La Merveilleuse visite* and, I'm now going to argue, *L'Air de Paris*.

L'Air's homo-eroticism comes close to that proposed by the journal *Arcadie*, the first number of which appeared in the same year.[9] There had already been the short-lived journal, *Futur*, from 1952 to 1955, but *Arcadie* was much more successful (though banned from display in kiosks), leading in 1957 to the establishment of social clubs in the French speaking world. Its founder, André Baudry, was very well connected in the arts and politics, but his message also astutely judged the temper of the times. He proposed the notion of homophilia, stressing the erotic ('understood in the widest sense of the word: physical, psychological, affective and intellectual' (*Arcadie* 71; quoted in Girard 1981: 49)) rather than the merely sexual; as Jacques Girard puts it, 'homosexual' was seen as 'designating precise, localizable and easily identifiable acts, whereas "homophile" related to "a global attitude which takes in the thousand nuances of human being"' (ibid.: 49–50).

Two things relevant here mark the conception of homophilia. One is the insistence that it 'must not be confused … with prostitution and effemi-nacy' (*Arcadie* 3, quoted in ibid.: 53). The Victor–André relationship could not be so confused – the film refuses the tarty iconography used on 'mauvais garçon' Lesaffre in *Thérèse Raquin* and implies the relationship's distinctness from the likes of Jean-Marc.

Second, as the quotes above suggest, there is something vague, evasive and intangible about just what homophilia is, not least in the equivocation about sex. This is caught in the use of the word 'amitié' (friendship), *Arcadie*'s key term for defining homophile relations, at times a euphemism but also an attempt to define something between lust and comradeship. The term was also important to Carné: Turk (1989: 60) quotes from his praise of friendship in his autobiography, linking it to Carné's oblique representation of homosexuality in such friendships as Xavier and Lucien in *Jenny* (1936). The ambiguity of the term is caught in a remark of Victor to Blanche in *L'Air*, that men's 'friendship pisses women off'. Throughout the film Blanche knows what the real erotic story is between Victor and André;[10] he presents as asexual camaraderie what she recognises as an erotically charged commitment.

The film, though, is not doing what Victor is doing. It may have counted on being misread as doing so. Male bonding, including the male couple, is a staple of French cinema (cf. Vincendeau 1993, Burch and Sellier 1996): as with the casting of Gabin (star of many such films), the homophilia of *L'Air de Paris* may have assumed it was thus gaining some generic protection. However, it is instructive to compare it with two male couple films released the year before, *Le Salaire de la peur* (*The Wages of Fear*) and *Touchez pas au grisbi* (*Grisbi*). Both of these, if anything, make even more of the central couple relationship. In *Le Salaire*, Mario (Yves Montand) effectively dumps Luigi (Folco Lulli), who has looked after him like a wife, for the fake glamour of Jo (Charles Vanel); there is an emotionally charged reconciliation scene between Mario and Luigi, but the strongest emotion is reserved for Jo's death in Mario's arms at the end of the long, perilous journey that constitutes the film's main action. In *Touchez pas au grisbi*, people remark on the fact that professional criminals Max (Gabin) and Riton (René Dary) 'have been together for twenty years'; the heart of the film is Max's sacrifice of his loot (the 'grisbi' of the title) to save the kidnapped Riton, who in the process is fatally wounded.

All three films put the emotional weight on the male couple relationship, although the men all have wives or girlfriends. However, there is much greater heterosexual conviction in *Le Salaire* and *Touchez pas au grisbi*. In the former, Mario and Luigi contrast with Jo and also Luigi's co-driver, Bimba (Peter Van Eyck), both of whom both explicitly say they are not interested in women; Mario, however, not only has a girlfriend, Linda (Vera Clouzot) but is also constantly eyeing women in the street, and the film ends with his delirious (and fatal) drive home, cross cut with Linda dancing in anticipation of his arrival, a clear suggestion of libidinal enthusiasm on both sides. Similarly in *Touchez pas au grisbi*, Max has a girlfriend, Betty (Marilyn Bufferd), and they both clearly take pleasure in their regular lunch and sex trysts. Linda and Betty are undoubtedly emotionally secondary to Jo and Riton, but there is genuine affection for and definite sexual satisfaction with the women in both cases. The same is not true of *L'Air de Paris*. The absence of children in the Victor–Blanche household (something underlined by having Blanche holding a baby, someone else's, the first time we see her in the film) and the fact that Victor's only mode of expressing affection is a light, mock punch to Blanche's chin both suggest this is a sexually undynamic marriage.[11] André and Corinne do clearly make love, though (partly for reasons of class difference) it seems not to have crossed his mind as a possibility when he first drives her home: he is all wide-eyed innocence, she worldly libidinousness when they stop outside her flat and she has to propose that he comes up. A later scene makes him more sexually forward, but opinions differ about how convincing Lesaffre's performance is at this point.

In short, if *L'Air* might just pass as an asexual male friendship film, it is certainly in no hurry to suggest the friends' heterosexuality. Moreover, unlike *Le Salaire* or *Touchez pas*, *L'Air*'s treatment of its central male couple draws much of its rhetoric from the treatment of heterosexuality in film. It's hard to imagine Mario or Max commenting to Jo or Riton on their 'beautiful smile', as Victor does to André. Lighting especially – both in two shots and in shot:reverse shot editing – reproduces the dynamics of screen heterosexuality. One scene, for instance, has Victor and André talking together on the latter's bed. Victor is screen right, wearing a black jacket, sitting with his body turned towards us on the edge of the bed, elbows on his knees (Figure 9.3). Light catches the top of his hair, his forehead and left leg, but André, who is stretched out on the bed, wearing a white shirt, is fully in the light. Victor talks about why he and some of the others love boxing, then asks André if he knows why he does. There is a cut to a different, closer angle: Victor's dark hair and jacket is on the extreme right of the screen; André, propped up one elbow now, turned towards us, catches to the full the frontal light that only illuminates Victor's turned away from us profile; he also has a strong light, coming from behind Victor, on his right shoulder, a top back light that catches and blondes his hair and, when he looks up into Victor's face, the light flashes in his eyes (Figure 9.4). This kind of differentiated disposition, used throughout the film with the couple, is exactly that used for heterosexual couples in film (cf. Dyer 1997: 132–140), with one qualification: the light on André is not softened. Whereas women in such set-ups are glowing, André is brilliant.

This brilliance may simply be a more 'masculine' lightness than soft focus glamour lighting, but it also relates to angel imagery. There is a long tradition of representing gay desire in the figure of the (male) angel in the international high gay culture that was very much a reference point for *Arcadie*. A French *locus classicus* of this is the early work of André Gide (discussed in a classic 1950s study by Jean Delay (1956: 492–519)), while in cinema we may note *Vingarne* (*The Wings*, Sweden 1916), *Mikaël* (Germany 1924), *Le Sang d'un poète* (France 1930), *Lot in Sodom* (USA 1930), *Teorema* (Italy 1968),

Figure 9.3 *L'Air de Paris*: André and Victor (frame enlargement).

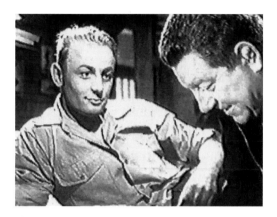

Figure 9.4 *L'Air de Paris*: André and Victor (frame enlargement).

Looking for Langston (GB 1989), related films like *Billy Budd* (USA 1962) and *Morte a Venezia* (*Death in Venice*, Italy 1971), and, most relevant here, the work of Carné himself: the sexually and morally ambiguous emissaries of the devil in *Les Visiteurs du soir*[12] (1942), the diaphanous clothes and white, white face of the pure lover Baptiste in *Les Enfants du paradis* (1943–4) and, most explicitly, the blonde, almost permanently half or completely naked angel of *La Merveilleuse visite*.[13] The whole tradition, and especially its denial of any compatibility between lust and innocence, is wickedly sent up in Lionel Soukaz' short film, *Le Sexe des anges* (1978).[14]

It is above all the brilliant light on André in *L'Air*, emphasising at once his physicality and his ingenuousness, that puts him clearly in this line of images of gay desire. This is reinforced by his not being socially located. Like Roland Lesaffre himself (as publicity emphasised), André is an orphan and has learnt boxing in the rootless anonymity of the military. He is first encountered on the railway line in Paris, rather, that is, than in a Paris neighbourhood. There is something strange about the way the film introduces him the first time he and Victor meet. They have both gone to a hospital where a mutual friend, one of Victor's boxers, has just died; Victor is standing talking to a registrar, when suddenly André's voice is heard and the camera moves back to reveal his presence – almost as if he has just landed there rather than having been physically present all along. The brilliant light and the lack of social location reinforce the overriding angelic characterisation: intense sexual appeal yet apparent lack of sexual awareness.

Vivid and sensual, the angel is unimpeachably spiritual. He may sometimes be another Waughian alibi, but he also expresses a longing for a form of sexual desire that is sinless and pure. He is the fantasy resolution of a conflict between lust and morality endured by generations of gay men. In some cases, he can also be the site for playing out the ambiguities and deceptions

146

of this resolution, but where this is not so, as with *L'Air de Paris*, his brilliance and vividness at once express the keenness of homophile longing and betrays its impossibility. After all, he does not exist. At the end of *La Merveilleuse visite*, the angel, besieged by uncomprehending townsmen, falls off a cliff and becomes a seagull. It is the only place for such unsulliable sensuality. *L'Air*'s angel, André, is of course not literally one, any more than the film is generically a fantasy. This creates especial problems for a film on the face of it so much about place.

L'Air de Paris seems to be a film insistently about Paris. Even before the credits, a song, 'La Ballade de Paris', is sung in the darkness by Yves Montand. He had introduced it with some success a year earlier; both it and the film's title told the first audiences that they were going to see a film about Paris. The credits reinforce this, with a series of postcard images of Paris to the accompaniment, mainly, of 'La Ballade' and another Montand success, 'Toi tu n'ressembles à personne', played by accordion and orchestra: nothing could be more 'Parisian'. The two main stars, Gabin and Arletty, have indelibly Parisian images (and accents), the first shot of the film is a railway sign indicating 'Paris 2 kilometres', locations (some studio recreations) include the area round the boulevard de Grenelle, the îles de la Cité and Saint-Louis and the Halles, all very familiar, there is an interspersed montage of postcard Paris and the films ends with Victor and André walking off towards Notre-Dame.

Yet the film also seems to undermine this Paris project. Blanche/Arletty spends most of the film saying she wants to leave Paris, André speaks with bitter irony about it ('it's got everything you need, the good Lord, cops ... and if that's not enough, you can always throw yourself in the Seine'), and when Corinne tells André she is marrying a rich man to help her career and, not least, Chantal's ailing antiques business, she says, 'That's life, that is, that's Paris'. Some of this may be generic: people in Paris films are always complaining about Paris.[15] Equally, some aspects of the faltering view of Paris – as compared to the Paris of accordions and postcard views – might be seen as in part registering changes in contemporary Paris, notably in its ethnic mix: Victor and Blanche live next door to an Italian family, André initially lives in an Arab hotel, and one of Victor's boxers, often prominent in the frame and especially fondly treated by Blanche, is black.

What makes these elements more unsettling is the way the film seems set on making Paris somehow insubstantial. The song sung in the dark at the beginning concentrates the audience on Paris, but also leaves it ungrounded in any imagery, while its gist is the problem of singing a song about Paris ('So many poets have written songs about Paris that I don't know what to say to sing its praises').[16] The accordion and postcards credits seem too insistently Parisian, especially when it turns out they have so little to do with the Paris of the film. The film's opening sequence takes place two kilometres from Paris (a sign tells us) on a railway track (as Corinne and André see each other for the first time, he working on the line, she looking down from a halted train), a moment of standstill in a site of transition, not quite yet in Paris proper.

One especially telling index of this undermining representation is the treatment of Victor/Gabin in relation to food. As Vincendeau points out, food is central to Gabin's image, as a man and as French (1993: 167–168, 177–178). *L'Air* denies him this. He is only once seen in a café (just after he first meets André); it is deserted and he is not known there – in other words, an impersonal space. Meals are often taken with the neighbouring family, where they eat Italian food; without telling Blanche and much to her annoyance, Victor hijacks their anniversary meal for a celebration of André's victory in the ring, except that André doesn't come and we don't see the meal. The only meal properly shown in the film is that of Corinne, Jean-Marc, Chantal and their associates in a bistro in les Halles, a sequence that does not include Victor/Gabin and which compares strikingly with the opening scene of *Touchez pas au grisbi*, where bourgeois slummers like this are expressly excluded from the restaurant that is virtually Max/Gabin's home. The very thing that grounds Gabin in his world – and archetypally Paris – in his other films is taken away from him here.

This desubstantialising representation of Paris goes hand in hand with the film's focus on a homophilic relationship. *L'Air de Paris* eschews showing us the gay Paris that did exist, despite the homophobic climate, the Paris described in Paul Reboux's open-minded survey *Sens interdits* of 1951, a Paris 'taken over by a pederastic elite', according to one commentator in 1953.[17] Even the homosexually obvious Jean-Marc is not placed anywhere in the city. In the racy sequence featuring Lesaffre in *Thérèse Raquin* discussed above, the proximity of the most important gay area of Paris, Pigalle, is rammed home by the sight of Sacré Coeur through the window, but Pigalle does not figure at all in *L'Air de Paris*.

Refusing to document this non-homophilic Paris, the film also cannot imagine any other locus for homosexuality. The film ends with Victor and André walking together towards Notre-Dame. It is a strange shot. Notre-Dame figures quite late in the credits sequence, seen in the distance, the frame dominated by a modern bridge; it appears in the sequence at the moment the music changes to a new melody in a jazzy arrangement, one that becomes associated in the film with the Paris of high fashion that the film rejects. Thereafter, Notre-Dame is only shown in order to place the flat where Corinne lives with Chantal. In other words, it has no meaning for the men or the film except a negative one. Moreover, it is shot, in this final image, with its flying buttresses fully lit and light flooding out of all the doors and windows of the Île Saint Louis quayside street down which the men walk – a magical look that at the same time underlines the impossibility of this happy ending. In short, the shot suggests that for Carné, there is no place for Victor and André, for homophilia, in Paris – or, this must mean, anywhere else. *L'Air de Paris*, a film so startlingly overt for its time, nonetheless portrays homosexuality as a love that does not even know its name, or place.

Acknowledgement

From Susan Hayward and Ginette Vincendeau (eds) *French Film: Texts and Contexts*, London: Routledge, 2000.

Notes

1 As in English, 'air' can refer, as it does in the title, to a song (discussed later in the chapter) and to ambience.

2 '...déséquilibrée, désorienté, et comme intérieurement trahie', *Le Parisien Libéré*, 30.9.54 (in Pérez 1994: 133).

3 Pérez (1994: 130) notes this. The main exception seems to be the right-wing journal, *Aspects de la France*, whose critic, Georges Hellio, referred to Victor being in the grip of 'a demon a teensy weensy bit equivocal' (1.10.54; in Pérez 1994: 133). Marcel Carné, in the context of a discussion of the lesbianism in the film, says that he was much attacked at the time, *Paris-Presse* referring to 'L'Air de Paris, an unbreathable air', evoking, so Carné presumably understands, the image of the airless decadence of lesbian milieux (Grant and Joecker 1982–3: 14).

4 It is possible that we are simply ignorant about gay representation in French cinema. There is as yet for the latter no equivalent to Vito Russo's *The Celluloid Closet* (1981) and recent research suggests that there is more to find out than even he knew about gay representation in Hollywood (leave alone elsewhere). The French language books on homosexuality and film (Garsi 1981, Philbert 1984) in fact have very little in them about French film (especially before the 1970s). It's possible that research might reveal that *L'Air* is less isolated than it appears.

5 The first such legislation since decriminalisation in 1791.

6 Burch and Sellier (1996) note that the issue of collaborationism commonly focused on questions of sexual relations between French women and German men; it would not be surprising if the same trope applied to gay men. One of the key witnesses in Marcel Ophuls' *Le Chagrin et la pitié* (*The Sorrow and the Pity* 1969) is a respected underground militant who emphasises the importance for him of coming out as gay in the film to counter the idea that gay men were all collaborationists.

7 'I've just had a crazy night' – but 'folle', the feminine form of 'fou' (crazy), is also slang for a camp gay man.

8 Alain seems to live with a woman, whom he addresses with extravagant terms of endearment – but he also calls her 'vous' and they have separate bedrooms. Jean-Marc on the other hand goes into raptures when he sees André and his mates at les Halles – 'They are splendid! Young Hercules!' – while the captain in *Fanfan la Tulipe* says that he'd love to see Fanfan (Gérard Philippe) do his swashbuckling stuff, throwing 'Wouldn't you?' to Fanfan's beloved (Gina Lollobrigida) with a distinctly libidinal moue.

9 *Arcadie* was the journal of an organisation of the same name. Given that the founder of both had wide connections and that, among others, Cocteau and the film critic Jacques Siclier were involved in it, it is unlikely that Carné did not at least know about *Arcadie*. Frédéric Martel notes that in 1968 some breakaway members of Arcadie 'took the view that the allusions to homosexuality in the films of Marcel Carné were no longer sufficient' (1996: 71), indicating at any rate the perception of a link between the world views of Carné and *Arcadie*.

10 Women's perceptiveness about sexuality between men is a recurrent motif in Carné: cf. Renée and Adrien in *Hôtel du Nord*, Garance and Lacenaire in *Les Enfants du paradis* and Delia and the angel in *La Merveilleuse visite*.

11 Absence of children would certainly not indicate sexual coldness in contemporary cinema, but it did by and large before the 1960s.

12 Cf. the discussion in Turk 1989: 206–212.

13 This would have been even more obvious had Carné been able to shoot the ending he wanted, in which the camera would be shown and on it the crew, all 'young and beautiful, just wearing trousers with a little heart on them [like the angel] and all of a sudden the camera flies off into the infinite . . . as if to say, even if no-one believes in this story, at least the crew did.' However, he couldn't film it because he couldn't get hold of any 'M. Muscle' types from Paris in time (Grant and Joecker 1982–3: 10).

14 Briefly described in Dyer 1990: 225–226.

15 I'm grateful to Ginette Vincendeau for pointing this out.

16 Vincendeau (1993: 151–152) points out that Paris songs (with accordion) are often important in Gabin films, sung by him either to an audience within the film or direct to camera. Here not only is it not Gabin singing in a Gabin film, but the voice is disembodied, not visually addressed to anyone.

17 Frederic Hoffet in his *Psychanalyse de Paris*, referenced in Copley 1989: 193. Pederasty (notably in the slang term 'pédé') was often used in the period to refer to all male homosexuality, not just that involving boys.

References

Billard, Pierre (1995) *L'Age classique du cinéma français*, Paris: Flammarion.

Burch, Noël and Sellier, Geneviève (1996) *La Drôle de guerre des sexes du cinéma français*, Paris: Nathan.

Cadars, Pierre (1982) *Les Séducteurs du cinéma français*, Paris: Henri Veyrier.

Carné, Marcel (1979) *La Vie à belles dents*, Paris: Éditions Jean Vuaret.

Copley, Antony (1989) *Sexual Moralities in France, 1780–1980*, London: Routledge.

Delay, Jean (1956) *La Jeunesse d'André Gide*, Paris: Gallimard.

Dyer, Richard (1977) 'Stereotyping', in Dyer, Richard (ed.) *Gays and Film*, London: British Film Institute, 27–39.

Dyer, Richard (1990) *Now You See It: Studies on Lesbian and Gay Film*, London: Routledge.

Dyer, Richard (1997) *White*, London: Routledge.

Garsi, Jean-François (ed.) (1981) *Cinémas homosexuels*, Paris: Papyrus (*CinémAction* 15).

Girard, Jacques (1981) *Le Mouvement homosexuel en France 1945–1980*, Paris: Syros.

Grant, Jacques and Joecker, Jean-Pierre (1982–3) 'Rencontre avec Marcel Carné: Cinéaste Fantastisque (sic)', *Masques* 16: 6–16.

Marrot, Henri (1962) '*Air de Paris*', *Image et son* 153–4, 3–4.

Martel, Frédéric (1996) *Le Rose et le noir: les homosexuels en France depuis 1968*, Paris: Éditions du Seuil.

Pérez, Michel (1994) *Les Films de Carné*, Paris: Éditions Ramsay.

Philbert, Bertrand (1984) *L'Homosexualité à l'écran*, Paris: Henri Veyrier.

Reboux, Paul (1951) *Sens interdits*, Paris: Raoul Solar.

Russo, Vito (1981) *The Celluloid Closet*, New York: Harper & Row.

Turk, Edward Baron (1989) *Child of Paradise: Marcel Carné and the Golden Age of French Cinema*, Cambridge MA: Harvard University Press.

Vincendeau, Ginette (1993) 'Gabin unique: Le Pouvoir réconciliateur du mythe', in Gauteur, Claude and Vincendeau, Ginette, *Jean Gabin: anatomie d'un mythe*, Paris: Nathan, 93–205.

Vincendeau, Ginette (1997) 'Paradise Regained', *Sight and Sound* 7: 1(NS), 12–16.

Waugh, Thomas (1996) *Hard to Imagine: Gay Male Eroticism on Photography and Film from Their Beginnings to Stonewall*, New York: Columbia University Press.

10

CHARLES HAWTREY

Carrying on regardless

The Wild West. A posse rides up to a redskin camp and asks for Chief Big Heap. The braves point to a wigwam. From within there is the sound of a toilet flushing, and out comes a thin, bespectacled figure who greets the posse, in a voice at once lascivious and ladylike, with 'Oh, hello'. It is Charles Hawtrey and this is *Carry On Cowboy* (Figure 10.1).

Hawtrey appeared in twenty-three of the thirty Carry On films and always introduced himself with this drawling, suggestive yet refined, 'Hello'. He did not give a fig for the circumstances or the appropriateness of this greeting. He was sometimes cast as a weed or even a fairy, but just as often as a rampant heterosexual or macho man. It didn't matter. He didn't change his style or manner one iota.

He was already a well established character actor before the Carry Ons started. Beginning in films in 1930 at the age of sixteen, he was not much out of work on stage and screen from then on. At twenty three, he was still playing one of Will Hay's schoolboys in *Good Morning Boys* (1937). He was the kind of person you got familiar with in British films, though you might not be able to name them – people like Richard Wattis and Joan Hickson, who were like loveable but odd and sometimes crotchety distant relations. But Hawtrey remained very much a bit player – blink and you'll miss him as, for instance, the station porter in Powell and Pressburger's very strange home front movie *A Canterbury Tale* (1944). It was only with *Carry On Sergeant* in 1958 that he really found the 'character' that was to make him not only recognisable but also a name.

It wasn't intended that *Sergeant* would be the first of a series, yet with Kenneth Williams, Kenneth Connor and Hattie Jacques, as well as Hawtrey, in the cast, the mould was cast. The series ran more or less annually until 1978 and Hawtrey was in the best of them – as an unsuitable recruit in *Sergeant*, a 'special constable' in *Constable* (1960), secret agent 000 in *Spying* (1964), Mark Anthony's father-in-law in *Cleo* (1964), the chief in *Cowboy* (1965), a lavatory attendant in *Screaming* (1966), the Duc de Pomm-frit in the Scarlet Pimpernel spoof *Don't Lose Your Head* (1966), private Widdle of the Indian army in *Up the Khyber* (1968) and the great Tonka,

Figure 10.1 Charles Hawtrey, *Carry On Cowboy* 1965 (BFI Stills, Posters and Designs).

leader of an otherwise all female tribe in *Up the Jungle* (1970). In nearly all the parts he is miscast; in all of them he is wonderful.

He is always 'on'. Quite often he isn't given much to do but stand around, but nonetheless he is perpetually animated. His eyes dart bird-like behind his wire rimmed glasses, he nods at everything people say, looks delighted or crestfallen – no actor ever gave better value on the reaction front. He really enters into the spirit and the fun of it.

His laughter is infectious. For someone with such a high pitched voice, his laugh was quite fruity, and it often gave the impression of being spontaneous and unrestrained. At the start of *Don't Lose Your Head*, he is an aristocrat about to be guillotined. He is quite unconcerned, however, lying in place, his neck in the blade shaft, reading a book and roaring with laughter. The book? Something by the Marquis de Sade. 'Priceless!' quips Hawtrey and goes on happily laughing while the executioner gets ready.

He is a perpetual delight. But was he gay? The words Catholic and Pope may spring to mind, yet the films are oddly ambiguous – he is both 'obvious' and yet not explicit. Even in his private life, though his sexuality is hardly in doubt, he was not what we would now call out. It was hardly a shock horror revelation when he was discovered to have, in the touching vocabulary of the tabloids, a twenty-year-old lad staying with him the night his house burned down in 1988, but hard gossip has not found its way into print. He certainly had a background in queer sensibility before the Carry Ons. He was in something called *Bluebell in Fairyland* in 1925, sang the surely inappropriate 'A Country Life for Me!' at the Italia Conti school in 1925, played one of the lost boys in a production of *Peter Pan* and, most imaginable of all, was a male 'wilting lilly' and a female secret agent in 1930s revues.

The films sometimes come on quite strong about his sexuality. In the James Bond Carry On, *Spying*, he is asked why he was given the odd number 000, when all the other spies have been given a final digit other than zero. He recalls that the people assigning the numbers looked at him and said 'oh-oh' (as in, 'What have we got here?') and then 'oh' (dragged out, as in 'dear me'). It's clear here that everyone has got his number. Similarly in *Screaming*, where he's a gents' lavatory attendant; when cute Jim Dale and Harry Corbett go visiting, their efforts at making eye contact with him look like cottaging; when he proudly declares 'I live in a man's world', the real meaning of the butch phrase is evident.

Yet just as often he is either asexual and 'innocent', or even explicitly heterosexual. The very title of *Carry On Camping* (1969) leads one to expect the Hawtrey character to be, well, camp, but he's introduced when he's in a camping equipment shop trying out a tent by strenuously snogging in it with a girlfriend. In *Henry* (1971), he is a positively (and heterosexually) randy lord, who is bedding Henry VIII's present wife (Joan Sims) while the king (Sidney James) is getting off with a chamber maid (Barbara Windsor). As always, in terms of being gay, Hawtrey both obviously 'is' and isn't.

What's wonderful is the way that, whatever the part, he just doesn't even try to be butch and macho. Delicious ambiguities ensue. In *Doctor* (1968) he plays a man whose wife is pregnant. He so identifies with her, and the female role, that it is he who goes to the ante-natal exercise sessions. In *Regardless* (1960) he has to act as a second for a boxing match, which involves him in rubbing down the boxer, played by the forgotten but gorgeous Joe Robinson. When Robinson starts to whinge because he's been hit, which is after all the point of boxing, Hawtrey accuses his opponent of being a bully – and goes into the ring himself to defend Joe's honour (Figure 10.2). There's not a breath of suggestion that Charlie and Joe might be sexually interested in each other or that Hawtrey's character is anything other than straight. Yet the moment you put Hawtrey in the part, the rubbing down and sympathising with a muscleman's sissy behaviour take on a whole new complexion.

One of the effects of all this is to send traditional masculinity up rotten. In *Sergeant*, he is one of an in-take of National Service recruits, compulsorily called up to enlist in the army (a war-time legacy that did not end till the late 1950s). Like several of the others, who include Bob Monkhouse as well as Kenneths Connor and Williams, the army needs to make a man of him. They fail, but mainly because he so wants to please that he exaggerates what they want to the point of hysteria. Asked to stand stiff and straight on parade, he does so so rigidly that he topples over. Required to bayonet a hanging dummy, he goes to it with a will, shouting and screaming archaic macho phrases like 'Have at you sir!' and so carried away with the

Figure 10.2 Charles Hawtrey and unidentifiable opponent, *Carry On Regardless* 1960 (BFI Stills, Posters and Designs).

viciousness of it all that it is only with difficulty that he is persuaded to stop. By acting so exactly as the army requires, he ends up showing how utterly ridiculous stiff, violent, normal masculinity is.

This mockery of masculinity is all the more fascinating in the context of films that often seem like hymns to sexism. The men are good natured slobs who want nothing other than to have it away; the women, unless they are Barbara Windsor, are harridans. If the men are worthless, at least they want to have a good time; the women are intent on seeing that neither they themselves nor anyone else has any fun. This can be engaging – Sidney James and Barbara Windsor have a relish for the vulgar that is positively life enhancing – but it can be dreary, in the remorseless sexism of men who fancy themselves, like Monkhouse in *Sergeant* or Leslie Phillips in *Nurse*, *Teacher* and *Constable*, and in the terrible misuse of talents like Joan Sims and June Whitfield. It's in this context that Hawtrey is such a tonic. He just sails plain through the unremitting heterosexual sexism, making straight masculinity look absurd and so making it look much more delightful to be a queen.

The unambiguous ambiguity of Hawtrey's sexuality works well in both upping the already obsessive innuendo stakes of the Carry On films and in undermining any vestiges of commitment to masculine values. But as a gay icon or role model? I have always loved him, yet he does embody one of the things that the Gay Liberation movement tended to disapprove of – the stereotype of the effeminate gay man. And no doubt much of the straight laughter at him is oppressive laughter. He confirms that gay men are ineffectual, trivial and, worst of all, like women. Yet for all the hatred that is expressed through the stereotype, it is also the case that Hawtrey was much loved – and anyway, I'll take the comparison with women as a compliment, thank you.

Besides, who cares what straights think? The most attractive thing about the turn to Queer in recent years is that it implies a rejection of worrying about what straights will think. In his way, Charlie was like that too. What I relish most about him is his utter disregard for what anyone else may think. He just gets on with being himself.

The definitive example is in the second Carry On film, *Nurse* (1959). He plays a patient who likes nothing better than to listen to the radio. His favoured listening? He likes classical music, a bit iffy still in 1959, and plays along with it, miming the piano part in concertos with such an unguarded ecstasy that he flings himself out of bed. He also loves *Woman's Hour* (as what sensible person does not?) and simply has to take the earphones off to share recipes with his boringly uninterested fellow patients. Most of all he adores *Mrs Dale's Diary*, the long established radio soap of the time. At one point he is sobbing uncontrollably and a nurse rushes up concerned, but one of the others tell her not to worry – it's just Charlie listening to Mrs Dale. He is not defiantly queer; he just loves what he loves.

This reaches its peak in *Constable* (1960), which has more and the best of Hawtrey than any of the others. His first appearance is unforgettable. There is squabbling among the constables at a local police station (including Kenneth Connor, Kenneth Williams, Joan Sims and Leslie Phillips, presided over by Sidney James). In comes Charlie in his police uniform, a huge bunch of flowers in one hand and a bird in a cage in the other. 'Hello!', he greets everyone and carries on as if it was the most natural thing in the world for policemen to come to work with flowers and a budgie (Figure 10.3).

Later he is teamed with Kenneth Williams. It is lovely to see these two queens together, but it also reveals the difference between them. Williams was always pretentious, difficult; what made him so funny – in Carry Ons and, sublimely, on the radio show *Just a Minute* – were his self-importance, extravagant delivery and general snottiness. There was certainly a great sense of fun, but he had none of Hawtrey's unconcerned delight. Williams's humour was obsessed with other people, with his superiority to them, with what they may think; Hawtrey was oblivious to them, though generous and friendly. Here in *Constable*, he and Williams have to stake out a department store where there has been a rash of shoplifting. Williams has the idea for them both to drag up, so as to pass unnoticed among the women shoppers

Figure 10.3 Sidney James, Kenneth Williams, Kenneth Connor, Leslie Phillips (hidden), Charles Hawtrey and Bobbie the budgie, *Carry On Constable* 1960 (BFI Stills, Posters and Designs).

... Both get dressed in smart but not glamorous clothes. From the way Hawtrey primps in front of the mirror, it's obvious he wants to look nice and enjoys looking nice, but neither he nor Williams is trying to be Shirley Bassey. Hawtrey's delight in the whole business is expressed in a classic comic line: 'You know I haven't done this since I was in the army – at a camp concert.' The intended punch line is the play on 'camp', but audiences are usually falling about before this, at the idea that where a man would nat-urally remember dressing as a woman is, of course, in the army.

Even funnier to me, though, is a line that comes a little later. They decide what names to give each other. Williams says he'll be Agatha, after his grandmother. He's in full drag and Hawtrey looks at him, and with a lump in his throat, says, 'If grandmama could see you now, she'd be so proud' (Figure 10.4). How wonderful to be able to think that a grandmother would take pride in a grandson dressed in women's clothes and obviously loving it. None but Charles Hawtrey could suggest such an innocent, unaggressive and unforced delight in transgression.

Acknowledgement

From *Attitude* May 1994.

Figure 10.4 Grandmama would be so proud: Kenneth Williams and Charles Hawtrey, *Carry On Constable* (BFI Stills, Posters and Designs).

11

ROCK

The last guy you'd have figured?

Near the end of *Lover Come Back* (1961) there's a scene where Rock Hudson goes into his apartment block wearing only a woman's fur coat (Figure 11.2). Throughout the film he's been observed by two older men and every time they've seen him it's been in some situation where it's looked like he was pursuing or being pursued by every attractive woman around. When the two men see him in the fur coat one turns to the other and says, 'Well – he's the last guy in the world I would have figured.'

The two men in *Lover Come Back* had the same difficulty as much of the world's press when Rock's homosexuality became public along with the news of his having AIDS. *People* magazine quoted his aunt Lela saying 'Never would we think that he would be that. He was just always such a good person.' The British dailies reached for their usual clichés – 'Legend that Lived a Lie', 'Secret Torment of the Baron of Beefcake', 'Rock Hudson's Jekyll and Hyde Existence' – emphasising the 'shock' his homosexuality would be to the women fans who had so 'thrilled' to his 'husky frame'. There was apparently nothing gay about Rock Hudson's star quality or his appeal. One paper even managed a back-handed compliment by suggesting that, contrary to popular opinion, Rock was a good actor after all because he had been such a convincing heterosexual.

The reasons it had been impossible to figure that Rock was 'a homosexual' were revealed by a predictable vocabulary. Rock could not be gay because, on the one hand, he was 'virile', 'muscular', 'square-jawed', 'masculine', and, on the other, he was 'nice', 'good', 'likeable'. The linking term in all this is 'clean-cut', that uniquely US men's style of antiseptic machismo. Difficult for the press (and television) to know how to handle this and at best it could mean acknowledging a shift in the perception of gay men: we can be nice *and* butch *and* homosexual after all. At worst, it could be presented as a monstrous deceit practised on the libido of millions of women. Cross either one of these views with the fact of AIDS and you get both the surge of fund-raising and sympathy for AIDS victims (because after all AIDS sufferers are nice, and real, men) and the reiteration of the idea that gay men cause AIDS (just as Rock deceived women sexually,

Figure 11.1 Rock Hudson.

Figure 11.2 Lover Come Back 1961: Rock Hudson (BFI Stills, Posters and Designs).

so gay men have infiltrated a deadly disease on the world through their sexuality).

Whether in the benign or malignant version, and many stages of uncertainty in between, what such views share is the idea that it is surprising to think that Rock Hudson was gay, that there was a contrast between how he seemed on screen or in public appearances and how he was in private, that there was nothing gay about Rock as performer or image. It is this, rather than the media coverage of Rock in the light of AIDS,[1] that I want to focus on here.

One can't altogether blame the media for assuming that their readers would be surprised that Rock was gay. In an obvious way, there was nothing gay or queer about the Rock we saw.

When it became known that Montgomery Clift, James Dean, Sal Mineo and others of Rock's generation were, to some degree or other, queer, it was not such a surprise, even to those who were not already in the know. Clift and the rest do fit the stereotype of the queer as a sad young man. Even their appearances – physically slight, with intense eyes and pretty faces – are of a kind that contrasts with Rock's large frame, slow eyes and classically handsome face. The difference is very clear when you see James Dean and Rock together in *Giant* (1956). Dean's Method style now looks mannered: arched torso, hunched shoulders, shifting eyes, staccato speech and a walk so oddly stiff it is reminiscent of gay porn star Jack Wrangler (whose walk I used to suppose was some bizarre version of butch though I gather it was in fact arthritic). By comparison Rock is still, straight, unfussy, just *there* in the classic manner of Hollywood stars. Dean's style connotes naturalism, an acting convention associated in the period with awkwardness and neurotic emotionality. Rock's style suggests a different sense of the natural, namely normality. His very stillness and settledness as a performer suggests someone at home in the world, securely in his place in society, whereas James Dean's style suggests someone ill at ease in the world, marginal and insecure. Easier, then, to see Rock's image, as carried in his performance style, as one expressing the security of heterosexuality, and Dean's the insecurity of gays' positions in society and/or their inherent neuroticism. (You'd have to work very hard indeed to see anything in the film of the supposed affair between Rock and James that Britain's shame, the *Sun*, said Elizabeth Taylor said was going on during the filming of *Giant*.)

Neither in looks nor in performance style does Rock conform to 1950s and 1960s notions of what gay men are like. But nor does he fit with the images of gay desire that are found in gay picture magazines and short films of the period. I do feel less certain about this than about him not being a sad young man; Rock must in fact have been a pin-up and heart-throb for countless gay men. I well remember seeing *Pillow Talk* (1959) when it first came out. There is a scene where Doris and Rock, both in (separate) baths spread across a split screen, are talking on the phone. Doris puts her leg up out of the bath and rests her foot against the wall in a typical cheesecake pose and so does Rock, their feet meeting at the split in the screen. The sight of that sturdy, hairy calf (all, in fact, that you can see) fed the fantasies of this already intensely voyeuristic teenager for several months thereafter. Yet Rock never became a favourite source of erotic fantasy for me and he really doesn't fit the gay pornographic imagination of the time.

The physique magazines and soft-core pulp novels centred predominantly on two types of desirable male: the youth and the muscle man. Rock was neither. The 'youth' type was identified above all by his crew cut, but also by imagery of jeans, biking gear, campus pennants or other talismen of what's now called youth culture. Tony Curtis, Tab Hunter, Marlon Brando and others fitted this and belong to gay iconography of the period, but Rock never did. In a *Saturday Evening Post* spread on him in 1952, he is at home, washing the car, listening to Frank Sinatra albums, eating ham and eggs. It's all very wholesome, unrebellious, normal, even a bit middle-aged – and naked. He's in shorts, or an après-shower towel, in almost all the pictures, and he has a really lovely body. But he is not the other desirable type, he is not a muscle man. He has a large, strong physique but the contours are soft, the look sleek; he never had much 'definition', was never 'cut', 'ripped' or 'shredded', to use the repellent vocabulary of 1980s bodybuilding. Even by the standards of the 1950s, Rock was not muscley, not like Steve Reeves or even, say, Jeff Chandler. If many of us did put Rock on our walls (or, more likely, would like to have done), it was because he conformed to more general notions of what an attractive man is; it was not a specifically queer taste, whereas Tony, Tab, Marlon, Steven and Jeff conform closely to 1950s queer imagery.

In terms of its relations to stereotypes of homosexual men and homosexual erotic imagery of the 1950s and 1960s, there is nothing especially queer about Rock Hudson's image. Does that mean there is nothing to say about it in gay terms?

We are most used to sensing a star's homosexuality with people like Montgomery Clift and others mentioned above. Despite the largely unambiguous heterosexuality of his roles, Monty always seems to be pushing at the boundaries of masculinity, his gayness troubling, inflecting, exploring what it means to be a man.[2] This was not Rock's way. He produced a flawless surface of conventional masculinity. Yet it is a surface strangely lacking in force and intensity. It's a sort of parade of the signs of masculinity without any real assertion of it. What's fascinating is the way this quality unsettles the apparently complacent heterosexuality of his films. If Monty seems to be trying out new roles for men, Rock, in effect if not in intention, seems to subvert the security with which ideas of masculinity and femininity, normality and heterosexuality, are held. This is especially exploited in two groups of films that were among his most successful, the sex comedies and the melodramas he made with Douglas Sirk, and it gives a fascinating resonance to his one 'art' movie, *Seconds*.

Rock's sex comedies feature not only the kind of gag which I opened with but also plots that revolve around sexual ambiguity. What often happens is that, for part of the film, Rock (sometimes deliberately, sometimes not) appears not to be full bloodedly heterosexual: he is woman-shy, or impotent, or a milquetoast, as a means of getting, usually, Doris Day to drop her defences.

In *Pillow Talk* (1959), for instance, Doris and Rock share a telephone line and loathe each other, she for his monopolising the phone with his woman-ising, he for her stuck-up attitude. They have however never met. When they do, he adopts a different persona, a shy Texan visiting New York, and she falls for it and him. On the phone, the womanising Rock casts doubts on his alter ego for not making a pass at her; Doris does not understand what he is getting at, until he reminds her that there are some men, 'that just, well, they're very devoted to their mothers, the type that likes to collect cooking recipes, exchange bits of gossip'. With this fascinatingly unmistakable sketch of the queer, he plants doubts in her mind, even though she dismisses it as a 'vicious' thing to say. Later she and Rock go to a nightclub. Giving her a quizzical look which only we see, he asks her to tell him about her job – 'must be very exciting working with all them colours and fabrics and all'. This interest in interior decoration, not mentioned by the womanising Rock, nonetheless triggers the doubts he's planted; she looks at him won-deringly and he brings a glass to his lips with his little finger raised (one more tell tale sign). Then when he dunks a chip, takes a bite and remarks, 'Ain't these tasty? – wonder if I could get the recipe – sure would like to surprise my ma when I get back home', she responds on cue and gets him to kiss her. His posing as a sodomite has paid dividends in his strategy of het-erosexual conquest.

A Very Special Favor (1965) goes further still. Here the woman in question is Leslie Caron, playing a psychiatrist who is trying to treat Rock's deliberately exaggerated priapism. This is in reality a scam set up by Leslie's father, Charles Boyer, who is worried that she may be frigid and hopes that Rock may be able to break her down. However, nothing works until, in the last ten minutes of the film, Charles and Rock hit on the idea of Rock's pretending to be, after all, a fag. He persuades a 'plain' secretary who adores him to disguise herself as a young man and, making sure Leslie knows when and where, checks into a motel with 'him'. The trick works and Leslie takes up the challenge to cure him of his inversion in the fashion made prominent ten years earlier in *Tea and Sympathy*, that is, by having sex with him.[3]

One film, *Man's Favorite Sport?* (1963) (Figure 11.3), turns the pretence

Figure 11.3 Man's Favorite Sport? 1963: Rock Hudson with limp fish between Paula Prentiss (left) and Maria Perschy (BFI Stills, Posters and Designs).

motif on its head. Here Rock is a celebrated expert on fishing, something the film's title, reinforced by title song, publicity and genre expectations, unmistakably equates with male heterosexuality. Enter Paula Prentiss, intent on persuading him to take part in a fishing competition as a publicity stunt. She dismisses his every argument against his participation until in desperation he takes her to a mechanical piano museum so that, under the cover of their noise, he can tell her the real reason. Unfortunately, and funnily, the electricity goes off just at the moment that she yells back the reason to him: 'You mean you've never been fishing in your entire life?!' It is in effect a moment of forced, embarrassed coming out. The rest of the film consists of Paula blackmailing him to take part (or else she'll out him) and then teaching him to fish (sexually converting him).

What is all this about? In *The Celluloid Sacrifice*, Alexander Walker suggests that 'the main aim of the sex comedy's sparring partners . . . is to make each other neurotically unsure of their gender, their sex appeal and their potency'. Rock pretending *not* to be a wolf in *Pillow Talk* puts Doris in a quandary:

Yes, he *is* the perfect gentleman, but is that really flattering to her as a woman? When he refrains from kissing her, is it just because he respects her or is she really not his type? Of course, he *looks* virile enough, but can one be quite sure? Maybe he dotes on his mother and collects cook-book recipes. And sure enough, Rock's *alter ego* acts as cissily as predicted, and Doris gets panicky. After making men keep their distance for so long, has she now fallen for one with no urge to come hither?

(1966: 221)

Walker sees the sex comedies as at heart misogynist. The humour of the man who pretends to be gay is at women's expense, a deceit especially unpleasant in *A Very Special Favor*, where the whole thing is orchestrated between father and suitor and even another pathetically enamoured woman is dragged into the plot. The sex comedies' misogyny may reach its nadir when, in *Man's Favorite Sport?*, Rock confesses to Paul that he doesn't even like fish, surely drawing on the widespread use of the term 'fish' to disparage women (a usage supposed to be especially common to queers, with their prissy repulsion from the female)? However, if the pretending-to-be-queer routines are at women's expense, they are also at gay men's, since the routines are funny because it is intrinsically funny to think that any man is a queer, especially one like Rock Hudson. The one thing that is not mocked by these routines is the heterosexual masculinity embodied by Rock, and presumably it was assumed that Rock's image was so indelibly heterosexual that he could get away with such stuff.

Or was it? The insistent return to this pretending-to-be-a-cissy routine also suggests a more elaborate scenario now that we know (and can say that we know) that Rock was gay. Here is this homosexual (Roy Scherer Jnr, Rock's real name) pretending to be this straight man (Rock Hudson) who's pretending to be a straight man (the character in the film) pretending to be a queer (for the sequence or gag in the film). The hysterical pleasures of confusion, so central to comedy and farce, are as delirious here as in, say, *La Cage aux folles* (1978), or the many versions of *Victor/Victoria*[4] to which, once you know he's gay, Rock's comedies come so close. These 1960s comedies have a reputation for blandness and safeness, for conventional sexual morality crossed with a complacent view of sex roles. Now they look much more interesting, bristling with sexual hysteria and gender confusion, more aware than they've been given credit for, of the instabilities of heterosexuality and normality.

Rock's other great popular success came earlier, in the series of lush, weepy dramas produced by Ross Hunter and directed by Douglas Sirk: *Magnificent Obsession* (1954) (Figure 11.4), *All That Heaven Allows* (1955) (Figure 11.5), *Written on the Wind* (1956) and *The Tarnished Angels* (1957). Originally dismissed as lachrymose tripe by the critics, they have since the 1970s

Figure 11.4 What's really there?: Rock Hudson and Jane Wyman, *Magnificent Obses-sion* 1954 (BFI Stills, Posters and Designs).

become canonical classics of film history. One of the characteristics of these films is the extraordinary sense of frustration and dissatisfaction in their central female characters. They move in rich, bland suburban interiors that have all the airless comfort and reassurance of a department store or a mail-order catalogue. They are stifled by the anaemic morality and pat emotional texture of their lives. What they need is . . . well, Rock. In these films, Rock figures as the promise of 'life', through his virility and sexuality certainly, but also by his association with nature. It is perhaps clearest in *All That Heaven Allows*. Here Jane Wyman plays a recently widowed suburbanite whose children and neighbours think she should marry a middle-aged, safe, 'undemanding' man. Rock plays the man who comes to prune her trees; he wears lumberjack shirts and reads Thoreau: he is 'natural man'. Jane falls in love with him and it is clear that what Rock embodies is seen as the answer to her restless, empty life.

Though it is possible to see all this in feminist terms, depicting the inade-quacies of life for women in bourgeois society and granting the intensity of female (sexual) desire, still the answer to the woman's problem does still seem

Figure 11.5 Still hoping: Hudson and Wyman, *All That Heaven Allows* 1955.

to be a tall, dark, handsome male – Rock. It is here, though, that the films become really interesting. For although Rock represents the values of natural masculinity, of 'real men', he doesn't really deliver. Marriage is always deferred, his virility is never really put to the test. We never see him 'saving' the woman from her plight, we only have the promise of it. In *Magnificent Obsession*, he will save her by restoring her sight – but the film ends before we know the outcome of his operations on her, finishing on her plaintive cry of 'Tomorrow!' There is a ready sexual implication to this cry. Before it, when Rock embraces her, she clings to him, but he tells her not to get 'too excited'. She smiles a wonderfully knowing smile, before saying almost coyly, 'Can I get excited tomorrow?' Yes, that excitement can be had tomorrow – but who does not know that tomorrow never comes? The ending of *All That Heaven Allows* is equally unresolved, with Jane, still not married to Rock, sitting by his bed where he lies, a cripple in a coma. There are two fairly indisputable phallic symbols in the sequence: outside a stag comes to the window; under the covers Rock raises one knee in what looks like a massive erection. These are over the top promises of virility and, after all, only symbols, not the real thing. Similarly, in *Written on the Wind* and *The Tarnished Angels*, the promise of deliverance Rock represents for Lauren Bacall and Dorothy Malone can only take place after the film is over, if at all.

Casting Rock adds to the intensity of this endlessly deferred gratification. He looks the part so perfectly – big, strong, good-looking – yet in the end all that he does is look the part. Had he the force, the heterosexual commitment, of a Clark Gable or a Steve McQueen, we know that, even if the films had ended in the same way, he'd still be up on his feet 'fulfilling' the woman before we'd left the cinema (or rewound the tape). With Rock in the part you can't be so sure and this is what gives the films their terrible sense of desolation. What women want is a real man, but the only real men around are but a promise of fulfilment, endlessly put off, never finally kept. You could see this as a critique of the very idea of the 'natural man', exposed as a sham that women would do well to turn their backs on. But I think the films do believe in the idea of, even the need for, virility, it's just that they don't really believe 'real men' exist anymore. The films are thus a tragic, rather than a feminist, view of the situation of women.

In both the comedies and the melodramas, Rock's presence throws into question the ideas and the viability of heterosexual masculinity. Perhaps the campy possibilities of this were not lost on the makers of *Dynasty* (who knows what they really thought they were doing?) when they cast Rock as a stud farmer and threat to Krystle and Blake's marriage. In the Denverian world where there is nothing but image, Rock brought all the weight and authority of a star image which had already given the game away: that there is nothing but image, that the ideas of heterosexuality and normality that *Dynasty* endlessly gestures towards have always been a sham and a mockery.

Knowing that Rock was homosexual can alter the dynamics of looking, confirming or bringing out the confusions of the sex comedies and the uncertainties of the Sirk melodramas in a way that unsettles their heterosexual affirmations. This is not at all the same as suggesting that Rock's sexuality was thus expressed in his performance. Only one film may do this, *Seconds*, a black and white Hollywood art film directed by John Frankenheimer.

One scene is quite astonishingly resonant. Rock calls on a middle-aged widow, telling her he is an old friend of her husband. She is surprised, 'My husband never mentioned...', her voice tailing away, leaving space for wonder about what sort of a friend this handsome stranger might have been. He asks if he can have one of her husband's water-colours as a memento, paintings that she never realised meant anything to her husband and that she no longer has. 'We shared an interest in art,' he tells her, to her astonishment. The last time he saw him he did some sketches, now he'd like to do a painting, could he have a photograph to help him? His remarks occasion sad reflections in her:

> He was a quiet man. The thing I most remember him for were his silences. It was as if he were always listening to something inside, some voice, he never talked about it, so I never knew what it was.

169

> He lived as if he were a stranger here. There was a look around his
> eyes as if he were trying to say something, I don't know what, a
> protest against what he'd surrendered his life to. I never knew what
> he wanted.

A mysterious and devoted younger male friend, artistic sensitivity, a longing
not expressed – it's hard to see this scene and not think that what's unsaid is
the husband's queer sexuality. Yet Rock is in fact the husband. The film has
a science fiction premise. For a price, a company offers tired middle-aged
businessmen a new life: a faked death and an entirely new face and body. In
the scene just described, Rock, bored and lonely in his new life, goes back to
visit his wife. Not only does she not recognise him in this new guise but nor
does she recognise her husband in his description of him. He has become
what he wanted to be (an artist) but she never knew he wanted to be that
and thus in every sense does not recognise him.

Later in the film, Rock has been caught by the company, annoyed at his
breaking his contract by getting in touch with his wife. As with others who
have broken the rules, he is sent to wait with all the other renegades,
hopeful that another body may come along so that he can be transformed
again. A man handing out pills looks at a young man and nods in the direction of Rock; the young man turns and looks directly at Rock, trying to
catch his eye. It turns out to be Charlie, the old colleague who first told him
of the scheme, who has himself been transformed and then disillusioned.
Rock does not recognise Charlie and nor do we, so that it just looks like one
man trying to pick up another, encouraged by a first man who knows one
when he sees one. Moreover, the idea of Charlie having drawn Rock into the
'seconds' scheme is also suggestive of the common model of queers recruit-
ing susceptible others to their way of life.

Hudson was known to be personally committed to *Seconds* and this was
generally interpreted at the time as a bid to be taken seriously as an actor;
but perhaps the story also appealed, even unconsciously, for these queer resonances. If so, it is a melancholy appeal. The scene with the wife is suffused
with regret, the new life offered by the company through Charlie's recruit-
ment is tawdry and desolate, and the film ends with Rock dying on the
operating table, his body to be used for some new recruit. The film may
suggest the idea of the gay Rock making a bid to escape the confines of his
straight image, but it also presents it as a bid too terrible to be undertaken.

Seconds is an exception. What Rock's films more typically do is unsettle
the dream of fulfilling heterosexuality. In turn, the visual treatment of his
illness also dislodged some of the dreams of a gay life California-style.

What dominated the press and television coverage were before and after,
BA and AA, pictures. Rock healthy, strong, gorgeous in stills from films
and in early pin-ups, side by side with Rock tired, haggard, tragic. One of
the most fascinating examples was the use of a highly touched-up recent

photo of him. Some papers (Italy's *Eva Express* for example (Figure 11.6) said it had been taken after he'd been to Paris for treatment, while others (Britain's *News of the World* for one (Figure 11.7)) said it had been taken 'just a couple of months' before the AIDS story finally broke. Either way it was put beside a picture of Rock ravaged by AIDS. This mix-up suggests the

Figure 11.6 Eva Express, cover 12.9.85.

171

Figure 11.7 News of the World, 18.8.1985.

way the juxtaposition of the 'beautiful' and the 'awful' Rock implies not only chronology (one following another) but also simultaneity, as if the two images were different sides of the same thing, two aspects of the condition of homosexuality.

Such a juxtaposition of beauty and decay is part of a long standing rhetoric of queerness. It is the Dorian Gray syndrome. It is a way of constructing queer identity as a devotion to an exquisite surface (queens are so good-looking, so fastidious, so stylish, so amusing) masking a depraved reality (unnatural, promiscuous and repulsive sex acts). The rhetoric allows the effects of an illness gotten through sex to be read as a metaphor for that sex itself.

If anything, this way of seeing gayness became even more prominent with the coming of AIDS, even if the style of the surface has changed. Now, as the pecs got bigger, the cadaverous effects of AIDS became even more familiar. The gay glossies set side by side ever more generously proportioned hunks with every more detailed, alarming and heart-rending accounts of AIDS sufferers. Jeffrey Weeks notes in *Sexuality and Its Discontents* the bitter irony of AIDS occurring at the end of a period when the image of gay men as effete was put to rest as a prevalent image:

> The cultivation of the body beautiful was a vital part of that [rejection of the effeminate image]. But AIDS is a disease of the body, it wrecks and destroys what was once glorified.

> (1985: 50)

This paradox, this contrast between a bland, even sexless, physical perfection and the raddled awfulness of sexual practice was not of course the reality of most gay men's lives. But it was a powerful and deeply-rooted imagery, encapsulated in the juxtapositions of Rock BA and AA. If Rock's death brought attention to AIDS, boosted fund-raising, made people realise that 'nice people' get AIDS, it was also used to reinforce venerable myths about queers.

Acknowledgement

From (expanded) *The Body Politic* 121, December 1985.

Notes

1　This is discussed in Bébout 1985.
2　Cf. Waugh 2000.
3　The pretending-to-be-gay motif surfaced later in Rock's career in a non-comic context in the TV mini-series *The Star Maker*, where he allows himself to be discovered by Brenda Vaccaro in bed with another man, so that she will think her daughter is safe with him, thus enabling him to make off with the girl later. (My thanks to Charlotte Brunsdon for telling me about this movie.)
4　Germany 1933, GB 1935 [*First a Girl*], Germany 1957, USA 1982.

References

Bébout, Rick (1985) 'August 12, 1985', *The Body Politic* 119: 31–32.
Walker, Alexander (1966) 'The Last American Massacre: Rock Hudson & Co', in *The Celluloid Sacrifice*, London: Michael Joseph, 214–232.

Waugh, Tom (2000) 'Montgomery Clift Biographies: Stars and Sex', in *The Fruit Machine*, Durham NC: Duke University Press, 93–100. (First published in *Cinéaste* 10: 1, 1979–80.)

Weeks, Jeffrey (1985) *Sexuality and Its Discontents*, London: Routledge.

Further reading

Babington, Bruce and Evans, Peter (1989) *Affairs to Remember: The Hollywood Comedy of the Sexes*, New York: Yale University Press, 197–215.

Lippe, Richard (1987) 'Rock Hudson: His Story', *CineAction!* 10: 46–54.

Meyer, Richard (1991) 'Rock Hudson's Body', in Fuss, Diana (ed.) *Inside/Out: Lesbian Theories, Gay Theories*, London: Routledge, 259–288.

Rappaport, Mark (1992) *Rock Hudson's Home Movies* (film).

12

READING FASSBINDER'S
SEXUAL POLITICS

Fassbinder's films tend to provoke political debate. In the second issue of *Gay Left* there was a review by Bob Cant of *Fox and his Friends* (1975).[1] Cant admired the film for its anatomy of 'the corruptive nature of capitalism' (not only at the general level of the film's showing that 'in a bourgeois society all relationships have economic overtones', but also in the way that, through the references to Hollywood and the scene with the GIs, the film brings out 'that West Germany – like most of Western Europe – is a neo-colony of American imperialism') and for its unflinching depiction of 'the jungle-like atmosphere' of 'the gay ghetto'. In the third issue of the journal, Andrew Britton wrote a reply to Cant's review, seeing the film as one whose 'version of homosexuality degrades us all, and should be roundly denounced'. Britton argued that the film does not deal with the impact of capitalist economic structures on human relationships but merely with a moralising view of '"filthy lucre"' and that '"people with money tend to be unpleasant"'. Moreover, the film fails, in his view, to deal with the specificities of homosexuality, both as this sexual orientation articulates with class (i.e. the different experience of middle-class and working-class gays; 'why and how the bourgeois gays depicted have come to acquiesce in the institutions of the society which oppresses them') and in the particular oppression that gay people suffer in society ('There is nothing in *Fox* to show that gayness is subject to ideological, social or legal constraints').

An echo of this exchange over *Fox*, though less focused since the writers were not specifically addressing each other, can be found in Elizabeth Wilson's account of *The Bitter Tears of Petra von Kant* (1972) in *Red Rag* and in Caroline Sheldon's remarks on the same film in her article in *Gays and Film*. Wilson sees *Petra von Kant* as 'less about lesbianism than about women's place in society' and argues that 'throughout the film Fassbinder relates the psychological constructs of relationships to the economic realities on which they are based'. Sheldon, on the other hand, places *Petra von Kant* in the 'freak show genre' of 'men's films about lesbians', alongside *Les Biches* (1967) and *The Fox* (1967). She sees it stressing the (implicitly inherent) 'unwholesomeness' of the women, and compares it unfavourably with *Fox and his Friends*, concluding that 'From this comparison it appears that male gay film-makers are no more sympathetic to lesbians than straight ones'.

These two pairs of exchanges crystallise the kind of debate that surrounds Fassbinder's films, especially in relation to sexual politics. Two themes in particular emerge – the relationship between class and sex politics in Fassbinder's films, and the 'unpleasantness' of the worlds the films depict. The divergence of views on these themes – which run through so much of the critical literature I shall refer to in this article – seems to me to be related to the ambiguity of the films themselves. This ambiguity can be located in the films' political perspective, which I want to designate as 'left-wing melancholy'. In the next section of this article I want to try to delineate this perspective as it informs Fassbinder's films, stressing its reactionary implications. In the final section, however, I want to move back from this analysis in a series of qualifications. In particular, I want to argue that the kind of debate exemplified by Bob Cant and Andrew Britton, Elizabeth Wilson and Caroline Sheldon, indicates the real effectivity[2] of Fassbinder's films, an effectivity that cannot be automatically read off from the films themselves, an effectivity moreover that the films do not, as it were, deserve.

The divergences of views outlined above are partly explicable by the ambiguity of the films at the level of dialogue and narrative. It would be very hard to determine what sense one is supposed to make of many of the films' endings, for instance. Why does Marlene leave Petra? Petra apologises to her for her habitual treatment of her; Marlene kisses Petra's hand, and the latter snaps, 'Not like that!', and it is at this point that Marlene starts to pack her bag. Petra's response to Marlene's gesture is the kind of opaque moment that sends literary-critical minded viewers into enthusiastic character speculation, but it is really anyone's guess as to what we are to make of it. Similarly – are we to believe Hanni and Franz when they declare at the end of *Wildwechsel* (1972) that theirs was not 'real love'? Do we believe Effi when, on her death bed, she acknowledges that Instetten was right to behave as he did? Most of us on seeing the films will probably be clear where we stand on such issues – I feel Marlene rejects Petra because she recognises that Petra is incapable of not seeking to control in relationships, that Hanni and Franz truly loved each other, that Effi's final declaration is ironic. But I don't think I could demonstrate these readings from textual evidence – the texts are, in this sense, open.

This tendency towards ambiguous narrative closure is, however, the limit of the films' openness. Elsewhere – in casting, *mise en scène*, composition, etc. – Fassbinder's films can be clearly situated under the rubric of 'left-wing melancholy'.[3] This is admittedly an imprecise term, referring broadly to a view of life that recognises the exploitativeness of capitalist society but is unable to see any means by which a fundamental change in this society can take place. This melancholy is left-wing – and not just a general despair at the human condition – because it sees the specifically (historically determinant) capitalist source and character of misery in contemporary society and observes how the weight of oppression lies on the working class. In its 'melancholy', however, it does not see the working class as the agent of historical change – instead it stresses the working class as the victim of capitalist society and/or as hopelessly complicit in its own oppression. The sexual-political version of this substitutes or adds, for the working class, women and gays. (Left-wing melancholy can also properly show how capitalism and patriarchy deform the lives of the middle classes, men and heterosexuals, even while recognising the advantages and power that these groups have.)

This left-wing melancholy shows itself most obviously in the emphasis on victims in Fassbinder's work. The central figure of many of the films (as of Douglas Sirk's melodramas) is a sufferer – Effi Briest, Franz (*Fox*), Emmi (*Fear Eats the Soul* (1974)), Petra von Kant. It is true that the social source of this suffering may be clearly spelt out – marriage, class, racism, in the case of these three films; and even when it is not so clear, there are none the less indications of a source of misery outside the individual character's personality. Men – in the constant reminder of them in the painting in her flat, in Petra's discussion of her marriage with Sidonie, in Karin's taunting of Petra with stories of men she has been with,[4] and, most tellingly, in the way that, following a phone call out of the blue from her husband, she ups and leaves Petra – are indicated as a source of Petra's unhappiness. In *Katzelmacher* (1969) – where Jorgos, the *Gastarbeiter*, who suffers most and whose nickname gives the film its title, is not treated as the central figure – male power over women is indicated both in details of the narrative where the men assert physical power over their girlfriends and in contrasting scenes between the men together (where they discuss how to assert their power) and the women together (where, overlit and with romantic piano music playing out of tune over, the discussion is romantic about men). More diffusely, Hanni and Franz in *Wildwechsel* are victims of the hypocrisies of familial sexuality (in the first sequence, with Hanni's mother's reluctant agreement to 'stay on in bed' on Saturday morning, despite what Hanni might think, an agreement then disappointed by the father putting the desires of his pubescent daughter, to be driven to school, before those, now awakened, of his wife), the tattiness of commercial teenage culture, the unpleasant factory conditions in which Franz works, and the incomprehensibility of the law (as Hanni and Franz are caught in the corridor between the courts, while off screen in the court itself their sentences are being decided).

One can show, then, that the social sources of suffering are indicated in the films. The problem is that what we see, what is dwelt on, is the state of being a victim itself. This emphasis is achieved by various means. Andrew Britton discusses the use of fate motifs in *Fox*, with their connotation of an inexorable destiny in which the protagonist is caught. In *Petra von Kant* it is through the use of long takes and prowling camera, particularly in the last third of the film, with Petra lolling on the floor clutching a gin bottle, the camera down there with her, insistently, painfully, for minutes on end. Most characteristic, perhaps, is the use of static compositions that suggest entrapment. Renny Harrigan (1977) details some of these in her article on *Effi Briest* (1974); other examples one might cite are: Hanni hopscotching in the bars across the corridor at the end of *Wildwechsel*; Emmi and Ali shot through the doors of the restaurant where they are celebrating their wedding, the walls crowding in on them from both sides of the screen, the shot held on them at the end of a sequence in which the disdain of the waiter has been made quite clear; and, also from *Fear Eats the Soul*, the moment when the Yugoslav woman, who has joined Emmi's cleaners' team and is now relegated below the previously ostracised Emmi, looks straight out to camera through the banisters (bars) of the stairs. These stylistic procedures may even function to express the victim state of protagonists who might not otherwise be perceived as victims. For example, the group in *Katzelmacher* might not appear victims in the narrative that we see – it is after all they who victimise Jorgos and, within the group, the men are clearly ascendant over the women. However, the shots of them grouped by a handrail in the street that recur throughout the film indicate the group's entrapment in a wider, hinted at mesh of social oppression. These shots are from different distances but always head-on and *static*; the characters are *rigidly* grouped (hence emphasising that they have been shaped as a group), with meaningless slight variations on the grouping from shot to shot; they are *contained* within the frame and around the rail; the harsh light and grainy texture of the image are oppressive. The repetition of the poses within the frame – the women leaning back with their left knee bent, the men sitting with their legs open – also expresses the rigidity of gender roles.

This dwelling on the victim state is not gloating. As Jan Dawson (1974) puts it, 'However refined or uncouth the characters ... they are ultimately united by the tremendous compassion with which they are observed'. Yet there is a problem with putting it the way Dawson does. The point-of-view on the characters is compassionate (or, rather more accurately in my view, pitying), but they are characters that Fassbinder has constructed – not singlehandedly, but with his collaborators and drawing on the available modes of representation in the culture. As Dawson puts it, it is as if the films are compassionate for people who already existed and happened to wander in front of the cameras; whereas the films are a construction of the character type 's/he about whom compassion/pity is to be evoked'.

There is what one might call an 'emotionalism' about the representation of these characters, so that the elements of criticism of society become marginalised in favour of the depiction and laying bare of suffering. The repeated use of female protagonists, though it is partly to do with the oppression of women, is also to do with, as Fassbinder says,[5] the idea that 'women can show their emotions more' and hence can be used for greater emotional expressivity; and also with the fact that the suffering woman, woman-as-victim, is a key icon of patriarchal culture. As Susan Brownmiller (1975) and Laura Mulvey (1975) have argued, one in the context of the culture of rape, the other in relation to the representation of women as sex objects in film, the image of female suffering is, in this culture, a beautiful image. This is in part by virtue of the tender care with which it is painted, sculpted or photographed, but crucially because it places the spectator in a position of power over the represented woman, power that inflates the spectator's ego even if at the same time evoking his[6] – real and genuine – compassion.

Fassbinder's *mise en scène*, his way of seeing, pins characters down in static takes, traps them between compositional bars. This both expresses entrapment and also distances the spectator, so that we are placed in relation to the films' characters in that position of superiority, albeit caring, that visitors to a zoo have in relation to the caged animals – they are separated from us, and trapped there for our contemplation. There is beauty too in Fassbinder's depiction of victims. Beauty is notoriously hard to define or indicate, and Fassbinder's films are also at times remarkable for their insistent ugliness; yet his choice of performers for central roles is also linked to two traditions of beauty (in film and the surrounding culture). The first, in some of his female protagonists, is the fairly conventional notion of what an attractive woman looks like in Western culture: white, young, even-featured, slim. Hanna Schygulla, featured in fourteen of his films up to and including *Effi Briest* (his sixteenth feature film), is most representative here, especially in *Effi Briest*, where the black and white photography of her in impeccable period clothes recalls that of *Vogue* photographers such as Richard Avedon. The second tradition of beauty is that evoked by various vaguely surrealist-inspired critics and cinéastes, most consistently in the magazine *Midi-Minuit Fantastique*. This is a celebration of the beauty of pain or ugliness in a women, often with frankly Sadeian implications. Fassbinder does not go so far as *Midi-Minuit*, but there remains a certain fascination with flawed, scarred or 'off' features, especially in characters who are both sympathetic and in other respects attractive, that is, young, elegant, sexy. Eva Mattes' slightly Mongoloid features (*Wildwechsel*), and the flattened face and thin lips of Irm Hermann (Marlene in *Petra von Kant*) are examples here, as in Fassbinder's (as Franz in *Fox*) bashed-in face and squinty eyes. (The films clearly establish these performers as characters who are, respectively, young, elegant, and sexy.) The last example reminds us that it is not only women who are beautiful victims in Fassbinder's films.

It's important to stress here that I am not claiming that Fassbinder's films – and much less Fassbinder the person – are *simply* patriarchal or bourgeois. Rather, the propensity for victims, while it may well be expressive of compassion or pity, is enmeshed in a visual and narrative rhetoric that bespeaks and tends to reinforce a bourgeois patriarchal way of seeing – that is, think-ing and feeling about – the oppressed. It also goes hand in hand with some other ideological characteristics of his work.

There is, to begin with, a problem over the films' definitions of class. The problem is partly that there is a preponderance of characters whose class position is marginal – lumpenproletariat (Franz, Emmi, the group in *Katzel-macher*) and even, if the term exists, lumpenbourgeoisie (Petra von Kant). These are important class positions, not to be ignored, especially in contemporary capitalist society with its commitment to unemployment and its need for a reserve army of labour (cf. Judith Mayne's remarks (1977) on Emmi and Ali in *Fear Eats the Soul*) – but they remain marginal, and, by definition, powerless. Moreover, when the films do come to deal with the central structures of capitalist society, they do so in rather odd, or displaced, ways. In *Fox*, Franz is exploited by his bourgeois friends but he is not exploited as a worker – he is exploited as a backer of Eugen's father's print-ing works. They are able to exploit him because of his working class/lumpen ignorance of capitalist ways (in particular, legalities), but the real relations laid bare are not those of the labour: capital nexus that underpins capitalism.

Another example is *Fear Eats the Soul*. Mayne argues that this shows how 'the development of capitalist society is marked by relentless and increased domination of the commodity form over all aspects of life'. She points both to aspects of narrative (e.g. Emmi's social reacceptance is represented by the attitude of her grocer, who recognises his need for her as a good customer despite her marrying an Arab; Ali's seeking comfort in the bed of Barbara, the owner of the bar where Emmi and Ali first meet, none the less shows, Mayne suggests, that 'Ali's relationship to Barbara is first and foremost that of customer and proprietor') and also to the way that Emmi and Ali's rela-tionship is constructed through the way others look at them, 'the interplay of objectifying stares': 'Emmi's relationship to Ali exists for the viewer through the disapproving gazes of her co-workers, neighbours, children and nameless figures in public places. (. . .) The context of Emmi and Ali's rela-tionship is, in a word, that of reification'. In this perspective, the film's analysis of capitalist society turns out to focus on the market as the key instance of capitalism, not the mode of production. (It also implies that before capitalism much was free that is now commoditised, whereas capital-ism replaces with the cash nexus the much worse oppression of feudal obli-gation.) This has two consequences for Fassbinder's films (though, because of the uncharacteristic delicacy of *Fear Eats the Soul*, the first of these does not apply to it) – the brutalisation of people at the hands of capitalist forces, and the absence of a recognition of labour (by which I understand the production and reproduction[7] of life by human activity) as a potential source of resis-tance and subversion.

The sense of brutalisation[8] comes through in the insistent crudity and vulgarity of many of the characters (though I would not want to go along with Roger Greenspun's self-revealing comment (1975) that 'It is impossible not to sympathise with Eugen's feelings [about Franz's lower-class vulgarities], since [Franz] never consents to use a handkerchief nor, after months of instruction from the accomplished Eugen, learns not to pour the red wine with the fish'). The seedy colour stock of *Wildwechsel* emphasises Hanni's garish taste in clothes and Franz's sallow complexion, while the opening scenes dwell on Hanni's mother picking at her complexion and her father, unshaven and gross in his pyjamas, demanding sex. That this can be seen as brutalisation is suggested by the long tracking shot of the chicken factory where Franz works, in which we see the whole process by which a vividly coloured live animal becomes a soapy white packaged foodstuff. (A brutalisation perspective tends always to stress industrialisation rather than capitalism as the source of workers' misery.) While there is a certain ironic romanticism in the treatment of Hanni and Franz's sex scenes, elsewhere in Fassbinder's work working-class sexuality, especially men's, is seen as immediate and purely genital (without any wider sensuality). This often revolves around discussions of penis size, in which the characters assume that foreign men (e.g. Jorgos) and working-class men (e.g. Franz in *Fox*) have bigger penises than other men, an assumption the films do nothing to question.

The brutalisation motif in Fassbinder's films obscures the humanity of the class of which the characters are representative, for the depiction could not signal ugliness and disgust if it did not assume a true, unbrutalised humanity somewhere else (in the audience?). Moreover, like the victim emphasis, it implies a model of human society which denies human practice. Fassbinder's films are politically depressing, not only because the characters are defeated but because, since we are to see them as beautiful victims, they don't even try. Hardly anywhere is there a notion of working-class, or women's, or gay, struggle, whether in the form of resistance (not being brutalised by the forces that seek to brutalise) or revolution (overturning those forces). In her discussion of *Effi Briest*, Renny Harrigan (1977) observes that 'Fassbinder has portrayed a passive, suffering heroine of the upper classes – there weren't many others available if the plot was to be at all realistic' – but this is to ignore precisely the story of women's resistance, of what women have been able to achieve within their subordination. It is not that one is calling for a glowing or sentimental model of how 'wonderful' the oppressed are, nor for films to deal only with those active in public politics or to deny the reality of defeat, but rather that it is politically necessary to recognise traditions of resistance and subversion, since they are the root of all other political struggle. To put it another way, the emphasis in Fassbinder's films on people as victims of society and history implies a model of social change that is unable to indicate how people can be actively involved in that process of change; it implies, in other words, a model that makes political struggle pointless.

181

Having said all that, let me now begin to retreat from it in a series of quali-fications. First, we are talking about the films, not the man. It is the rhetoric that earns them the indictment of left-wing melancholy; and there is no unproblematic connection between this and Rainer Werner Fassbinder's intentions or political credentials. I stress this not only because I reject any easy equation of a person's thoughts and feelings and the signification of the art s/he is involved in producing, but also because this body of films is widely seen and talked about (relatively) and does address questions of sexual politics. For these reasons, I'd rather have Fassbinder on my side, and I don't want to jeopardise this by calling him names just because I find the films themselves problematic.

Second, there are worse things in this world than left-wing melancholy. We are living in a period in which capitalist recession is not visibly being greeted by working-class revolutionary struggle (though there's always plenty of resistance), and which is for artists and intellectuals a retreat from the hopes of May 1968. Moreover, Fassbinder is living in a wealthy country of quite exceptional political repression, which has seen, as in Britain, a dis-turbing resurgence of fascist politics (with considerable working-class support). On the terrain of sexual politics itself, I acknowledge the force of a line Petra von Kant is given to say: 'People need one another, but haven't learnt how to live together'. This line gets its resonance from what has hap-pened to the sexual political movements: partial and precarious victories at the level of civil rights, equal pay and so on, accompanied by the virtual col-lapse of the wider aims of liberation in the face of the narrower blandish-ments of permissiveness. In this context, left-wing melancholy, while it is a fatal political attitude, is also an understandable one.

Third, one of the weaknesses of the films' politics, which the Cant-Britton, Wilson-Sheldon exchanges highlight, is their failure to articulate adequately class and sexual politics. *Fear Eats the Soul* comes nearest to it, but *Effi Briest* and *Fear of Fear* do not explore the class specificities of their female protagonists' oppression, while on the other hand neither *Petra von Kant* nor *Fox* show any awareness that gays are oppressed as gays. Yet, serious as this weakness is, one has to acknowledge that no one else has cracked this particular political nut – neither in films, nor very much in political theory or practice. Fassbinder is better at showing the class dimen-sion (and this is how Ruth McCormick, for instance, appropriates his work, treating the sexual representations as unproblematic metaphors for class relations), but if one compares *Fox* to a film that is very good on gay oppres-sion, *Hunting Scenes from Lower Bavaria* (*Jagdszenen aus Niederbayern,* Germany 1968), one sees very clearly how difficult it is to combine both politics. *Fox* is silent on gay oppression; but *Hunting Scenes from Lower Bavaria*, in terms of class, makes Fassbinder's melancholy view of working-class vulgarity seem positive – not only does *Hunting Scenes* dwell on the coarse sexuality and physical crudeness of its peasant characters, it explicitly compares them to pigs (through a shot of them pursuing the gay protagonist which has the same sickly-sweet music over as was earlier piped into the vast sheds where the pigs are penned). The film is also pretty suspect in its representation of women – yet it remains one of the few films to show quite clearly how male gay oppression works (and does not put the cause of gay suffering in gays' own emotional inadequacy). Set side by side, *Hunting Scenes* and *Fox* show how very hard it is still for anyone to work out the articulations of class and gender/sexuality, respecting both their specificity and their interdependence.

Fourth, there does seem to be a shift taking place in Fassbinder's work, certainly if his contribution to *Germany in Autumn* (1978) is anything to go by. In some ways, this is the most insistently ugly of any of his films that I have seen. Fassbinder as performer wears a shirt that is too tight for, and hence emphasises, his podgy stomach; he is sick, sniffs cocaine, shouts at Armin, bursts into tears; a long-held, low-angle shot of him and Armin at a table emphasises the empty beer bottles and overflowing ashtrays. There is nothing attractive about the situation or the character – yet it is moving in a way different from the compassion displayed/evoked in the earlier films. Partly, no doubt, this is because one recognises Fassbinder as Fassbinder, and this makes the sequence the most unambiguous coming out in his work. Coming out is always a difficult and moving occurrence, and even more so in the context of so 'heavily' political a film as *Germany in Autumn*. What adds to this quality is the sequence's ending, where Armin, who has no political sympathies with the Fassbinder 'character' and has been pretty well abused throughout the sequence, comforts his sobbing friend. It is a moment in which the strength of tenderness – and in the face of squalor – is acknowledged, perhaps for the first time in Fassbinder's work.

Fifth, it is important to see how some, at any rate, of the problems of Fassbinder's work stem from it being the work of a gay film-maker. This dimension is present not only at the level of subject matter, but also in the elements of camp sensibility in his work. Jack Babuscio's discussion (1977) of *Petra von Kant* highlights the way that Fassbinder's much commented on distanciation techniques spring from the emphasis in camp on artifice, theatricality and 'the ironic functions of style'. Much of the rhetoric of Fassbinder's films is camp. As Manny Farber and Patricia Patterson (1975) put it: 'All of his appetites (for the outlandish, vulgar and banal in matters of taste, the use of old movie conventions, a no-sweat approach to making movies, moving easily from one media to another, the element of facetiousness and play in terms of style) are those of camp and/or Warhol.'

Camp is an enormously ambiguous phenomenon, ambiguous in its own right as a particular sensibility, and even more so in its relation to the homosexual sub-culture. On the one hand camp is relentlessly trivialising, but on the other its constant play with the vocabulary of straight society (in particular, the excesses of male and female role-playing) sends up that society in a needlingly undermining way. In the last analysis, gay politics and culture are going to have to move beyond the limitations of camp; but we still have to appreciate how central and almost instinctive a feature of the male gay sub-culture it is, how much many gay men feel at home – for once in their lives – with the camp sensibility. Fassbinder's work is caught up in these ambiguities, and I feel I want to defend his involvement in camp even while acknowledging its problems. The latter include the extreme ambivalence of his/camp's depiction of women, of which Christiane Maybach/Hedwig (Franz's sister in *Fox*) is the clearest instance. Are we to enjoy her strength and commonsense, her warmth, her unabashed vulgarity, or is it her fleshy physicality, her streaked peroxided hair and slobbering lips? Either way she is 'too much', and camp enjoins us to enjoy *both* aspects. Moreover, and this is the real difficulty with camp, the films go into a world where the camp sensibility is barely known or understood, where the dangerous play of ambiguities is read as either gay bad taste, trivialisation and woman-hating or else a depiction of the awfulness of women. None the less, one still has to recognise that it is Fassbinder's camp that has allowed him to develop the kind of foregrounding techniques which critics have usually preferred to ascribe purely to Brechtianism.

Finally, discussion of camp already leads us to the issue of 'reading', of how these films are appropriated by their audiences. This cannot be construed from an analysis of the films themselves, though the ambiguities of Fassbinder's work are already enough to indicate that his films will be very differently understood by different members of the audience, according to both their structural position in society (class, gender, race, sexual orientation, etc.) and their political orientation. What is clear is that Fassbinder's films are eminently suitable for further debate. This is already evident in the Cant–Britton, Wilson–Sheldon exchanges and in the variety of views argued in the various articles I have referred to. At the critical level, Fassbinder's films tend to get discussed in terms of their sexual politics – they put this question on the agenda of critical debate. At the level of German film culture too, one can see that Fassbinder's films are part of a wider involvement with sexual politics evidenced by such films as *The All-Round Reduced Personality*, *Hunting Scenes from Lower Bavaria*, *The Lost Honour of Katharina Blum*, *Ich liebe dich ich töte dich*, *The Left-Handed Woman*, *Armee der Liebenden*, *Shirin's Wedding* (lesbian films remain a significant absence). It is also my experience that Fassbinder's films often provoke better discussion of sexual political issues than some films that I would argue are more ideologically acceptable. I remember a discussion in a gay liberation group about *Fox*, which centred on the adequacy with which the film dealt with sexual and class politics. The issue of the relationship between these two politics was one that this group was usually reluctant to discuss (many considering it irrelevant), and *Fox* provided the occasion for one of the most productive engagements with the issue that I can remember. At the levels of critical debate, film-making and political use, Fassbinder's work has been *effective* in stimulating debate and thought – even if one does still have to recognise how it is also appropriated by film festivals and art cinema marketing as formalism or apolitical cynicism. That political effectivity – limited though it is – may be far more important than the films' own political despair. In the end, it is not so much what the films say that matters, but rather what people do with what they say.

Acknowledgement

From Rayns, Tony (ed.) *Fassbinder*, London: British Film Institute, 1979.

Notes

1 Since this article is centrally about the take-up of Fassbinder's films in the English speaking world, I have throughout used the English or German titles of the film discussed, according to which was the more widely used. The relevant original titles are as follows:

Bitter Tears of Petra von Kant, The	*Die bitteren Tränen der Petra von Kant*
Fear Eats the Soul	*Angst essen Seele auf*
Fox and His Friends	*Faustrecht der Freiheit*
Germany in Autumn	*Deutschland im Herbst*

2 By effectivity, I do not mean 'effect', which implies a direct impact from the film onto the audience and/or society at large. Rather I want to emphasise the way the films can be taken up, used, made to do political work through discussion, critical debate and so on.

3 The term is associated with Walter Benjamin, who used it to describe the poetry of Erich Kästner and the Neue Sachlichkeit. See Benjamin 1974.

4 Here Fassbinder falls into one of the stereotypical scenes in films with lesbian characters; cf., for example, *Tystnaden* (*The Silence*, Sweden 1962) or *The Killing of Sister George* (GB 1969).

5 In an interview in the book for which this essay was written.

6 This representation addresses a male spectator, invites him to take up the position described. This does not mean that all men necessarily accept the invitation, nor does it tell us how women place themselves in relation to such representations.

7 By production, I understand the means by which material existence is maintained in society, and by reproduction I understand not only procreation but also the means by which social relations are maintained.

8 I'm not sure where the term 'brutalisation' comes from, but it can be located in the kind of social criticism represented by E. A. Shils, Ortega y Gasset and the Orwell of *1984*.

References

Babuscio, Jack (1977) 'Camp and the Gay Sensibility', in Dyer, 40–57.
Benjamin, Walter (1974) 'Left-wing Melancholy', *Screen* 15: 2, 28–32.

Britton, Andrew (1976) 'Foxed: A Critique of *Fox*', *Gay Left* 3: 16–17; reprinted in *Jump Cut* 16 (1977), 22–23.

Brownmiller, Susan (1975) *Against Our Will*, London: Secker and Warburg.

Cant, Bob (1976) 'Fassbinder's *Fox*', *Gay Left* 2: 22; reprinted in *Jump Cut* 16 (1977), 22.

Dawson, Jan (1974) 'Rainer Werner Fassbinder: the Prodigal Prodigy', *The Listener* September.

Dyer, Richard (ed.) (1977) *Gays and Film*, London: British Film Institute.

Farber, Manny and Patterson, Patricia (1975) 'Fassbinder', *Film Comment* 11: 6, 5–7.

Greenspun, Roger (1975) 'Phantom of Liberty: Thoughts on Fassbinder's *Fist-right of Freedom*', *Film Comment* 11: 6, 8–10.

Harrigan, Renny (1977) 'Women Oppressed!', *Jump Cut* 15: 3–5.

Mayne, Judith (1977) 'Fassbinder and Spectatorship', *New German Critique* 12: 61–74.

McCormick, Ruth (1974) 'Fassbinder and the Politics of Everyday Life', *Cinéaste* 8: 2.

Mulvey, Laura (1975) 'Visual Pleasure and Narrative Cinema', *Screen* 16: 3, 6–18.

Sheldon, Caroline (1977) 'Lesbians and Film: Some Thoughts', in Dyer, 5–26.

Wilson, Elizabeth (1975) 'How Much Is It Worth?', *Red Rag* 10, 6–9.

Further reading

Crimp, Douglas (1982) 'Fassbinder, Franz, Fox, Elvira, Erwin, Armin and all the Others', *October* 21: 63–82.

Dyer, Richard (1990) *Now You See It*, London: Routledge, 90–96.

Kuhn, Anna (1984) 'Rainer Werner Fassbinder: The Alienated Vision', in Phillips, Klaus (ed.) *New German Filmmakers*, New York: Frederick Ungar, 76–123.

La Valley, Al (1994) 'The Gay Liberation of Rainer Werner Fassbinder: Male Subjectivity, Male Bodies, Male Lovers', *New German Critique* 63: 109–137.

MacBean, James Roy (1984) 'Between Kitsch and Fascism: Notes on Fassbinder, Pasolini, (Homo)sexual Politics, the Exotic, the Erotic and Other Consuming Passions', *Cinéaste* 13: 4, 12–19.

Moltke, Johannes von (1999) 'Camping in the Art Closet: The Politics of Camp and Nation in German Film', in Cleto, Fabio (ed.) *Camp: Queer Aesthetics and the Performing Subject*, Edinburgh: Edinburgh University Press, 409–432.

Perlmutter, Ruth (1989) 'Real Feelings, Hollywood Melodrama and the Bitter Tears of Fassbinder's Petra von Kant', *Minnesota Review* NS 33: 79–98.

Watson, Wallace Steadman (1996) *Understanding Rainer Werner Fassbinder: Film as Private and Public Art*, Columbia SC: University of South Carolina.

Waugh, Tom (2000) 'Rainer Werner Fassbinder', in *The Fruit Machine*, Durham NC: Duke University Press, 43–58. (First published in *The Body Politic* 29, 1976–77.)

13

IDOL THOUGHTS

Orgasm and self-reflexivity in gay pornography

What makes (gay) pornography exciting is the fact that it is pornography.

I do not mean this in the sense that it is exciting because it is taboo. The excitement of porn as forbidden fruit may be construed in terms of seeing what we normally do not (people having sex), what is morally and legally iffy (gay sex) or what is both the latter and, in Britain, not that obtainable (pornography itself). All of these may constitute porn's thrill for many users, but they are not what I have in mind here.

Nor do I mean that the category 'pornography' makes pornography exciting because it defines the terms of its own consumption and is moreover a major player in the business of constructing sexual excitement. Pornography does indeed set up the expectation of sexual excitement: the point of porn is to assist the user in coming to orgasm. However, it is also the case that no other genre can be at once so devastatingly unsatisfactory when it fails to deliver (nothing is more boring than porn that doesn't turn you on) and so entirely true to its highly focused promise when it succeeds. In this pragmatic sense, porn cannot make users find exciting that which they do not find so. Yet in a wider sense, pornography does help to define the forms of the exciting and desirable available in a given society at a given time. The history of pornography – the very fact that it has a history, rather than simply being an unvarying constant of human existence – indicates that excitement and desire are mutable, constructed, cultural. There can be no doubt at all that porn plays a significant role in this, that it participates in the cultural construction of desire. However, this too is not what directly concerns me here.

When I say that it is the fact that it is porn that makes porn exciting, I mean, for instance, that what makes watching a porn video exciting is the fact that you are watching some people making a porn video, some performers doing it in front of cameras, and you. In this perception, *Powertool* (1986) is not about a character meeting other characters in a prison cell and having sex; it is about well-known professional sex performers (notably, Jeff Stryker) on a set with cameras and crew around them; it's the thought and evidence (the video) of this that is exciting. Now I readily concede that this is not how everyone finds porn exciting. For many it is the willing suspension of disbelief, the happy entering into the fantasy that *Powertool* is all happening in a prison cell. I shall discuss first how a video can facilitate such a way of relating to what's on screen, and it may indeed be the most usual way. Yet I do not believe that I am alone or even especially unusual in being more turned on by the thought of the cameras, crew and me in attendance. I shall look at this phenomenon in the rest of the article, focusing especially on the videos of the gay porn star, Ryan Idol. I shall end by considering the apparent paradox of such self-reflexive porn: that it is able to indicate that it is 'only' porn and yet still achieves its orgasmic aim.

Gay porn videos do not necessarily draw attention to their own making. By way of illustration, let me consider one of the more celebrated scenes in gay porn, the subway sequence which forms the last part of *Inch by Inch* (1985).

A subway draws up at a station; a man (Jeff Quinn) enters a carriage of which the only other occupant is another man (Jim Pulver); after some eye contact, they have sex, that is, in the matchlessly rigorous description of *Al's Male Video Guide* 'suck, fuck, rim, titplay' (1986: 132); at the next station, another man (Tom Brock) enters the carriage but the video ends, with a title informing us that 'the non-stop excitement continues ... in the next Matt Sterling film, coming February 1986'.

This sequence unfolds before us as an event happening somewhere of which we are unobserved observers. In other words, it mobilises the conventions of realism and 'classical cinema'. The first term indicates that what we see we are to treat as something happening in the real world. The second refers to the ways in which a film or video places us in relation to events such that we have access to them from a range of vantage points (the many different shots and the mobile camera that compose a single sequence in such cinema), while not experiencing this range as disruptive or impossible; a special feature of this cinema is the way it enables the viewer to take up the position of a character within the events, most obviously through the use of point-of-view shots and the shot/reverse shot pattern. Videos do not really give us unmediated access to reality, nor do viewers think that they do. What I am describing are particular (if commonplace) ways of organising narrative space and time in film and video (between which I make no distinction for the purposes of this discussion).

The realism of the *Inch by Inch* sequence is achieved most securely by the use of location shots taken in a subway. These open the sequence and punctuate the action five times, reminding us of a real life setting that had really to exist in order to be filmable. The interior of the subway carriage could be a set – it looks very clean and the graffiti are too legible and too appropriate ('SUCK', 'REBELS', 'BAD BOYS') to be true – but the accuracy of the seating and fittings, the harsh quality of the lighting and the fact that all four sides of the carriage are seen, suggest either an unusually expensive set or an actual carriage rented for the occasion. The lack of camera or set shake suggests that the lights passing outside are indeed passing rather than being passed, but the care with which this is done is itself naturalistic. The high degree of realism in the setting is complemented by filmic elements associated with realism, such as hand-held camera and rough cutting on action. Further, the sound gives the appearance of having been recorded synchronously with the action, so that the grunts, heavy breathing, gagging, blowing and dialogue ('Suck that cock', 'That feels good') don't sound like they've been added later, as is more usual with porn videos.

The performances too suggest a realism of genuine excitement. Both performers have erections most of the time (by no means the rule in porn) and their ejaculations, partly through the skill of the editing but also in some longer takes, seem to arise directly from their encounter. This compares favourably with the worked-for quality betrayed in much porn by the sudden cut to an ejaculation evidently unconnected to what the performer was doing in the immediately preceding shot. To such technical realism we may add a quality of performance, a feeling of abandonment and sexual hunger (especially on the part of Jim Pulver), unsmiling but without the grimly skilled air of many porn performances.

The quality of abandon relates to the idea of the real that all the above help to construct. This is a notion that anonymous sex, spontaneous, uncontrolled sex, sex that is 'just' sex, is more real than sex caught up in the sentiments that knowing one's partner mobilises or sex which deploys the arts of sexuality. As John Rowberry puts it, 'The sensibility of wantonness, already considered anti-social behaviour when this video was released, has never been more eloquently presented' (1993: 93).

The rules of classical cinema are used in the sequence with exactly the degree of flexibility that characterises their use in Hollywood. The first, establishing interior shot of the carriage shows both Jeff and Jim and thus their position in relation to one another (Figure 13.1.1). Both sit on the same side of the carriage and the camera is positioned behind Jim's seat pointing along the carriage towards Jeff. The first cut is to a medium close-up of Jeff (Figure 13.1.2), with the camera at pretty much the same angle towards him as in the establishing shot – thus the spatial dislocation is only one of relative closeness and not one of position; it may be said to resemble the activity of the human eye in choosing to focus on one element out of all those before it; in short, we almost certainly don't notice the cut but go along with its intensification of the situation, allowing us to see the lust in Jeff's eyes.

The next cut is to Jim (Figure 13.1.3). The direction of Jeff's gaze in the previous shot, as well as the continuing effect of the establishing shot, do not make this sudden change of angle disturbing. Moreover, although the camera is at 45 degrees to Jim, just as it was to Jeff, and although Jim is looking to his right off-screen and not at the camera, just as Jeff was looking

Figures 13.1.1–13.1.4 Inch by Inch 1985: Jeff Quinn (left in 13.1.1) and Jim Pulver (frame enlargements).

to his left off-screen, nonetheless we treat the shot of Jim as if it is a shot of what Jeff sees, as a point-of-view shot. I think this is true despite one further discrepancy, namely that, although Jeff's gaze is clearly directed at Jim's face (and still will be in the next shot of him (Figure 13.1.4)), nonetheless this shot of Jim is a medium shot from a lowish angle, which has the effect of emphasising his torso (exposed beneath an open waistcoat), the undone top button on his jeans and his crotch; in other words, Jeff, in the shot on either side of this, is signalled as looking at Jim's face (even, it appears, into his eyes), yet this shot, if taken as a point-of-view shot, has him clearly looking at Jim's body. Yet such literal inaccuracy goes unnoticed, because of the shot's libidinal accuracy – it's not Jim's eyes but his chest and crotch that Jeff wants.

These few shots show how very much the sequence is constructed along the lines of classical cinematic norms, how very flexible these norms are, and in particular how they can be used to convey psychological as much as literal spatial relations. Such handling characterises the whole sequence, which it would be too laborious to describe further. However, the sequence, like much porn, does also push the classical conventions much further than is normal in Hollywood, perhaps to a breaking point.

Linda Williams, in her study of (heterosexual) film/video pornography, *Hard Core: Power, Pleasure and the 'Frenzy of the Visible'*, discusses the way that the genre has been propelled by the urgent desire to see as much as possible of sexuality, by what she calls 'the principle of maximum visibility' (1989: 48). Two aspects of this are particularly relevant here.

One is the lengths to which porn goes to show sexual organs and actions. Williams lists some of the ways that this has operated 'to privilege close-ups of body parts over other shots; to overlight easily obscured genitals; to select sexual positions that show the most of bodies and organs . . . to create generic conventions, such as the variety of sexual "numbers" or the externally ejacu-lating penis' (ibid.: 49). These are what a friend of mine calls 'the plumbing shots' and are presumably what made John Waters remark that porn always looks to him 'like open-heart surgery'. The camera is down on the floor between the legs of one man fucking another, looking up into dangling balls and the penis moving back and forth into the arsehole; or it is somehow hov-ering overhead as a man moves his mouth back and forth over another's penis; and so on. Such spatial lability goes much further than classical norms, where the camera/viewer may, in effect, jump about the scene but will not see what cannot be seen in normal circumstances (even in actual sex one does not nor-mally see the above, because one is doing them). Very often the editing of these sequences betrays gaps in spatial and temporal continuity, ignored, and caused, by the 'frenzied' (to use Williams's suggestive term) will to see. The moment of coming is sometimes shot simultaneously from three different camera positions, which are then edited together, sometimes one or more in slow motion. Such temporal manipulation through editing again breaks the coherence of classicism. Devices like this may work because – as in the 'incor-rect' shot of Jim described above – they are in tune with the libidinal drive of the video. But they may also draw attention to the process of video making itself, so that what the viewer is most aware of is the cameraperson down on the floor, the performer's climax shot from several cameras, or the editor poring over the sequence, things that may spoil or may, for some, enhance the excitement of the sequence.

The other aspect of the 'principle of maximum visibility' of interest here, and central to Williams's book, is showing what is not, and possibly cannot be, seen in actual sexual intercourse, most famously the ejaculating penis. Here the difference between straight and gay porn is especially significant. As Williams discusses, much of the 'frenzy' of heterosexual porn is the desire to show and see what cannot be shown and seen, female sexual pleasure, something of no concern to gay (as opposed, of course, to lesbian) porn. Equally, the oddness of showing the man ejaculating outside of his partner's body is less striking in gay porn; withdrawal to display (especially when involving removing a condom, or ignoring the fact that in the fucking shots he has been using one) is odd, but much (probably most) actual gay sex in fact involves external ejaculation (and did so even before AIDS).

Yet the insistence on seeing the performers' orgasm is an interesting feature of gay porn too. As in straight porn, it brings the linear narrative drive that structures porn to a clear climax and end (cf. Dyer 1992), as well as relating to the importance of the visible in all male sexuality. Within gay sex specifically, seeing another's orgasm is also delightful because it is a sign that the other is excited by one and is even a sort of gift, a giving of a part of oneself. Such feelings are at play in come shots in gay porn. Additionally, one may see come shots as a further dimension of a video's realism. Come shots are rarely, if ever, faked; we really are seeing someone come. This is happening in the story and fictional world of the video, but it's also happening on a set. Its conventionality, its oddness when involving withdrawal, the often disruptive cut that precedes it, all draw attention to it as a performance for camera. This breaks classical norms, but it is the foundation of the excitement of pornography that I want to discuss in the next section.

If gay porn, like straight, runs the risk of disrupting its own illusionism, some of it has been happy to capitalise on this. Most gay porn is like the subway sequence in *Inch by Inch* (though less accomplished in its deployment of codes of realism and classicism), but a significant amount is not. In its history (not much shorter, according to Waugh (1996), than that of the straight stuff), gay film/video porn has consistently been marked by self-reflexivity, by texts that have wanted to draw attention to themselves as porn, that is, as constructed presentations of sex.

This may be at the level of narrative: films about making porn films (*Giants* 1983, *Screenplay* 1984, *The Next Valentino* 1988, *Sex, Lies and Video-cassettes* 1989, *Busted* 1991, *Loaded* 1992, *The Idol Maker* 1997, *Shooting Porn* 2000), about taking porn photographs (*Flashback* 1980, *Juice* 1984, *Bicoastal* 1985, *Make It Hard* 1985, *Rap'n about 'ricans* 1992); about auditioning for porn films (*The Interview* 1981, *Abuse Thyself* 1985, *Screen Test* 1985); about being a live show performer (*Le Beau mec* 1978, *Performance* 1981, *Time Square Strip* 1982, *The Main Attraction* 1989); about having sex in porn cinemas – just like the patrons (*The Back Row* 1973, *Passing Strangers* 1977, *The Dirty Picture Show* 1979). It may be at the level of cinematic pastiche or intertexual reference (*The Light from the Second Storey Window* 1973, *Adam and Yves* 1974, *The Devil and Mr Jones* 1974, *Five Hard Pieces* 1977, *Cruisin' 57* 1979, *Gayracula* 1983, *Early Erections* 1989, *Single White Male* 1993, *The Cockpit Club* 2001[1]). It may be a display of a star, someone known for being in porn (*Best of the Superstars* 1981, the *Frank Vickers Trilogy* 1986–89, *Deep Inside Jon Vincent* 1990, *Inside Vladimir Correa* 1991); or more specifically a film about being a porn star, showing him on the job (*Inside Eric Ryan* 1983, *That Boy* 1985). There are even successful films that are histories of gay porn (*Good Hot Stuff* 1975, *Eroticus* 1983). Where the film does not refer to film

192

porn as such, it may well refer explicitly to the psychic elements necessary for the production of porn: narcissism (e.g. a man making love to his own mirror image (*Le Beau mec* 1978, *Pumping Oil* 1983)), exhibitionism (e.g. a bodybuilder fantasising posing nude (*Private Party* 1984)), voyeurism (*Le Voyeur* 1982, *On the Lookout* 1992), and dreaming and fantasising themselves, two of the commonest motifs in gay porn films, resulting in elaborate narrative structures of flashbacks, inserts, intercutting and stories within stories. All of these elements of content can be supplemented by the form of the film itself. The *Interview* films (1989–) for instance have the subject talking to the off-screen but heard director while stripping, working out and masturbating. *Roger* (1979) cuts back and forth between long shots and close-ups of the action (Roger masturbating), using different shades of red filter, the rhythmic precision of the cutting drawing attention to itself and hence to the film's construction of a celebration of its eponymous subject.

I am far from claiming that this tradition of self-reflexivity is characteristic of most gay porn. If the list I have given (itself very far from complete) is impressive, it constitutes but a drop in the ocean of the massive gay film/video porn business. Yet the tradition is there and encompasses many of the most successful titles. The self-reflexive mode would not be so consistently returned to, did it not sell – and it would not sell if it did not turn people on. Moreover, it is not unreasonable to assume that some people (like me) take pleasure in even non-self-reflexive porn by imagining the rehearsals, the camera and crew, by focusing on the performers as performers rather than as characters.

I want to examine gay porno self-reflexivity by focusing on the work of one highly successful contemporary porn star. Ryan Idol (Figure 13.2) is a young man who must have blessed his parents and perhaps God that he was born with so appropriate and serviceable a name.[2] Few stars can have got their own name so often into the title of their videos (*Idol Eyes* 1990, *Idol Worship* 1992, *Idol Thoughts* 1993[3]) or had it used as the basis for so many puns in magazine feature spreads ('Ryan Idol, Yours to Worship' (cover, *Advocate Men*, July 1990); 'Idol Worship' and 'Pinnacle' (cover and feature title, *Advocate Men*, March 1993); 'Richard Gere was My Idol – So to Speak', *The Advocate Classifieds*, 18 May 1993)). Ryan seems to have no existence, no image, other than that of being the subject of sexual adulation. What is exciting about him is that he is a porn star.

There is with all movie stars a potential instability in the relationship between their being a star and the characters they play. When the fit is perfect – Joan Crawford as Mildred Pierce, Sylvester Stallone as Rocky Balboa – we do not, except in a camp appreciation, sit there thinking that we are seeing a movie star baking pies by the score or becoming World Heavyweight Champion; in so far as the discrepancy worries us at all, we resolve it by seeing the role as expressive of personality qualities in the star – in the case of Joan and Sly, for instance, variations on notions of

Figure 13.2 Ryan Idol's *Idol Thoughts* heads up Catalina Video's Spring 1994 releases.

working-class advancement. There is, in other words, a set of cultural categories to which both role and star image refer, beyond that of simply being a very famous performer in movies. Porn stars – like, to some extent, musical stars – cannot mobilise such reference so easily; they are famous for having sex in videos.

There can be an element of wider social reference in porn stars' images. The extremely successful Catalina company has created an image of the California golden boy, with no existence other than working and making out. This is an image that seems to offer itself as stripped of social specificity, a sort of pornographic utopia uncontaminated by class, gender or race, although it is of course highly specifically white, young, US and well fed. Residually, gay porn stars are still generally given social traits. Jeff Stryker, for instance, perhaps the biggest star of the 1980s and 1990s, is repeatedly associated with working-class iconography, through roles (a mercenary in *Stryker Force* 1987, a garage mechanic in *The Look* 1988, a farm boy in *The Switch is On* 1987) or accessories in pin-ups (spanners, greasy jeans). This is often reinforced by the idea of him as an innocent who, willingly but almost passively, gets into sexual encounters (as in his gaol videos, *Powertool* 1986 and *Powerful II* 1989, or the farm boy in the city narrative of *The Switch is On*). It would however be hard to say anything even as broadly definite as this with Ryan Idol, even though he has played a lifeguard (*Idol Eyes* 1990), college quarterback (*Score Ten* 1991), naval officer (*Idol Worship* 1992) and pilot (*Idol in The Sky*). Even these roles in fact play upon the one clear role that he has, being a porn star.[4]

The sense of his not offering anything but himself as body is suggested by his readiness to play with different body images in his many porn magazine spreads. In *Advocate Men* in July 1990, he has almost bouffant hair with a still boyish face and body. This look is capitalised on in the spread in the November 1991 issue of the short-lived *Dream*, which seemed to be addressing itself to men and women, straight and gay simultaneously; unusually for an Idol spread, there are no shots with erections, he is posed on black satin sheets and his expression is one of practised but unsullied yearning. Before that (at least in terms of publication, if not actual shoot), in *Mandate*, June 1990, the hair is cut much shorter at the sides, the top more obviously held stiffly in place with spray, he uses a leather jacket as prop, and poses more angularly, which, together with harder directional lighting, makes him look both more muscley and more directly sexual. Something similar is achieved in *Jock*, December 1991, though with more tousled hair and the fullest sense of social reference (a locker-room and football gear, part of the publicity for *Score Ten*). By 1993, however, there was a more radical alteration of the image, and in two, almost simultaneous forms. His hair is long and Keanu Reeves-ishly floppy now and his body less defined. In *Advocate Men*, March 1993, he poses by a pool, more in the 'art' style of a gay photographer like Roy Dean than this magazine's usual house style. In *Mandate*, June 1993, he is sweaty, with grease marks on his body, a much raunchier look, which is picked up in his pictures in *The Advocate Classifieds* for 18 May 1993, which have some residual boxing iconography. In the features and photospreads accompanying the release of *Idol in The Sky*, featured in five gay glossies between January and July 1997, Ryan's body is now slacker and hairy and the poses more macho mature, with splayed legs and chewing on a cigar.

There are continuities in this imagery, but these serve to emphasise him qua porn star. The thong tanline is unchanging, a tanline associated with exotic dancers, that is, sex performers. More significantly, he consistently poses in ways that relate very directly to the viewer. He holds his body open to view, his arms framing rather than concealing it, his posture, especially from the hips, often subtly thrust towards the camera (especially notable in shots lying on his side in *Dream* or seated in *Torso*, December 1991). This sense of very consciously offering the body is reinforced by the fact that he almost invariably looks directly, smilingly, seemingly frankly, into the camera, and has an erection. The only variation in the latter is that it is more often free standing or lightly held in the early photos, more often gripped and pointed in the later ones. There is absolutely no sense here of someone being observed (as if voyeuristically) as they go about their business nor of someone posing reluctantly, embarrassedly, just for the money. That impression is reinforced by interview material: 'I'll do maybe one or two adult films, mostly as an outlet for my exhibitionism' (*Advocate Men*, July 1990: 48), 'Ryan reveals that he likes showing off his big body. "I like doing it and I like watching it," he says' (*Prowl*, June 1991). In *Ryan Idol: A Very Special View*, 1990, scripted by Ryan himself, he talks in length about the pleasures of posing for photographs and of being an exotic dancer.

His magazine spreads, a vital component of any porn star's image, construct him as nothing other than a porn star, and this is echoed by the information on his life. Porn stars are seldom given an elaborate biography, but there is usually an implication of something in their lives other than pornography. Though Ryan has not made so many videos, he has done very many photo spreads and personal appearances. Interviews with him give the impression that that is what his life consists of, the more so with the establishment of the Ryan Idol International Fan Club (which included a 'hot line', a co-star search, a 'Win a Date with Ryan Contest', and a sales catalogue, including posters, T-shirts, pictures, 'paraphernalia' and cologne; in short, 'We're offering [the fans] many, many ways to get closer to Ryan Idol' (*The Advocate Classifieds*, 18 May 1993, 51)). *A Very Special View* offers a day in the life of a porn star, but unlike other such videos featuring, for instance, Vladimir Correa or Jon Vincent, Ryan's day does not consist of sexual encounters but a photo shoot, a strip show and doing solos for us. His career even has its own narrative dynamic, to do with the gradual extension of what he does on camera. In all his videos he does solos and in most he is sucked off; in *Idol Eyes*, the penis in the close-ups of him fucking Joey

Stefano is in fact another porn star's, David Ashfield's, as subsequent coverage revealed; but in *Score Ten* he did his own stunt work and, with a fanfare of publicity, in *Idol Thoughts* he sucks someone else off. Subsequently there were rumours, and talk of high level negotiations, that Ryan would finally be fucked, but it did not come to pass. This trajectory, itself following the pattern of many porn narratives, is part tease, keeping something in reserve for later in the career, but also part play with the question of sexual identity – Ryan makes straight porn videos, was 'open' in early interviews ('I share my lovemaking equally with women and men', *Dream*), though much less equivocally gay later ('"Do you enjoy sucking dick?" "What do you think? I think it's a turn-on. And I think that question is pretty much answered in *Idol Thoughts*"', *Advocate Classifieds*). Such fascination with the 'real' sexual identity of porn stars in gay videos is a major component of the discourse that surrounds them, and the idea that Ryan might 'really' be straight excites or exercises many viewers (though one might wonder what is so straight about getting your cock hard under the gaze of other men). In any case, the fact that one has no guaranteed knowledge of his sexual object choice contributes to the sense that with Ryan sex is performance rather than identity.

His videos further emphasise his existence as porn star. Only three are actually about him being a porn star (*A Very Special View*, the footage in *Troy Saxon Gallery II* 1991 and *Idol Thoughts* 1993) but the rest all play with the idea of his having his being in the pleasures of looking. In *Idol Eyes* he spies on others having sex but is first really turned on by looking at himself in the mirror, getting into different outfits in front of it and masturbating at his own image. His voice-over talks about his learning to get off on men through getting off on himself (a casebook statement of one of the Freudian aetiologies of homosexuality as an extension of narcissism). Similarly in *A Very Personal View* he jacks off looking at himself in the bathroom mirror, saying in voice-over: 'Nothing wrong with that – I do enjoy being with myself – sometimes it's much more exciting – especially when someone . . . might be watching' (a rider I'll return to). In *Score Ten* he masturbates in front of a fellow student, posed on the bonnet of a car with the student inside, so that he, Ryan, is framed and kept distant by the windscreen. *Idol Worship* has him strip off and masturbate in the control room of the ship he commands, all the while telling the crew not to look, to keep their eyes on their instruments, orders which they obey. *Trade Off* (1992) begins with neighbours Ryan and Alex Garret spying on each other and then out jogging; at one point, Ryan stops in his run to answer a phone in a public phone box, a voice tells him to strip and jack off, here on the public highway ('You know you like to be looked at') and he does so as Alex looks on; when they finally meet, they masturbate in front of one another, with none of the body contact one might anticipate. Thus we have voyeurism (*Idol Eyes*, *Trade Off*), exhibitionism (*Trade Off*), narcissism/self-looking (*Idol*

Eyes, A Very Special View), display (*Score Ten*), denial of looking (*Idol Worship*), a series of entertaining plays on what is at the heart of porn: looking, showing, being looked at.

A Very Special View is a more sustained exploration of this, especially in the opening and closing solo sequences. In the first, Ryan is discovered by the camera when he wakes up and masturbates; this is accompanied by a voice-over in which he says he does this every morning and how he enjoys it. The treatment is for the most part classical; we are invited to imagine that Ryan doesn't know we are there and has added the commentary later. Yet even here Ryan teases us with the knowledge that he does know we are, as it were, there.

The sequence is in two parts, the first on the bed, the second in the bathroom. At the end of the first, Ryan is pumping his penis hard and glances at the camera momentarily and then again on a dissolve to the bathroom sequence. It is in the latter that Ryan makes the remark in voice-over quoted above, that it can be more enjoyable to make love to oneself, 'especially if someone might be watching'. Earlier in the sequence he has evoked the possibility of another person being present:

> There's no better way to start the day than to stroke my cock and bring myself to a very satisfying orgasm. Come to think about it, there is one better way and that would be to have someone working on my hard cock as I awake and slowly, slowly getting me off.

This comment runs the risk of reminding the viewer of what is not the case, that he is not in bed with Ryan sucking him off. The later comment alludes to what is the case, that someone is watching him – the camera/us. This immediately precedes his orgasm, so that what is in play as he comes is the fact of looking and being looked at.

When we first see him in the bathroom, he is looking at himself in the mirror, and several other mirrors duplicate his image. He masturbates in the shower, but a close-up towards the end makes it clear that he is still appraising himself in the mirror. When he comes, he looks straight ahead, head on to the camera. But is he looking at the mirror or the camera, at himself or us? Either or both, for our pleasure in him is his pleasure in himself and vice versa.

The last sequence plays much more strongly on the presence of the camera and Ryan as image. He goes into a friend's bedroom to have a rest. He strips to his briefs and gets on the bed, then turns to the camera, saying 'Do you want to see?', a rhetorical question in a porn video, and takes off his briefs. The sense of him as a performer is emphasised by the mirrors in the room. Not only do they connote display, narcissism and exhibitionism, they are also the means by which we see the cameraman from time to time. Perhaps this is an accident – 'bad' video-making – but with a star like Ryan it is entirely appropriate. What is he but someone being filmed? At two points we see an image of him which the camera draws back to reveal has been a mirror image; any distinction between the real Ryan and the image of Ryan is confounded.

Most remarkable though is Ryan's constant address to the camera. Once again he runs the risk of reminding us of other, unavailable possibilities: 'Imagine it anyway you want', he says, but of course should we wish to imagine having sex with him, we have to imagine something other than what we are seeing. But for the rest he talks entirely about the situation we are watching. He speaks of his control over his penis ('I make it do what I want'), an obvious asset in a porn star. He draws attention to the narrative structure of the sequence, its progress towards orgasm, by saying that he is about to come, but won't do it just yet, how he likes to hold off for as long as possible. He even draws attention to the porn viewing situation, by saying twice that he wants the viewer to come with him, something porn viewers generally wish to do. The shouts that accompany his orgasm are punctuated by glances to the camera, still conscious of our intended presence, still reminding us that he is putting on a show for our benefit.

There are further, more convoluted and virtual demonstrations of the pleasures of being in porn in *Idol Thoughts* (1993). This consists of a series of episodes linked by Ryan as 'porn star Ryan' going through his mail and phone messages. He remembers having sex with someone who has left a message, imagines others having sex when reading a letter from one of those involved and also imagines having sex with Tom Katt, a partner proposed in phone messages from his agent. If the first two of these are presented as real-life encounters, they are also at once fantasy material (memory, imagination) and real performances for the camera – the ontological conundrums of porn are already present with a vengeance. Ryan also jacks off into a pair of briefs sent to him by a fan, which he then puts into an envelope to post back, suggesting the fantasy of tangible if displaced contact with a porn star; this is all the more complicated here because it is a reassurance of contact (Ryan really will come into your briefs, it won't just be any old sperm stains they'll come back with) in the context of what is after all only a film and also because we have the pleasure of seeing Ryan do it, which the fan would only have if he too bought the video. Another section has Ryan playing with himself as he watches a video of two other men having sex; we see both the video Ryan sees and the men videoing each other (that is, making the video Ryan sees) – and indeed, we are not sure when we are watching the video or the making of the video (is the latter in fact already part of what Ryan is watching?). The video within a video seems intent on confirming that porn stars like to have unpaid for sex with each other, but like to go on doing so in a context of pornographisation (videoing each other), and meanwhile we know that what we are seeing must in fact be a paid for performance.

With the final section of *Idol Thoughts*, however, even the reference to

sexual activity outside of pornographic performance disappears. Throughout
the film there have been messages from his agent about the possibility of
Ryan working with Tom Katt (a star of pretty much his own magnitude)
and the final sequence gives us the much heralded moment when Ryan sucks
another star. It is overdetermined as a fantasy about porn (rather than just
being a pornographic fantasy). Immediately before it, Ryan takes a photograph of Tom and rubs it against his cock, thus literally masturbating with
the pornographic image itself. The sequence begins with Tom sucking Ryan
and then, when the great moment arrives, there is an overhead shot of Ryan
smiling knowingly up at Tom/the camera before taking Tom's cock into his
mouth; the dramatic camera position and pause with smile signal the
significance of this moment in Ryan's pornographic career. The sequence
ends with both men posed like statues, first Ryan standing and Tom kneel-
ing, then vice versa (Figures 13.3.1–13.3.3); they come in turn over each
other's chests, set pieces of display, clearly and not just expediently separate
in space and time from the preceding fucking, the apotheosis of this
encounter between stars. After the sequence we return to Ryan alone in his
room, answering his agent's phone message about working with Tom but
looking at us and saying, 'I want him!' This declaration may or may not

Figures 13.3.1–13.3.3 Idol Thoughts: Ryan and Tom posing to come (frame enlargements).

have been shot after shooting the scene with Tom, but for the spectator Ryan's desire to have Tom has already happened, either in the order in which the film has unfolded or in the fact that the scene has now been shot (because here it is in the film). The declaration could be taken as a coming out as gay, in so far as Ryan is definitely only Ryan in this video and is saying he wants Tom, but even more it is a declaration of the desire to be in an important porn scene with an important porn star, the desire to make porn, to be a porn star.

In emphasising here self-reflexive gay porn, I not only don't want to give the impression that it is the more common form, but also don't want to suggest that it is superior to less or un-self-reflexive examples. Intellectuals tend to be drawn to the meta-discursive in art; since what they themselves do is a meta-activity, they take special comfort from other things that are meta, like self-reflexive art. Yet it interests me that so viscerally demanding a form as pornography (it must make us come) can be, and so often is, self-reflexive.

According to much twentieth-century critical theory, this ought not to be so. It has long been held that work that draws attention to itself – cultural constructs that make apparent their own constructedness – will have the effect of distancing an audience. A film that draws our attention to its processes of turning us on ought not to turn us on; you shouldn't be able to come to what are merely terms. As Linda Williams puts it, pornography has a problem:

> sex as spontaneous *event* enacted for its own sake stands in perpetual opposition [in porn films] to sex as an elaborately engineered and choreographed *show* enacted by professional performers for a camera.
>
> (147; Williams's italics)

Yet, as I have tried to show, in much gay porn, at any rate, the show is the event.

This is a piece with much gay culture. Being meta is rather everyday for queers. Modes like camp, irony, derision, theatricallity and flamboyance hold together an awareness of something's style with a readiness to be moved by it – *La Traviata*, *Now Voyager* and 'Could It Be Magic' (in Barry Manilow's or Take That's version) are no less emotionally compelling for our revelling in their facticity. The elements of parody and pastiche and the deliberate foregrounding of artifice in much gay porn are within this tradition. Episodic films like *Like a Horse* (1984) and *Inch by Inch* move from one obviously constructed fantasy to another – from a jungle encounter to a non-place, abstracted leather sequence to an Arab tent, from a studio rooftop to a studio beach to a studio street – without for a moment undermining their erotic charge. This is characteristic of the way we inhabit discourse. We are constantly aware of the instability of even our own discourses, their hold on the world still so tenuous, so little shored up by a network of reinforcing

201

and affirming discourses, and yet our stake in them is still so momentous. We see their deliberation but still need their power to move and excite; it's thus so easy for us to see porn as both put-on and turn-on.

This, though, is not mainly what is at play in the Idol oeuvre. For here there is no sense of putting on a fantasy, no sense of performing anything other than performance. The idea of sex as performance is generally associated with male heterosexuality, and the element of working hard to achieve a spectacular orgasm is certainly present in much gay porn. Yet performance in the Ryan Idol case means much more display, presentation, artistry, the commitment to entertainment – literally a good show. It is a construction of sexuality as performance, as something you enact rather than express.

Gay men are as romantic and raunchy, as expressive and essentialist, as anyone else. Yet much facilitates a perception of (gay) sex as performance. Owning to one's gay identity – itself so fragile a construct – is perilous: seeing sexuality as performance rather than expression is appealing, since it does not implicate that compelling notion, the self. At the same time, dominant culture does little to naturalise our sexuality, making it harder to see gay sex acts as a product of pure need. We are less likely to think of gay sex in terms of biology than of aesthetics.

Paradoxically, there is a kind of realism in pornographic performance that declares its own performativity. What a porn film really is is a record of people actually having sex; it is only ever the narrative circumstances of porn, the apparent pretext for the sex, that is fictional. A video like *A Very Special View* foregrounds itself as a record of a performance, which heightens its realism. It really is what it appears to be.

This realism in turn has the effect of validating the video, and the genre to which it belongs. By stressing that what we are enjoying is not a fantasy, but porn, it validates porn itself. As Simon Watney has argued (1987), the importance of doing this in the age of AIDS could not be greater. And by specifically celebrating masturbation, videos like Ryan's also validate the very response that porn must elicit to survive, that is, masturbation. The most exciting thing of all about porn is that it affirms the delights of that most common, most unadmitted, at once most vanilla and most politically incorrect of sexual acts, masturbation.

Acknowledgement

From (revised) *Critical Quarterly* 36: 1, 1994.

Notes

1 These films refer respectively to *A Star is Born*, Garbo, Cocteau and Brando movies, *The Devil and Miss Jones*, fifties stag movies (and *Five Easy Pieces* of

course), *American Graffiti*, *Dracula*, educational television documentaries, *Single White Female*, *Fight Club*.

2   Before he was Ryan Idol he was, equally fortunately, Marc Anthony Donais in *Playgirl* (February 1989).

3   Though *Idol Gods*, which he referred to in an interview in 1997, never got made.

4   In 1997, he also appeared, fittingly, in the long-running stage play about gay pornography, *Making Porn*.

References

Al's Male Video Guide (1986), New York: Midway Publications.

Dyer, Richard (1992) 'Coming to Terms', in *Only Entertainment*, London: Routledge.

Rowberry, John (ed.) (1993) *The Adam Film World Guide* 14: 11, Los Angeles: Knight Publishing.

Watney, Simon (1987) *Policing Desire: Pornography, AIDS and the Media*, London: Methuen/Comedia.

Waugh, Tom (1996) *Hard to Imagine: Gay Male Eroticism in Photography and Film from Their Beginnings to Stonewall*, New York: Columbia University Press.

Williams, Linda (1989) *Hard Core: Power, Pleasure and the 'Frenzy of the Visible'*, Berkeley/Los Angles: University of California Press.

Further reading

Burger, John R. (1995) *One-Handed Histories: The Eroto-Politics of Gay Male Video Pornography*, New York: Harrington.

Fung, Richard (1988) 'Looking for My Penis: The Eroticised Asian in Gay Video Porn', in *Bad Object Choices* (ed.) *How Do I Look?*, Seattle: Bay Press, 148–160.

Merck, Mandy (1993) '*More of a Man*: Gay Porn Cruises Gay Politics', in *Perversions*, London: Virago, 217–235.

14

HOMOSEXUALITY AND HERITAGE

A camera pans down the façade of Barcelona Cathedral and comes to rest; bells toll as a square, black car draws up; a man in a white suit gets out and opens the door for an older woman in black, whom he leads towards the cathedral as the camera rises again; extras in black, white or beige 1920s costume mill about in front of the grey cathedral; a horse and carriage passes by. This is the opening shot of *Un Hombre llamado 'Flor de Otoño'*;[1] the man is the protagonist, Lluis, the woman his mother and they are at once established as part of the spectacle of heritage. This presentation of a well-lit, well-dressed world continues with scenes of Lluis at dinner in the well appointed bourgeois flat he shares with his mother. Then he leaves after coffee and we next see him in bed with a man, Alberto, in a sleazy part of town. It is dark and tacky, homosexual, the antithesis of heritage. Yet the trajectory of the film is to effect a reconciliation of heritage and homosexuality. Moreover, and surprisingly, given its middlebrow respectability and focus on a homophobic past, heritage cinema in general has been surprisingly hospitable to homosexual representation. This is the subject of this chapter.

The term 'heritage cinema' is used to indicate a run of mainly European films made since the 1960s.[2] Internationally celebrated examples include *Novecento* (*Nineteen Hundred*, Italy 1976), *Angi Vera* (Hungary 1978), *Chariots of Fire* (UK 1981), *Gallipoli* (Australia 1981), *Het Meisje met het rode haar* (*The Girl with Red Hair*, Netherlands 1981), *Mephisto* (Germany 1981), *Fanny och Alexander* (Sweden 1982), *A Room with a View* (UK 1985), *Jean de Florette/Manon des sources* (France 1986), *Miss Mary* (Argentina 1986), *Rosa Luxemburg* (Germany 1986), *Babettes gaestebud* (*Babette's Feast*, Denmark 1987), *My Left Foot* (Ireland 1989), *Daens* (Belgium 1992) and *Belle époque* (Spain 1993). This is only the tip of the iceberg of what is also not a very tightly defined kind of filmmaking, chronologically or formally.

To take chronology first. There have long been period films and literary adaptations in most national cinemas, but with a few exceptions they have tended to play up romantic, adventurous or melodramatic possibilities and have not prized notions of fidelity to sources. Equally there have always been films explicitly addressing ideas of national patrimony and identity, but these have not necessarily used heritage cinema modes. The style began to crystallise from the late 1940s on, notably in the work of David Lean (*Great Expectations* 1946, *Oliver Twist* 1948, *Lawrence of Arabia* 1962), Jacqueline Audry (*Gigi* 1949, *Olivia* 1951, *Le Secret du Chevalier d'Eon* 1960), Luchino Visconti (*Senso* 1954, *Il gattopardo* [*The Leopard*] 1963, *La Caduta degli dei* [*The Damned*] 1969) and Volker Schlöndorff (*Der junge Törless* 1966, *Michael Kohlhaas, der Rebell* 1969).

The formal characteristics of such films include the following: the use of a well known literary source, and/or key historical moments (the French Revolution, the Italian Risorgimento, the World Wars), periods (Edwardian, Fascist) or occasionally the lives of writers and artists; these texts, moments and figures most often drawn from the past 150 years; a conventional film style, with the pace and tone of art cinema without its propensity for symbolism, intellectual talk or noticeable directorial styles; settings and costume based upon meticulous research, presented in pristine condition, brightly or artfully lit. It is this last, the sense of the attentive and tasteful display of historically accurate dress and decor, a museum or antiques aesthetic, that brings these films into the orbit of the heritage industry which came to frame leisure and cultural sites in the 1980s and 1990s. The view of the past that heritage cinema offers is at once straightforward and tangible, and it is this that distinguishes it from other filmic approaches to history in the period, be they, to take only queer-related examples, deconstructive (*Ludwig – Requiem für einen jungfräulichen König* [*Ludwig, Requiem for a Virgin King*] Germany 1972, *Looking for Langston* UK 1988, *Swoon* USA 1991, *Forbidden Love* Canada 1992), poetic (*Satyricon* Italy 1969, *Caravaggio* UK 1986, *Edward II* UK 1991) or camp (*Desperate Remedies* New Zealand 1993, *Stonewall* UK 1995).[3]

Heritage cinema has been notably hospitable to homosexual subject matter (though in this chapter, written for this book, I focus on male instances). It already figures in Lean (*Lawrence of Arabia*), Audry (*Olivia, Le Secret du Chevalier d'Eon*), Visconti (*La Caduta degli dei*) and Schlöndorff (*Der junge Törless*), with Visconti (*Morte a Venezia, Ludwig*) and Schlöndorff (*Coup de grâce, Un Amour de Swann*) continuing to produce queer themed work into the main period of heritage cinema. In some cases, the homosexuality is very marginal (*Barry Lyndon, La Nuit de Varennes*) or equivocal (*Becket, Orlando*), but for the most part these are films that deal centrally and definitely with homosexuality.[4]

Despite the precedents, homosexual heritage films only appeared in anything approaching critical mass from the end of the 1960s (as of course did heritage cinema more widely). This forms part of the increase in gay filmic representation in the period, itself made possible by the impact of the gay movements, these in turn part and parcel of the liberalisation of attitudes on matters sexual and the increasing mass commodification of sexuality in the 1960s and 1970s. The emergence of 'gay' was part of what made homosexual heritage films possible. Some (*Another Country*, *Las cosas del querer*, *Una giornata particolare*, *Un Hombre llamado 'Flor de Otoño'*, *Maurice*, *Meteoro ke skia*, *Nous étions un seul homme*, *Älskande par*) seem pretty clearly inspired by a gay or sexually liberal political agenda. With arguable exceptions (*Ludwig*, *Le Maître de musique*, *Morte a Venezia*, *Redl ezredes*), they all take a broadly positive view of homosexuality – which is to say that they take such a view while depicting pasts that did not.

To approach this, I want to make a distinction between history and heritage. History is a discipline of enquiry into the past; heritage is an attitude towards the legacy of the past. Both have to deal with what comes down to us, what is left over, from the past. However, whereas historical enquiry uses an examination of the left-overs to try to understand what happened in the past and why, a heritage sensibility values them for their own sake, savours the qualities and presence of dwellings, costumes, artworks, objects. Heritage cinema could be used – and, I will argue in the case of homosexual heritage was importantly used – as a vehicle to explore issues of history, but its main impulse is towards appreciating the things of the past and telling stories of what it was like to live among them. In this perspective homosexual heritage cinema is about envisaging homosexual men among the attractions of pastness.

History

The gay movement was founded on the notion that homosexual is an identity; its assertion of the rights and worth of people who practised same-sex sex was based on the idea that we were a kind or community of persons. One aspect of making this claim was to demonstrate that this identity had a past. History could give substance to what might seem an ephemeral present identity, either by affirming we'd always been around in some shape or form or by showing how our identity has emerged out of the past. George Chauncey, Martin Duberman and Martha Vicinus evoke what is at stake in their introduction to a 1989 collection of articles on lesbian and gay history:

> Because the history of homosexuality has been denied or ignored, ... gay people's hunger for knowledge of their past is strong. Having struggled to create a public sphere for themselves in the world today, they seek to reclaim their historical presence. For many, gay history helps constitute the gay community by giving it a tradition, helps women and men validate and understand who they are by showing them who they have been.

(12)

The practice of gay history suggested a number of things to look for in the past. The first was simply the presence of homosexuals in the past and this, as I shall show next below, is also part of the appeal of homosexual heritage cinema. However, while historical scholarship also explored the nature of gay oppression and the profound, even perhaps incommensurable differences in the manifestations of 'homosexuality' in the past,[5] homosexual heritage was more inclined to cherish in the past antecedents of the practices and beliefs of gay liberation: being yourself, coming out, heroism. I deal with this in the later part of this section.

Duberman, Vicinus and Chauncey's collection is titled *Hidden from History*. Professional historians had been unable to see or acknowledge lesbians and gay men in the past; gay history had to show that we were there. This is also something that heritage cinema does. Just by having homosexual stories in heritage dress, gay men become part of the wider historical panorama constituted by heritage cinema itself: we too were around in the 1910s and 1920s (*Céleste, Coup de grâce, Un Hombre llamado 'Flor de Otoño', Der junge Törless, A Month in the Country, Nijinksy, Redl ezredes, Valentino*), there was a gay experience of World War Two (*Le Dernier métro, The Dresser, Europa, Europa, Mediterraneo, Nous étions un seul homme, Voor een verloren soldaat*). Sometimes this insertion of gay men into history is more pointed. *Una giornata particolare* and *Gli occhiali d'oro*, both films set under fascism, state that gay men too were victims of the regime, explicitly bringing out parallels and differences between their situation and that of, respectively, women and Jews;[6] *Europa, Europa* hints at possibilities of understanding between Jews and queers under Nazism.[7] Other films deal specifically with gay oppression (*Maurice, Meteoro ke skia, A Month in the Country*, the Wilde films); somewhat ambivalently, *Il conformista* relates the rise of fascism to homosexual repression (Marcello becomes a fascist to evade recognition of his homosexual desires),[8] while *Another Country* links 1930s communism to rebellion against homophobia (Guy becomes a communist spy as a means of getting back at a society that outlaws homosexuality[9]).

The last example also indicates the way that homosexual heritage cinema may point to antecedents to gay liberation itself. These are most often manifested in two of the cardinal principles of the gay movement: being oneself and coming out.

Being oneself meant realising and living out one's sexual nature, with the sense that this is 'what you really are'. In heritage cinema characters may know themselves to be gay from the start of the film (*Carrington, Las cosas del querer, Le Dernier métro, The Dresser, An Englishman Abroad, Ludwig, Nijinksy, Älskande par*, Charlus in the Proust films, *Un Amour de Swann* and *Le Temps retrouvé*); Edvard in *Det forsømte forår* provides a complex example, as he looks back from a present, in which he knows himself to be gay, at himself as an adolescent, when he appears to have no inkling of it. Very commonly though there is a narrative of realisation. It may be a slow realisation that may not even be articulated as such (*Nous étions un seul homme*, *Voor een verloren soldaat*) or gradual acceptance of what the character always knew about himself (*Another Country*, *Wilde*). Or there may be a moment of realisation: Frits in *De Avonden* understands the nature of his feeling for Wim after the latter dies; only at the end of *Il conformista* does Marcello, meeting up by chance with the chauffeur from his childhood, begin to confront the fact of his homosexuality. Sometimes it takes other characters to recognise the main character's homosexuality: Lord Risley (*Maurice*) perspicaciously invites a baffled Maurice to meet some (queer) friends 'whom, if I'm not mistaken, would interest you'; Redl (*Redl ezredes*) seems startled when a young man makes a pass at him in a brothel; an old man in make-up on the vaporetto near the beginning of *Morte a Venezia* seems to feel an appalling affinity with the soberly dressed Aschenbach, and Tadzio seems to understand the nature of Aschenbach's interest in him before he does himself. It can be that we find out but the character himself doesn't seem to: in *Mountains of the Moon*, there is a scene where Speke cradles and kisses with frenzied passion the sick Burton, but it is never alluded to or expanded upon in the rest of the film. Occasionally, as in *Morte a Venezia*, realisation may not be welcome. *Maurice*, on the other hand, is not so much about the eponymous hero discovering he is homosexual as working out what this truly means: the film is a journey towards enlightenment, moving through a variety of definitions of homo-eroticism (Christian sin, aesthetic sickness,[10] Greek idealisation, psychiatric illness) before arriving at a Carpenterian[11] natural sexuality in the arms of the game-keeper Alec.

The process or moment of realisation may be purely internal, but commonly it also involves declaration or what would now be called coming out. This ranges from the coded and indirect (at the end of *De Avonden*, Frits gives a New Year's speech about his hopes for a future leading 'the Other life', explicitly the life of a writer but also clearly, to us, his life as a gay man) through the private (Lluis in *Un Hombre llamado 'Flor de Otoño'* goes in drag to his mother's bedroom at night to tell her about himself) to the brazen (in *Meteoro ke skia* Napoleon and Cleon stroll languidly and obviously queer through a busy public park, subject to a stream of mocking comment). Characters may be outed by others (Redl is entrapped and thereby exposed; Birk in *A Month in the Country* learns of Moon's homosexuality from a man he meets in a pub), with variable results (in the case of Redl and Moon, enforced suicide and friendly acceptance respectively).

The moment of coming out can be given further resonance. Gabriele's outburst to Antonietta in *Una giornata particolare* that, yes, he is 'un frocio', a fairy, a queer, is especially effective for being shouted against the sound that has been continuous throughout the film, a radio broadcast covering Hitler's state visit to Rome – Gabriele's vocal declaration of homosexuality is pitted against the aural embodiment of homophobic fascism. In *Las cosas del querer*, Mario is rehearsing a song of unrequited love in an empty theatre; half-way through he turns and faces the on-stage pianist, the straight Juan, and addresses the song to him, making a clear declaration of love; here the character's sexuality itself is not a revelation, but the force of feeling in his delivery of the song (tears in the eyes, crack in the voice) and the abandonment of the public enactment of love (facing the auditorium) in favour of the private avowal (facing up stage and shown in close-up) are an assertion performed within the confines of a supposedly heterosexual love song.[12] The motif of declaration is twisted in *Another Country* by having Guy use flamboyant homosexuality not only as a defiance of the repressiveness of a homophobic establishment but also as a cover for his spying on behalf of communism – who would ever think someone so blatantly gay, such an obvious high risk, would be a spy, or, as he puts it, 'What better disguise than total indiscretion?'.

Both realisation and declaration are heroic and for the most part homosexual heritage cinema contents itself with these small acts of courage from the past. *Un Hombre llamado 'Flor de Otoño'*, however, not only embodies all the historical impulses discussed so far – putting gays back into history, being oneself, coming out – but also makes homosexual bravery the centre of the film. Much of the plot concerns Lluis's political activities against the dictator Primo de Rivera in 1920s Barcelona; he fights alongside trade unionists and anarchists but also explicitly in the name of 'a revolution in which we can be ourselves [that is, gay] twenty-four hours a day' (and not just, as the film shows it, at night); together with his boyfriend Alberto and another gay friend, the boxer Kid Surroca, they perform various acts of sabotage until they are betrayed in the act of blowing up a train carrying the dictator and are executed. In one incident, Lluis, a drag artiste, uses his cross-dressing skills to distract the guard of a small arsenal they wish to rob; he dresses as a peasant woman, hysterically giggling 'No' as he rolls in the grass with Alberto, counting on the guard's voyeurism and delight in seeing a woman taken against her declared wishes, and thus enabling Surroca to knock the guard out: Lluis's drag has served the cause of democracy.

At the end of the film, the trio are called to execution from their shared cell. Lluis, hitherto always smooth chinned, has several days' growth of beard. In a gesture surely modelled on Marlene Dietrich's at the end of *Dishonored* (USA 1931), he picks up a compact and firmly, carefully applies lipstick; he hugs Surroca, then kisses Alberto fully on the lips and they go to their deaths with his arm around Alberto; the camera remains and tracks along the floor of the cell and comes to rest on the compact and lipstick. The lipstick gesture affirms that he is a martyr to gay revolution as much as anarchism. Lluis/Flor de Otoño is a hero on the side of anti-dictatorship in a film made (1977) in the first flush of the demise of Franco (1975); he is part of the history of the struggle for democracy in Spain, but the film insists that he be understood to be so as a queer and in the name of queers.

Heritage

In such ways heritage cinema can put homosexuals into history. This though is not its primary impulse. What is at issue is, rather, heritage, our belonging in what is handed down as cherishable from the past.

One dimension of this is the importance of queers in the source material of the films, the literary heritage from which most of the films are drawn. As John Hill points out, the 'literary standing of the original is ... a part of the heritage which the heritage film displays' (1999: 78), and not the least powerful aspect of heritage cinema from a gay perspective is the strong presence of lesbian and gay authors in its sources. Heritage cinema would be extraordinarily diminished without the following (not all of them with evident gay content): Paul Bowles (*The Sheltering Sky*), Colette (*Gigi, Becoming Colette*), Rudi van Dantzig (*Voor een verloren soldaat*), Sergei Diaghilev (*Nijinksy*), E. M. Forster (*Howards End, Maurice, A Passage to India, A Room with a View, Where Angels Fear to Tread*), Henry James (*The Bostonians, The Europeans, Portrait of a Lady Washington Square, The Wings of the Dove*), Agnes von Krusenstjerna (*Älskande par, Amorosa*), Napoleon Lapathiotis (*Meteoro ke skia*), Thomas Mann (*Bekenntnisse des Felix Krull, Morte a Venezia, Tonio Kröger*), Marcel Proust (*Un Amour de Swann, Céleste, 102 Boulevard Haussmann, Le Temps retrouvé*), Gerard van Reve (*De Avonden*), Arthur Rimbaud and Paul Verlaine (*Una stagione all'inferno, Total Eclipse*), Umberto Saba (*Ernesto*), Vita Sackville-West (*Portrait of a Marriage*), Gertrude Stein (*Waiting for the Moon*), Lytton Strachey (*Carrington*), Oscar Wilde (*The Trials of Oscar Wilde* [UK 1960], *Forbidden Passion, Wilde, An Ideal Husband*), Virginia Woolf (*Mrs Dalloway, Orlando*) and Marguerite Yourcenar (*Coup de grâce*). Some films (*De Avonden, Meteoro ke skia*) link homosexuality and cultural capacity through the notion of poetic sensitivity; *Meteoro ke skia* also places its poet hero in a European decadent, primarily gay tradition including Wilde (Napoleon writes a poem about Wilde and Bosie, and he and Cleon gaze at a photograph of them together), Cavafy (Cleon is part of a group seeking to rehabilitate his reputation) and Lautréamont (Cleon reads from *Les Chants de Maldoror*). All of this is in line with the impulse in early gay history towards uncovering a lineage of great men and women of the past who were homosexual. The appeal of this is evoked by the title of the book *Plato, Shakespeare, Walt Whitman and Me* and discussed by Chauncey, Duberman and Vicinus (1989: 3):

> It has long been reassuring for gay people, raised in a society offering them no positive images of themselves, to claim gay heroes, ranging from Sappho, Julius Caesar and Shakespeare to Willa Cather, Walt Whitman and Gertrude Stein, and much of the earliest work by historians simply sought to establish in a more scholarly fashion the homosexuality attributed to certain respected historical figures.

More important still than this affirmation of the place of queers in cultural patrimony is the look of the films and how gay men fit in. Here I want to concentrate on clothes, defining pleasures of heritage spectacle and also primary means for the presentation of gay masculinity.

This could be a concern with gay cultural history, exploring the historical association of homosexuality and sartorial taste. Heritage cinema has occasionally shown an interest in this. Norman, the eponymous *Dresser*, has stereotypically a queer's job; Guy Burgess in *An Englishman Abroad* is concerned to persuade Coral Browne to get him some clothes from a shop in Jermyn Street in London, the *ne plus ultra* of English male elegance (and with a very ambiguous role in gay history); Lacenaire in *L'Elégant criminel* is, as the title implies, defined in part by his stylishness; both *Un Amour de Swann* and *Le Temps retrouvé* model Charlus on the many portraits of one of great gay arbiters of male taste, the Count Robert de Montesquiou-Fezensac[13] (Figures 14.1 and 14.2).

However, this is not the main way in which clothes work in homosexual heritage cinema. Rather they exploit the wider expressive potential of male period clothing.

Figure 14.1 The Baron de Charlus (Alain Delon) eyes a footman in *Un Amour de Swann* 1983 (BFI Stills, Posters and Designs).

Figure 14.2 James McNeill Whistler: *Robert, Comte de Montesquiou-Fezensac*
(Copyright The Frick Collection, New York).

Since the eighteenth century, which is to say in the period covered by heritage cinema, men's clothes have deployed a much more limited vocabulary than women's: jacket and trousers as the basis of the ensemble, fabrics highly restricted, cut more important than pattern or, especially, colour (Buzzacarini 1992, Chenoune 1993). This narrow semiotic range has often been interpreted as indicating emotional repression, as, in J. C. Flügel's influential 1930 formulation, a 'great masculine renunciation' in the name of the values effective in the pursuance of business and power: straightforwardness, sobriety and restraint.[14]

One could well imagine how this might be used in heritage cinema to express homosexual repression and liberation, and indeed sometimes it is. Repression: Redl's many buttoned military jackets are always fully done up, squeezing his slightly podgy frame, suggesting someone ill at ease and anxious about giving himself away (in terms of class as well as sexuality) (Figure 14.3). Liberation: the eponymous hero of *Ernesto* removes his stiff collar when he has sex with the labourer at the start of the film and thereafter begins to wear light coloured, and eventually, patterned waistcoats with his black suit.

Figure 14.3 Redl ezredes 1984: buttoned-up Alfred Redl (Klaus Maria Brandauer) with his fatal seducer, the loosely-scarved Alfredo Velocchio (László Gálffy) (BFI Stills, Posters and Designs).

Quite commonly, heritage films suggest the danger for queers of trying to draw on colours and fabrics beyond the normal male range. Wilde (in *Wilde*) in cream frock coat and purple or green buttonhole is, most people seeing the film will know, clearly riding for a fall. *Meteoro ke skia* (Figure 14.4) emphasises the distinctiveness of queer dress, dwelling in close-up and at length on Napoleon's dressing and undressing, notably in a scene where he changes from hated, conscript's army gear to civilian clothes in exquisitely modulated greys; in the park scene alluded to above, he is an obvious queer, with his tight white trousers, large, loose white shirt and blowsy pink rosette at the neck.

Things do not need to go so far as this. *Morte a Venezia* (Figures 14.5 and 14.6) signals Aschenbach's decline into queerdom through slight but telling departures from the strictest of male attire that he has worn for most of the film. His first apprehension of Tadzio may be read as – or we may take him to read it as – a simple delight in beauty. It is surprising, partly because it is apparently simple, un-striven-for, unlike the disciplined beauty of his music, and partly because Tadzio is a boy. However, it is only gradually that the erotic dimension of this is borne in on the apparently happily heterosexual Aschenbach. At one point he follows Tadzio down a boardwalk to the beach and the latter, in a striped, buttock-clinging tank swimsuit, swings

Figure 14.4 Meteoro ke skia 1985: Napoleon (Takis Moschos) (left) and Cleon (Georgos Kentros) (BFI Stills, Posters and Designs).

Figure 14.5 *Morte a Venezia* 1970: Aschenbach (Dirk Bogarde) before Tadzio (BFI Stills, Posters and Designs).

Figure 14.6 Morte a Venezia: Aschenbach after Tadzio (BFI Stills, Posters and Designs).

round the posts of the boardwalk, looking at Aschenbach on each turn, his expression ambiguous but at least suggesting that he knows he is the object of Aschenbach's gaze and perhaps understanding better than Aschenbach its erotic charge. Aschenbach, dressed in standard male summer white suit, veers off the boardwalk, confused, sweating. The film cuts at once to a close up of him looking at Tadzio picking out 'Für Elise' on the hotel piano. Aschenbach now for the first time wears a dark bow tie with hollow spots. It is rather floppy, unlike the tightly knotted, narrow ties he has worn hitherto, and this floppiness goes along with the white handkerchief flouncing out of his breast pocket, a marked contrast to the handkerchief we have earlier seen him carefully fold and put in his pocket to show disciplined peaks. There is nothing extravagant about the bow tie and white handkerchief, yet they already mark a departure from the strictest discipline of male costume. By the time Aschenbach has submitted to the suggestions of the barber, and had his hair dyed and his face made-up, his clothes have edged much closer to the queer. Furtively following Tadzio, his governess and sisters through the streets, he now wears a large red band round his beige straw hat and a red tie with a diamond pin; when he skulks in the shadow of a portico, the pin glints in the dark with something approaching vulgarity. He is now in thrall to queer desire; when he dies on the beach gazing at Tadzio, hair-dye runs grotesquely down the side of his face. A move into more expressive clothes signals a decline into abject queerdom.

Homosexual heritage can express through clothes ideas of the repression and the dangers of the expression of queer desire. However, it does not do so so very much. This is perhaps because one of the defining pleasures of the films is looking at men wearing nice clothes. If all that the clothes expressed was restriction and discomfort, they would be a lot less pleasurable to look at, to imagine yourself touching or wearing. In any case, it is wrong to think of the restraint of male clothing as necessarily repressive and uncomfortable. Stiff collars and fully buttoned up jackets, waistcoats and shirts may express this, but, as Anne Hollander (1994: 8) suggests, the jacket-and-trousers ensemble, especially in the form of the suit, is also redolent of ease and grace. For instance:

> The separate elements of the costume overlap, rather than attaching to each other, so that great physical mobility is possible without creating gaps in the composition ... languid sprawling will cause the costume to disarrange its easy fit into attractively casual folds which form a fluid set of grace-notes for the relaxed body, and which also obligingly resume a smooth shape if the wearer must quickly get up and stand straight.

The masculine beau ideal of self-control and social conformity is one that, clothes promise, men can be at ease with, be at home in.

To have homosexual characters dressed like this was a declaration that gay men too could form part of graceful, decorous masculinity. Queer masculinity had characteristically been represented as something abnormal, informed by ideas of sickness (queers as emaciated, cadaverous, pale or just plain weird looking) and effeminacy (plucked eyebrows, prissy lips or exaggerated feminine fleshiness). In heritage cinema on the other hand, queers were shown as indistinguishable from other nicely turned out, worth looking at men.

Good-looking clothes also facilitate the exploration of what men may find attractive in each other. Here I would like to contrast two films, *Ernesto* and *Maurice*. Both represent relationships between an eponymous middle-class protagonist and a working-class lover – an unnamed labourer in *Ernesto*, Alec in *Maurice*. In both cases it is the working-class character who knows what he wants, the middle-class one who has to find out. However, and centrally through the use of clothing, *Ernesto* constructs attraction between men over-whelmingly in terms of difference, while *Maurice* moves it towards sameness. In the process, both also suggest different models of queer social integration.

Ernesto (Figures 14.7 and 14.8) opens with a systematic class contrast. The camera, in a very low position, shows sacks, bales of straw and a workman's trousers (grey serge, loose, untailored, dirty); someone in smart black trousers and shoes, with a polished cane, enters from the right and starts walking, the camera tracking with him until finally he goes down a slope and comes into full view: Ernesto, in black suit with bowler hat, stiff white collar and pale grey-blue tie. His class position is emphasised by the contrast with the background (black on beige/cream/oatmeal) but so is his youth, since his pretty, fine features and soft skin stand out in his staid clothes. A few shots later in a waist-up framing, he moves along a group of labourers, selecting those to whom he'll give employment that day, among them the man who will be his first lover. Again he stands out pure black, young, fastidious against the mainly off-white, collarless shirts and, where worn, loose dark waistcoats of the labourers. Class and youth are expressed through the clothes, but this then takes on an erotic charge in the sequences between the labourer and Ernesto. The former's clothes and appearance emphasise a rougher textured male pulchritude: he wears off-white, lightly stitched shirts or ribbed button-top vests, the buttons undone pulling open across his hairy chest; he has black hair, short on the sides but long, wiry and unruly on top; he seems to burst out of his clothes, embodying a fully masculine, wholly unrepressed homosexual desire. Ernesto, as we've seen, wears black suits and stiff white collars; his wavy hair is pomaded into neatness; he is hairless (and we are told has not even started shaving yet) – his is the smooth, sleek, neat beauty of the feminine. That the contrast is not only of class and age but also of gender is made explicit when the labourer refers to himself as the man (and relates this to his role as penetrator in sex).

When Ernesto becomes a man (he shaves, goes with a female prostitute, wants to penetrate the labourer), he meets a boy, Ilio, at a concert. Ilio has longish, fair hair and very soft features, and is not only younger than Ernesto

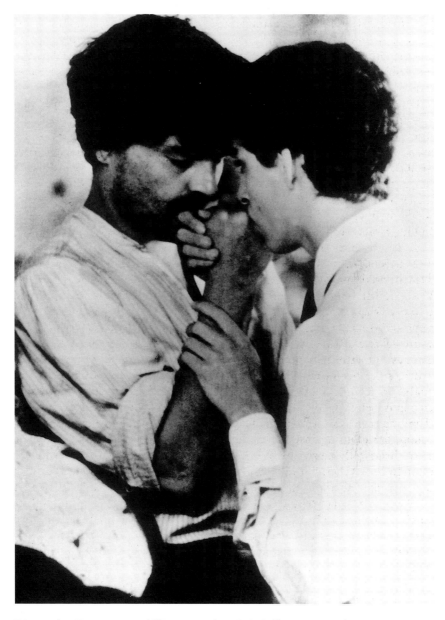

Figure 14.7 Ernesto 1978: difference as class (BFI Stills, Posters and Designs).

Figure 14.8 Ernesto: difference as sexual position (BFI Stills, Posters and Designs).

but comes from a much wealthier family. As if this isn't enough, the gender equation (higher class + younger = more feminine) is reinforced by the fact that he has a twin sister, Rachele; towards the end, Ilio and Rachele swap clothes and the latter, now dressed as a boy, tries to seduce Ernesto, although he remains fixated on Ilio at a dressing table putting on make-up. If Ernesto's sexual preference is not in doubt (he continues to desire the bio-logical male), it is also clear that he now desires the feminine man. What's more, he will probably marry Rachele because that's just what you do: the films ends with him at a party set up for him to announce his engagement to Rachele; he looks about desperately for Ilio and then turns to the camera and shrugs his shoulders. The film retains then its insistence on difference (and indeed gender difference) as a structuring principle of male homosexual desire, but implies that it can be maintained alongside conforming to the social organisation of heterosexuality.

The relationship between Maurice and Alec looks at first as if it is of a piece with that between Ernesto and the labourer. Alec's dark ruffled hair, rough textured collarless shirts, loosely knotted neckerchiefs, heavy, cruddy boots and dirty leggings contrast with Maurice's fair, floppy but close-to-the-head hair, stiff white collars, tightly knotted black ties and featureless dark shoes (Figure 14.9). The contrast is most marked when they meet in

Figure 14.9 Maurice 1987: dress and difference (BFI Stills, Posters and Designs).

the garden, Alec in his gamekeeper's gear, Maurice in dinner jacket; that night, Alec climbs into Maurice's bedroom and they make love. Thereafter, however, clothing (and lack thereof) makes them look more alike: naked in bed together, then both in identical whites for a cricket match, and then, when he comes to visit Maurice in London, Alec wearing a neat blue suit of the same cut as Maurice's (Figure 14.10). Class, or at any rate wealth, difference is still registered – Alec's suit is of a somewhat harsher blue and it hangs more stiffly – but similarity is the more marked, notably in tracking shot over their neatly folded clothes as they lie in bed together in a rented room, one man's set indistinguishable from the other's. They are thus integrated with each other and into a conventional masculinity.

At the end of the film Maurice leaves the space of his class, represented by Clive's country house, for Alec's, the boathouse. His symbolic departure from his place in society is underlined by the final image of him as an undergraduate waving and then turning away; this image is imagined by Clive as he looks out from his bedroom window and the film ends on his looking into the darkness, counting the cost of having opted for his proper place in society through marriage. Thus in plot terms, Maurice and Alec are not integrated into society; however, not only is their choice seen as the better one by dwelling upon Clive, included in society but excluded from the realisation of his true feelings, but also visually, through clothes, Maurice and Alec are integrated into the graceful masculinity of the heritage aesthetic.

Ernesto and *Maurice* both involve adapting (in different ways) to decorous masculinity. Such conformity at the level of costume makes it feels like the men are integrated at the level of the film's social world, even though the former involves keeping up married appearances and the latter separating from the world. This is characteristic of homosexual heritage. Exceptionally, and to return finally and again to where we started, *Un Hombre llamado 'Flor de Otoño'* achieves an integration of unmanly queenliness into its *mise en scène* even while depicting a society that deals ruthlessly with homosexual rebellion.

The film begins, as indicated above, by underlining the separation of the bright heritage world of assumed heterosexuality and the dark world of queers. Lluis performs a drag act at nights under the stage name of Flor de Otoño (Autumn Flower); when he laments that he, Alberto and Surroca cannot be themselves twenty four hours a day, Alberto tells him he can only expect to be Flor de Otoño from eleven till two at night (in the drag club). This exchange takes place during a long take of the three grouped together round a dressing table, all reflected in the table's mirrors. Surroca has been hitting a punch bag and stands bare chested in boxing shorts; Alberto is getting dressed, allowing us to appreciate the detail of his clothes, the button flies in the oatmeal tweed suit trousers, the rather stiff collar that has to be turned down after he has done up his tie, the latter consisting of vertical blocks of colour in the cream, beige and ochre range, rather short and

Figure 14.10 Maurice: dress and sameness (BFI Stills, Posters and Designs).

tucked into his suit waistcoat; Lluis is applying make-up, disguising his eyebrows, pencilling in other, higher ones. Surroca and Alberto dress within the codes of straight masculinity – bare chest, respectable suit – albeit with a pleasure in the care and display of that masculinity. Lluis on the other hand adopts a style that is understood within and by the film to be a queer one. Part of the trajectory of the film is Lluis's insistence on bringing that style into the rest of his life, which is also the film bringing it into the *mise en scène* of heritage.

In one sequence Lluis is hauled out of the club while still in drag, beaten up and left outside the door of his flat, his assailants ringing the bell so that his mother will find him and his humiliation will be complete; however, he runs off before she can open the door. But later, in the full drag of a smart señora (nothing vulgar or showbizzy, in other words dressing heritage not camp), he goes to see his mother in her bedroom in the middle of the night to tell her about himself. He insists that she keep the light out as he speaks, and the half light on him as he speaks is appropriately reminiscent of the confessional. Eventually however she insists on putting the light on. He has by this point taken off his (woman's) hat and wig, affirming his homosexual identity as a man in women's clothes. She tells him to come to her and they embrace, the camera tracking back along her bed to where he has left the hat and wig. There has thus been a gradual progress of queer into heritage, from avoiding being seen at all when dumped outside the flat through the half-light of confession to the fully lit embrace of an unequivocally gay self-presentation amidst full, but unflashy and uncluttered, period trappings. Very homosexual, very heritage.

Heritage cinema depicts past worlds in which homosexuality was illegal, mocked, despised and persecuted, in which gay men thought of themselves as queers. Yet it depicts these worlds, including being homosexual in them, as attractive. Several commentators, notably Andrew Higson (1993) and John Hill (1999), have argued that there is a defining contradiction in (British) heritage cinema between ostensible social critique and loving spectacle – the story and dialogue may condemn the worlds depicted but the look and texture of the films celebrate them. Yet perhaps the films are doing no more than evoke the contradictoriness of the past itself. Against the odds, there were also for queers love and sex and friendship, acceptance and tolerance, and you could still dress well and look good. Beyond this, what I have been trying to show is that, especially through clothes, homosexual heritage cinema does something quite specific with the contradiction between critique and spectacle: it produces the utopian pleasure of a vision of integration even in homophobic societies of the past. It imagines queers having been gay all along.

APPENDIX

Gay and lesbian heritage cinema

Gay

Amour de Swann, Un (Swann in Love)	France	1983
Another Country	UK	1984
Avonden, De (The Evenings)	Netherlands	1990
Bawang Bie Ji (Farewell My Concubine)	China	1993
Barry Lyndon	UK	1975
Becket	UK	1964
Bekenntnisse des Felix Krull (Confessions of Felix Krull)	Germany	1958
Blunt: the Fourth Man	UK	1977
Caduta degli dei, La (The Damned)	Italy	1968
Carrington	UK	1995
Céleste	France	1981
conformista, Il (The Conformist)	Italy	1969
cosas del querer, Las (The Affairs of Love)	Spain	1990
cosas del querer 2, Las (The Affairs of Love 2)	Spain	1996
Coup de grâce (aka *Der Fangschuss*)	Fr/Ger	1976
Dernier métro, Le (The Last Metro)	France	1980
Dresser, The	UK	1983
Elégant criminel, L'	France	1990
Englishman Abroad, An	UK	1983
Ernesto	Italy	1978
Europa, Europa	Fr/Ger	1991
Forbidden Passion	UK	1980
forsømte forär, Det (Stolen Spring)	Denmark	1993
giornata particolare, Una (A Special Day)	Italy	1977
Hombre llamado 'Flor de Otoño', Un (A Man Called Autumn Flower)	Spain	1977
junge Törless, Der (Young Törless)	Germany	1965
Ludwig	Italy	1972
Maurice	UK	1987
Mediterraneo	Italy	1991
Meteoro ke skia (Meteor and Shadow)	Greece	1985
Month in the Country, A	UK	1987
Morte a Venezia (Death in Venice)	Italy	1970
Mountains of the Moon	USA	1990
Le Maître de musique (Music Teacher, The)	Belgium	1988
nome della rosa, Il (Name of the Rose, The)	Italy	1986
Nijinksy	USA	1979
Nous étions un seul homme (We Were One Man)	France	1979
Nuit de Varennes, La	France	1982
occhiali d'oro, Gli (The Gold Rimmed Spectacles)	Italy	1988
102 Boulevard Haussmann	UK	1991

Orlando	UK	1992
Redl ezredes (*Colonel Redl*)	Hungary	1985
Sergeant, The	USA	1968
Sheltering Sky, The	Italy/UK	1990
stagione all'inferno, Una (*A Season in Hell*)	Italy	1971
Temps retrouvé, Le (*Time Regained*)	France	1999
Tonio Kröger	Germany	1964
Total Eclipse (aka *Rimbaud Verlaine*)	UK	1995
Valentino	UK	1977
Voor een verloren soldaat (*For a Lost Soldier*)	Netherlands	1992
We Think the World of You	UK	1988
Wilde	UK	1998
Älskande par (*Loving Couples*)	Sweden	1964

Lesbian

Aimee und Jaguar	Germany	1999
Amour de Swann, Un (*Swann in Love*)	France	1983
Amorosa	Sweden	1986
Avskedet (*The Farewell*)	Finland	1980
Banquière, La (*The Banker*[15])	France	1980
Becoming Colette	USA/France	1992
Belle époque	Spain	1993
Berlin Affair, The	It/Ger	1985
Bostonians, The	UK	1984
Chanel solitaire	France	1981
Color Purple, The	USA	1985
conformista, Il (*The Conformist*)	Italy	1969
Coup de foudre (*At First Sight*, aka *Entre Nous*)	France	1983
Dernier métro, Le (*The Last Metro*)	France	1980
Desert Hearts	USA	1993
Egymásra nézve (*Another Way*)	Hungary	1982
Extramuros (*Beyond the Walls*)	Spain	1985
Fried Green Tomatoes at the Whistle Stop Café	USA	1991
Getting of Wisdom, The	Australia	1977
Heavenly Creatures	N. Zealand	1994
Henry and June	USA	1990
House of the Spirits, The	Port/US	1994
Julia	USA	1977
Kvinnorna på taket (*Women on the Roof*)	Sweden	1989
Novembermond (*November Moon*)	Germany	1984
Oranges Are Not the Only Fruit (TV serial)	UK	1989
Orlando	UK	1992
Portrait of a Marriage (TV serial)	UK	1990
Rainbow, The	UK	1988
Religieuse, La (*The Nun*)	France	1965

Sister My Sister	UK	1994
Temps retrouvé, Le (*Time Regained*)	France	1999
Waiting for the Moon	USA	1987
Yo, la peor de todas (*I the Worst of All*)	Argentina	1990
Älskande par (*Loving Couples*)	Sweden	1964

Notes

1 See appendix for a listing of this and other gay and lesbian heritage films, including translations of titles.

2 Discussions of the term include Higson 1993, Monk 1995, Hill 1999, Vincendeau 2001.

3 I also exclude a number of other titles for being too grim (*Die Zärtlichkeit der Wölfe* [*The Tenderness of Wolves*] Germany 1973, *Salò* Italy 1975, *Aclà* Italy 1992, *Bent* UK 1998), too exotic (*Il fiore delle mille e una notte* [*Arabian Nights*] Italy 1974), too exuberant (*The Group* USA 1966, *Alexandria Why?* Egypt 1978, *Adieu Bonaparte*, Egypt 1984), too over the top (*The Music Lovers* UK 1971, *Salome's Last Dance* UK 1988) or about too recent history (*Prick Up Your Ears* UK 1987, *The Krays* UK 1990, *Les Roseaux sauvages* France 1994, *Backbeat* UK 1995).

4 Discussions of specific films include Arroyo 2000 (*Las cosas del querer*), Finch and Kwietniowski 1988 (*Maurice*), Turk 1998 (*Total Eclipse*), Waugh 2000 (*Ernesto*, *Maurice*, *Meteoro ke skia*, *Nous étions un seul homme*).

5 Cf. Bravmann 1997, Gowing 1997.

6 In *giornata*, Gabriele, a man who has just lost his job on account of his homosexuality, and Antonietta, a worn-down wife and mother of six, get to know each other when the block of flats they both live in is deserted because everyone else has gone off to see Hitler's parade through Rome; both, the film suggests, are oppressed by the regime's masculinist values. In *occhiali*, Eraldo, a heterosexual Jewish student, befriends an older gay dentist, Dr Fatigati; as the regime's grip tightens, Eraldo perceives the similarities between his situation as a Jew and Dr Fatigati's as a queer.

7 The Jewish protagonist of *Europa, Europa*, Solomon, passes as a Nazi during the War. When a fellow soldier, Robert, tries to seduce him, he, Robert, realises Solomon's racial identity from his circumcised penis. However, even though nothing develops sexually between them, Robert does not betray Solomon's secret, averring that 'not all Germans are the same' (i.e. prejudiced).

8 Marcello is propositioned as a boy by the family chauffeur; horrified at the desire awakened in him by this, he shoots the chauffeur and believes he has killed him; as an adult, he becomes a secret agent for the fascist regime, seeking in conformism an escape from the trauma of the childhood incident and what it might tell him about himself.

9 To put it more complexly, Guy wants to get back at his school, an embodiment of ruling-class values, whose all-male composition simultaneously facilitates homosexual sex and punishes homosexual love.

10 Suggested by Clive's shamed admission that he likes Tchaikovsky's *Pathétique* symphony, a by-word for queer culture: 'sweet water from a foul well, as they say'.

11 Edward Carpenter (1844–1929) was a middle-class socialist and early advocate

of gay rights; his relationship with working-class George Merrill was a living embodiment of his ideal of male sexual comradeship; E. M. Forster, author of *Maurice*, was one of the couple's many visitors.

12 For further discussion of the film, see Arroyo 2000.

13 As Ginette Vincendeau reminded me, this is at variance with the rather grotesque and fleshy descriptions of Charlus in the novel itself.

14 Stella Bruzzi (1997: 53–55) discusses the way this works in her account of *The Age of Innocence* (USA 1993).

15 The French title indicates that the banker in question is female.

References

Arroyo, José (2000) 'Queering the Folklore: Genre and Re-presentation of Homosexuality and National Identities in *Las cosas del querer*', in Marshall, Bill and Stilwell, Robynn (eds) *Musicals: Hollywood and Beyond*, Exeter: Intellect, 70–79.

Bravmann, Scott (1997) *Queer Fictions of the Past: History, Culture and Difference*, Cambridge: Cambridge University Press.

Bruzzi, Stella (1997) *Undressing Cinema: Clothing and Identity in the Movies*, London: Routledge.

Buzzacarini, Vittoria de (1992) *L'eleganza dello stile: duecent'anni di vesti maschile*, Milan: Lupetti.

Chauncey, George, Martin Duberman and Martha Vicinus (1989) 'Introduction', in Duberman, Martin, Martha Vicinus and George Chauncey (eds) *Hidden from History: Reclaiming the Gay and Lesbian Past*, New York: Penguin, 1–13.

Chenoune, Farid (1993) *Des Modes et des hommes: deux siècles d'élégance masculine/A History of Men's Fashions*, Paris/New York: Flammarion.

Finch, Mark and Kwietniowski, Richard (1988) 'Melodrama and *Maurice*: Homo Is Where the Het Is', *Screen* 29: 3, 72–83.

Flügel, J. C. (1930) *The Psychology of Clothes*, London: Hogarth.

Gowing, Laura (1997) 'History', in Medhurst, Andy and Munt, Sally R. (eds) *Lesbian and Gay Studies*, London: Cassell, 53–66.

Higson, Andrew (1993) 'Re-presenting the National Past: Nostalgia and Pastiche in the Heritage Film', in Friedman, Lester (ed.) *British Cinema and Thatcherism: Fires Were Started*, London: UCL Press.

Hill, John (1999) *British Cinema in the 1980s*, Oxford: Clarendon.

Hollander, Anne (1994) *Sex and Suits: The Evolution of Modern Dress*, New York: Knopf.

Martin, Richard and Koda, Harold (1989) *Jocks and Nerds: Men's Style in the Twentieth Century*, New York: Rizzoli.

Monk, Claire (1995) 'The British "Heritage Film" and its Critics', *Critical Survey* 7: 2, 116–124.

Turk, Edward Baron (1998) 'Le "Film maudit" d'Agnieszka Holland, *Rimbaud Verlaine* et sa réception', *Iris* 26: 163–176.

Vincendeau, Ginette (ed.) (2001) *Literature/Film/Heritage*, London: British Film Institute.

Waugh, Tom (2000) *The Fruit Machine*, Durham NC: Duke University Press. (Includes discussions of *Ernesto*, *Maurice*, *Meteoro ke skia*, *Nous étions un seul homme*).

INDEX